THE STRESS ANSWER

ALSO BY DR. FRANK LAWLIS

Mending the Broken Bond

The ADD Answer

The IQ Answer

THE STRESS ANSWER

Train Your Brain to Conquer

Depression and Anxiety in 45 Days

DR. FRANK LAWLIS

VIKING

VIKING
Published by the Penguin Group
Penguin Group (USA) Inc., 375 Hudson Street, New York, New York 10014, U.S.A.
Penguin Group (Canada), 90 Eglinton Avenue East, Suite 700, Toronto, Ontario,
Canada M4P 2Y3 (a division of Pearson Penguin Canada Inc.)
Penguin Books Ltd, 80 Strand, London WC2R 0RL, England
Penguin Ireland, 25 St. Stephen's Green, Dublin 2, Ireland (a division of Penguin Books Ltd)
Penguin Books Australia Ltd, 250 Camberwell Road, Camberwell, Victoria 3124, Australia
(a division of Pearson Australia Group Pty Ltd)
Penguin Books India Pvt Ltd, 11 Community Centre, Panchsheel Park,
New Delhi – 110 017, India
Penguin Group (NZ), 67 Apollo Drive, Rosedale, North Shore 0632, New Zealand
(a division of Pearson New Zealand Ltd)
Penguin Books (South Africa) (Pty) Ltd, 24 Sturdee Avenue, Rosebank,
Johannesburg 2196, South Africa

Penguin Books Ltd, Registered Offices: 80 Strand, London WC2R 0RL, England

First published in 2008 by Viking Penguin, a member of Penguin Group (USA) Inc.

1 3 5 7 9 10 8 6 4 2

Copyright © Frank Lawlis, 2008
All rights reserved

Drawings by Jackie Aher

A NOTE TO THE READER: Every effort has been made to ensure that the information contained in this book is complete and accurate. However, neither the publisher nor the author is engaged in rendering professional advice or services to the individual reader. The ideas, procedures, and suggestions contained in this book are not intended as a substitute for consulting with your physician. All matters regarding your health require medical supervision. Neither the author nor the publisher shall be liable or responsible for any loss, injury, or damage allegedly arising from any information or suggestion in this book.

LIBRARY OF CONGRESS CATALOGING IN PUBLICATION DATA
Lawlis, G. Frank
The stress answer : train your brain to conquer depression and
anxiety in 45 days / Frank Lawlis.
p. cm.
Includes bibliographical references and index.
ISBN 978-0-670-01973-1
1. Depression, Mental—Popular works.   2. Anxiety—Popular works.   3. Neuroplasticity—
Popular works.   4 Stress (Psychology)—Popular works.   I. Title.
RC537.L39   2008
616.85'2706—dc22   2008022146

Printed in the United States of America

To my sister, Nanciruth,
who showed me courage
and taught me how to laugh

Contents

Acknowledgments

There is always too large a number of people dating back to my infancy to recognize for their significant contributions to my books, and I apologize to those I may leave out. My first acknowledgment will always go to my wife, Susan, whose support and professional advice are always available to me as I search for the perfect word or the evidence to back up my conclusions. She is a wonderful partner in climbing my mountains of thought.

Dr. Phil McGraw will also always be on my top list of acknowledgments. His friendship and support have long been the centerpiece for my ambitions and schemes for making the world a better place to be. His loyalty will always be a quality I consider it a privilege to have.

I have discovered the magic of wordsmith Wendy Leonard's work as she has consulted on the completion of this book. She brought to the task not only her superb writing skills, but also her wealth of psychological research and knowledge. Thank you, Wendy, for a job well done. Sandy Bloomfield was a tremendous help in the final surge for completing the project.

Of course, this entire set of clinical conclusions and approaches could never have been assembled without the consultation and support of Dr. Barbara Peavey and our staff at the PsychoNeuro-Plasticity Center in Lewisville, Texas. We have learned from every patient we have seen, and we continue to break new ground in this crowded world of confusion as we strive to understand and treat individuals who need guidance through their suffering.

Jan Miller, my agent, and Shannon Miser-Marven have been with me from the beginning of this self-help series. They have been my guides when I got lost and served as boosters whenever I became discouraged. Along with this wonderful array of super people has been Carolyn Carlson of Viking. For some mystical reason she seems to understand my purpose for doing what I do, and has always been there making things happen without getting bogged down with the small stuff of the business of publishing books. My readers Ross Franks and Erica Chupp were of great assistance in making the book readable.

Preface

I've shared with many people that as an infant I was labeled "mentally defective due to severe brain damage," and many responses have been condescending comments about the lack of sophistication in diagnosis at that time. What I experienced was a blur of very frustrating challenges as I struggled to keep up with my peers, and I learned to bury my failures and embarrassments behind a smile and a good-natured joke or two.

To tell the truth, I did not know the letters of the alphabet until I was in the fifth grade, and I often hid when the teacher asked someone to recite the letters and apply them to some word-finding technique. The letters would jump around in my head and start to melt into one another. I couldn't tell a *b* from a *d* or a *p* from a *q*. I was a phonetic mess until I was a freshman in high school when a gifted teacher, Mr. Beasley, explained how letters sound. Maybe it was because little was expected of me, or because the teachers knew my parents were teachers and assumed too much, but I always felt like a freak about to be discovered.

Perhaps it was through music or my art teacher, but as time passed I started seeing things a little differently. I began to teach myself a personal language about symbols and how they could bring meaning to me in new ways. I discovered that if I allowed my brain to process things and events, they would usually evolve into meaningful parts. I trusted my mind to unravel solutions instead of closely following the methods taught by the teacher. Instead of solving math problems according to the book, I let each problem become its own process. Most times I would arrive at the right answer using my own path to get there. That plasticity I learned as a way to engage my brain still works for me, and I get much satisfaction from explaining this to others so that they, too, can find their own paths to the answers in life.

Brain plasticity merely means the flexibility of the brain to change—not only according to how we use it, but in response to demand. The brain, like every other organ and muscle, will atrophy and shrink without proper use, or it can become stronger and healthier with proper nurturance. Until just a few years ago, we had only indirect evidence of what the brain was doing, but now we can use new technology to calculate real change as well as to observe how some individuals have "rewired" their systems to recover from disabling conditions. I have been given the opportunity in this book to acquaint you with some of the basic approaches you can adopt in your personal life to utilize this newly found power. I am sure that in the coming generations new techniques will evolve that will take us into a completely new concept of health care in tune with these principles.

Awareness of how healing works continues to develop. I have seen plans for a device that would be used to evaluate neurological functioning based on your complaint, in order to "write" a prescription to reprogram your body functions via brain activity. This device would use your brain to bring your body back into appropriate balance—not merely to bring your functions into harmony, but to maximize your unique abilities for personal goals and contributions. With a special computer, you would undergo a process similar to a complete X-ray of your body, checking on how your brain and organs were performing. A wide range of therapies would be used, including some that are available today, but also including some that are not. For example, some medications might be needed to activate unused internal resources. You might also want to nurture your musical abilities or mathematical skills. Or you might actually need to operate at a slower pace and enjoy a vacation period to experience life more fully. Do you understand the implications of what we're discussing here? *Star Trek* technology would be realized in a way that would forever change life as we know it.

The applications in this book may be crude compared to later technology, but they are light-years ahead of the methods we use today for dealing with anxiety and depression. Rather than avoiding or "adjusting" to life sentences of impairment we can understand why we are what we are. Instead of treating symptoms, the concept of brain plasticity approaches the direct neurological complex at the core of the problems. By retraining the brain we grow stronger. For example, the symptom of a lack of concentration can be applied to every disorder in the *Diagnostic and Statistical Manual* of psychiatric diagnoses. In the realm of brain plasticity, lack of concentration signals the need to train the brain to shift its strengths to this area and broaden its competencies. As the brain expands its capabilities, new skills can be gained.

These new approaches are not independent from the contributions of existing mental health practices, which are all relevant and actually support the overall concept. I have spent most of my career learning interventions, starting with Rogerian human-potential approaches, the psychoanalytic psychodynamic model, and Adlerian developmental concepts, and continuing with behavioral modification, body/mind therapies, and a wide range of approaches that have yet to be defined. I have found that every one of them has facilitated my understanding of how the brain works. Every scientific therapy (and some nonscientific) has a right to claim a part of this great triumph in health care. The challenge is to know specifically how these tools can be integrated for the objects of brain function and health.

My purpose in life has always been to find ways of relieving suffering for my fellow beings on this earth, and this book has become a core part of that mission. For generations mental distress and torment have gone unhealed in spite of all the collective human wisdom we have had access to. But I am excited—and overwhelmed at times—to realize a revolutionary step in mental health care can help change that. I didn't invent the idea of brain plasticity and our ability to improve our mental capacities, but I recognize the

immediate applicability of the concept to this important realm of
the human condition.

Being something of a maverick in the mental health field, I am
accustomed to being criticized for being open to new ideas and
changes in the field. But instead of attacking the messenger, I would
hope that readers will approach the principles with an open mind
and study them to determine their validity on a personal level. I
hope that you consider the many routes to mental wholeness I have
presented in this book as possible answers to your frustrations and
stresses. I can assure you that none has been offered without having been observed hundreds of times to work quickly and
effectively.

I have also taken an innovative step by including interpersonal
stress in the brain plasticity arena. Why? Because interpersonal
stress is perhaps the most dangerous kind. It has been the locus of
conflict leading to human crises that range from divorces to wars,
which in turn has brought about heightened worldwide stress
overall.

As with any other book I have written, I am giving you a promise of hope by going through the exercises on a step-by-step basis.
I have attempted to emphasize those exercises that you can use
without the expense and trouble of seeking outside help, but of
course you should utilize what resources you have. To avoid seeking expert help when it is necessary only restricts your health.
Some exercises may not work as you might hope, but others may
change your life significantly for the better. Give yourself the chance
to open the doors to a new future of joy and excitement as you discover who you are—and more important, what you can become.

THE STRESS ANSWER

1

Maria's Story:
From Victim to Dragonslayer

Maria started her life not too differently from the rest of us. She had ten fingers and ten toes. Her body had no apparent maladies, and as far as anyone could tell, her brain was the same as any other baby's. She was instantly adored by her parents, who doted on her and expected nothing less for her than a future filled with hope, joy, and success.

Indeed, during Maria's first few years on the planet, she felt safe and comfortable in her world. Her mother tied beautiful ribbons of yellow or blue in her silky black hair, prompting warm and approving coos from all who beheld her. Her room was filled to the brim with books, dolls, and toys, and she had closets filled with lovely clothes. What more could a little girl ask for?

TECTONIC SHIFT

Maria's idyllic life began to crumble at the age of four, when her uncle moved into the family home after he was fired from his job. Short of money but eager to "help do his part," her uncle offered to babysit Maria so his brother and sister-in-law could have some much-needed time alone. Without giving it a second thought, Maria's parents accepted this seemingly gracious offer, and began to go out regularly on Saturday nights.

Left alone with her uncle (let's call him Bill) each week for hours at a time, Maria was caught up in the abhorrent process of pedophilic seduction. Using his exceptional charm, plying her with gifts, and taking her on "secret" outings—the classic tools of the pedophilic trade—Bill lavished her with attention that ultimately (and tragically) culminated in years of sexual abuse. As part of his sexual abuse ritual, Bill would take Maria downstairs to the laundry room in her home. He would have her help him cleanse the hard, cold folding table (upon which the abuse always took place) with an ammonia-based window cleaner–which Bill called "magical blue." Like a highly charged loving association gone terribly wrong, the smell of ammonia-based cleaners can still turn Maria's stomach to this day.

Part of what makes Bill's (or any pedophile's) seduction process so evil and spiritually damaging is how he methodically makes his victim (in this case, Maria) not only believe that this is how love and caring are supposed to be expressed, but also that everything must be kept secret, or else the love, gifts, and special treatment will cease. Why does this work? Research on the developmental processes of the brain and the way in which a young child builds the concept of morality has suggested that it's usually not until the child is older that he or she realizes this relationship is wrong. Prior to that realization, the child enjoys the special attention that is given in "payment" for the abuse; and while that's perfectly understandable, it nonetheless leads to tremendous guilt and shame—thus making the ultimate "telling" even more difficult.

THE TELLING

When Maria reached the age of eleven, she understood, for the first time, that Uncle Bill was abusing her sexually. As is so often the case, when she finally got the nerve to tell her mom what was happening, her mom refused to believe her. So, Maria told her dad . . . who also didn't believe her. But apparently her mother really *did* believe her, because Maria heard her parents fighting behind closed doors night after night about whether to kick Uncle Bill out of the house (which never happened). Feeling guilty, confused, and horribly responsible for upsetting the family dynamic, Maria "confessed" that she probably misunderstood Uncle Bill's actions; so, despite her self-disgust, the sexual abuse continued until she was almost fifteen years old. No, Bill didn't stop willingly, and her mom didn't intervene. Driving alone in a drunken stupor one day, Bill was killed in a car accident. No one ever discussed what had taken place, and even after he was gone, the unspoken code of silence continued.

National Sex Offender Registry

The National Sex Offender Registry website—coordinated by the Department of Justice—enables every citizen to search the latest information from all fifty states, the District of Columbia, and Puerto Rico for the identity and location of known sex offenders. Here is the website: http://www.fbi.gov/hq/cid/cac/registry.htm

Source: The Federal Bureau of Investigation (FBI) of the U.S. Department of Justice.

INTO THE STORM

Raised in a relatively religious household, Maria began to believe that her willing participation with her uncle would forever condemn her to hell. So, when she was about thirteen and boys naturally began to take notice of her, instead of enjoying the first blushes of puppy love, she felt a sense of repulsion, mingled with feelings of intrigue—which got all twisted up with perfectly normal adolescent hormone-driven desires. In an attempt to provide herself a modicum of self-protection, she began to overeat, literally building a wall around herself. Like a self-medicating drug, her eating behaviors became addictive, swirling into what I call a depressive storm, or downward mental spiral, which consumed both her body and mind.

Depressive storms are only one of many types of stress storms, a term I've coined to describe what happens when your brain circuits (or neurocircuits) go on overload, causing signals to get crossed and spiral out of control. Logic and rational thinking go out the window as your brain gets stuck in a mental ditch, with the engine revving and wheels spinning, but no forward movement. These storms can be caused by everything from chronic stress to trauma, as in Maria's case.

Maria's gut-wrenching guilt triggered one depressive storm after another, and her life was ruled by her misery. Anything that reminded her of her shame, her raw sexual needs, the distortion of her ever-growing body, or the smell of ammonia would drive Maria inside her home for weeks on end, where she ravenously consumed candy, chocolate, and ice cream and smoked cigarettes, all while listening to heartbreaking country-and-western songs. As the years dragged on, however, she did succeed in pursuing one avenue of constructive behavior: she decided to earn her college degree online, and successfully managed to complete 75 percent of her college degree in business administration. The remaining 25 percent, however, had to be completed in person and on campus.

Having to force herself to be seen in public and afraid of either ridicule or unwanted advances, she kept her time in public to an absolute minimum. Fortunately, because she was exceptionally smart, she successfully completed her degree. But when it came time to land a job, her lack of self-confidence betrayed her: any time she was recruited for a professional position she wanted (and was qualified for), she was enveloped again in her depressive stress storm. In fact, she would become so tongue-tied during the interview process that no one had a chance to evaluate her strengths. Sometimes, she didn't even show up for the interview.

When she was successfully hired as a receptionist (a fine job, but far below her qualifications), people in upper management quickly recognized the tremendous additional value she could provide the company, and offered her a managerial position in Human Resources. She would have to be interviewed by the vice president, but was assured that that was only a formality and the job was already hers. Maria turned the offer down flat. She feared the V.P. might ask about her past—and that was something she couldn't handle. She resigned her receptionist job the following week and spent the next month behind closed doors, alone and eating her pain away.

SILENT SCREAM

One of Maria's friends successfully persuaded her to see a psychotherapist. After getting a referral from her primary care physician, Maria began to have a faint sense of hope. However, despite her genuine engagement in the therapeutic process with a caring, qualified psychotherapist, any solutions or coping mechanisms lost all relevance the moment she started sliding into her usual mental "lockup." There was minimal improvement—but there was a new diagnosis: clinical depression.

Controlled by the stress storms that regularly overwhelmed her, Maria was unable to grab hold of the life she deserved. She imagined her stress as a grotesque black dragon with piercing all-knowing eyes that blocked the door to her future. In the rare instances when opportunity did knock—and the door would creak open just a hair to allow the faintest light to shine through—the dragon would slam the door shut with a hellacious roar, sending Maria silently screaming back to her small, dank dungeon. This would be her life forever . . . unless she could face the dragon and defeat him.

The story of Maria is one of the oldest stories in clinical psychology, and one that most of us can relate to. You may not have suffered at the hands of a sexual predator, but most of us have experienced some moment of shame or deep devastation early on in our childhood. Being able to forgive ourselves for dreadful circumstances beyond our control can be a struggle for any of us—and that is particularly true when an early onset of fixation depressive stress storms has diminished our brain's optimal neuropathway responses. For some of us, forgiving our parents for their transgressions can be even more difficult—because it's their job to protect us. The sad truth is, I've yet to meet a patient in a depressive stress storm who didn't suffer from guilt or shame as a child, which in turn has caused them a life riddled with pain.

YOU'RE NOT ALONE

It's estimated that more than 90 percent of us will have a bout with depression at some point in our lives. For some of us this experience may be unbearably debilitating. Almost all of us will have serious anxiety bouts that will restrict us from enjoying life's opportunities. Equally disturbing (if not more so), the interactions between our emotional stress and our body can exacerbate, and even initiate, serious chronic diseases such as type 2 diabetes, cardiovascular disease, and chronic pain, and may lead to premature death.

THE PROMISE

You may be relieved to learn that, ultimately, Maria's story was a happy one. What happened? In my view, the transformation didn't happen by will or insight, but rather, by divine intervention. Some might call it a miracle of circumstance, and others might call it grace, and surely, still others would say it was just dumb luck.

One day shortly after her twenty-seventh birthday, Maria was walking along the sidewalk, minding her own business en route to her car, after filing some work-related documents at the local court-house. But instead of turning left at the corner and proceeding to the parking lot, she turned right—and found herself opening the door of a Marine recruiting office. As she surveyed her surround-ings, she found herself thoroughly entranced by the impressive uniforms the women wore and the confidence they all seemed to share. She began thinking about their brave acts, and soon, Maria began imagining herself in such a role.

A uniformed, gray-haired woman with intense hazel eyes turned to Maria and said, "You are to become a true leader in service to your country. Are you ready?" Astounded that someone would be talking to her with such assurance, Maria could only stare back at this woman. Finally, she asked, "Who are you?" The woman quickly responded, "I'm Sergeant Patricia, but my name is not what matters right now. What does matter is why you are here. I truly believe that you could make a fine Marine and serve your country proudly. And yes, you would look good in that uniform, but what I want you to do is give me an answer right now." With that statement, the woman gently but reassuringly touched Maria on the shoulder. It was like a magic source of power that sparked Maria's mind, body, and soul.

EXCEEDING EXPECTATIONS AND BEYOND

Maria signed up that very morning, dedicating herself to something far greater than she was. Although she was overweight and clumsy—and didn't believe she had an aggressive or authoritative bone in her body—somehow she knew she would exceed her own expectations. And she did. She learned to march in step with her peers and to recite words of strength and honor that became so embedded in her brain, she would never again doubt the power within her, or the resources on either side of her.

Extremely demanding to say the least, the process of becoming a Marine was a godsend to this directionless young woman. With tremendous focus, hard work, and consistency, Maria evolved to become a physically and mentally fit Marine, earning her the right to join the corps.

Maria began to feel as if she was a brand-new person. She could feel her spirit awaken inside her, and it wanted to soar. For the first time since she was a small child, Maria felt that she could capably handle whatever came her way. The depressive storm lifted, and the dragon was finally vanquished. In time, Maria was promoted to a personnel director in a marketing firm and she continued to excel. She released her emotional baggage to the Universe, and the twinkle in her eyes attracted the supportive husband of her dreams. *Semper Fidelis.*

Her experience might seem mystical, but it can be explained scientifically: the discipline process employed by the Marines catalyzed changes in Maria's brain. The inherent capacity of the brain to bend and reformat its processing (based on new information and demands) had begun, allowing new realities to begin to form. *And new realities can form entirely new neuropathways in your brain.* Thus, with these (new and improved) resources, the debilitating storms can be deleted from the "program"—because the brain simply no longer operates that way anymore.

Sadly, not all Marias find their paths. It takes courage to break out of the familiar story that someone else may have written for you and to begin to write your own instead. You may be stuck in a similar stress cycle. You may even have accepted this diminished reality as your lot in life. But you have a choice now that goes beyond becoming a psychotherapy patient for the rest of your life. Maria would say, "Just do it and the mind will respond. It's a promise given to you. All you have to do is do it, and you will see and believe the treasures that await you. This I know for sure."

We all have issues from our past that have caused us shame and pain, which continue to alter how our brain processes events in our adult lives. But you don't have to remain a victim—especially now, when our society is undergoing a revolution in the mental health field unlike any we've ever known, with the promise of knowledge and tools unlike any we've ever had before. But it all starts with you.

You can reteach your brain to conquer the vicious cycle of self-destruction, and put the principles of transformation to work in your life. You really can make this happen . . . And I can help this process.

2

The Technology and Information Revolutions
for Brain Revitalization

Stress is a powerful force that can stand in the way of one's health and happiness. Stress isn't some esoteric concept. Stress lives inside us, residing in our souls.

Maria was lucky that she stumbled onto a way to reclaim her life. However, not everyone who needs a brain adjustment should be heading over to the local recruitment office to get it. So what does that leave in the way of options? To most people, it means calling in the pros. The problem is that mental health professionals—despite their extensive education and expertise—aren't always the answer. Plus, old-school theories and past technologies haven't proven sophisticated enough to develop and test programs at the intensity level that people like Maria need if they are ever going to break free of the stress storms ruling their lives. For those caught in the vortex of these storms, good advice, support, and willpower simply aren't enough. And for far too long, little has changed in the tools and instruction we've been given to deal with this onslaught.

But that is all changing, and in a big way. A veritable revolution is taking place that is transforming the mental health field. Actually, two revolutions are taking place at the same time—one in technology and another in information access. There is an amazing correlation between these two arenas. It seems the more we advance in the technological realm, the more information is available to be explained and applied in everyday language. And the best part is, you don't need to know organic chemistry or read Latin to learn how to apply most of the techniques and approaches directly to yourself or a loved one—I've already done the work for you. All you need is commitment to the process. Imagine . . . in just 45 days, if you use the step-by-step method explained in this book, *you can learn how to help your brain do its job better.* These could be the best weeks of your life as you discover the keys to your stress issues and resolve them once and for all. Maria changed her world and started on a new path when she headed for boot camp—think of this process as boot camp for your brain.

Although some of the more dazzling technology is still on the horizon, enough information is accessible today so that no one should feel stuck in a life that he or she is unhappy with. But that wasn't always the case.

SOME BACKSTORY

In the Dark Ages (500–1000 A.D.) it was generally believed that illnesses of the mind and body (and bad fortune, for that matter) either were caused by demons or were punishments for one's sinful behaviors. These superstitious habits of self-blame persisted for centuries. Enter Sigmund Freud in the late 1800s, a psychiatrist and neurologist who endeavored to create a more scientific approach. Freud introduced such groundbreaking concepts as the ego, the unconscious, and dream interpretation. Further, Freud helped lay down the foundations of the field of psychology, including terminology and diagnostics (tests) for generations of mental health professionals to come.

Only recently, starting in the 1950s, were biochemical medications invented to treat emotional distress. First MAOIs (monoamine oxidase inhibitors) such as Iproniazid, and from the 1970s on, SSRIs (selective serotonin reuptake inhibitors) such as Prozac positively affected depression and anxiety, thereby helping to improve the

lives of many people. However, it's the current technological revolution that is finally bringing stress management up to the level of
the rest of medicine.

MEDICAL APPROACH TODAY AND BEYOND

Think about the current process when you go to a medical professional for help. Suppose you have a stomachache and you explain
your pain to a doctor. After taking a medical history and conducting a physical exam, the doctor (hopefully) sends you for X-rays
and blood tests, perhaps stool samples and other related assessments. In the final analysis, the process would be to *triangulate* the
results, that is, to ascertain how the clinical signs fit the lab results
to determine your diagnosis and choose the best treatment.

However, if you go to a doctor for mental stress issues, there
aren't tests to triangulate, because you can't see thoughts on X-rays,
and there's no identifiable virus or bacteria for stress (well, not yet
anyway). So instead, you're stuck with a trial-and-error approach,
as was the case with Maria. Thus, the "proper" or "best" course of
treatment up to this point has been based mostly on guesswork,
albeit educated guesswork. However, exciting advances in technology are changing all that. We are now finding ways to see a
thought—or at least the process of a thought—which can help
medical professionals triangulate a diagnosis.

One of the greatest breakthroughs in understanding how the
brain works has emerged with the advent of the concept of brain
plasticity (also called neuroplasticity). This field of research has
demonstrated that (contrary to popular belief) your brain is *not*
permanently hardwired by the time you're five, but rather is able to
change physically, chemically, and anatomically in response to your
thoughts, experiences, and behaviors throughout your lifetime!
That's powerful information. This suggests that we can alter—and
therefore potentially heal—our brain by directing the organization
of stress thoughts (e.g., through mental training) in a step-by-step
method!

Today, we have (and you can benefit from) a set of evaluations and diagnostic tools that are not unlike what other forms of medicine have been using for many years. We can evaluate and measure the degree of healing. We can triangulate which protocols will best serve to optimize your quality of life. This is possibly as great a leap forward in public health as the discovery of antibiotics and vaccines.

IN THE EYE OF THE STORM

Have you ever been in the annoying situation where you couldn't remember the name of one of your own family members? Have you been confused or frustrated at your inability to find simple solutions for an everyday problem? Some days, do you just find yourself overwhelmed with too many tasks and feel you're losing control? Do you sometimes wonder if your brainpower is slipping away? Are you still experiencing conflict in a personal relationship you had years ago, perhaps with a parent who still interferes with your life? Are you at odds with your wife, husband, or child because you can't resolve issues that are really minor when you think about them objectively? Are you bored and feeling trapped in a life without real happiness? Are you getting in your own way because of the negative thoughts that run on a continuous loop in your brain?

If any of these descriptions apply, you may be suffering from the downward spiral of stress storms.

You know you're in a stress storm when you can't rationally talk yourself through a mind-set you know is irrational. For example, you know (in reality) your family will be perfectly fine on a trip or excursion, but your mind nevertheless keeps swirling into images of fear and feelings of desperation and maybe even panic. You can't stop thinking that the plane is going to crash. Or perhaps you find yourself falling into a depression, but there's no logical reason as to why you're feeling that way. In fact, you may even have just accomplished something great, but the next morning you don't want to get out of bed because you're so down. Maybe you return to your house twenty times because you're afraid you left the door unlocked. These are signs and symptoms that your brain is locked in a cycle you feel you have no control over—these are stress storms.

A WINDOW TO THE BRAIN

There are many dynamics to stress storms. I was raised on the great plains of West Texas, and some of the most vivid memories I have are the dust storms and "northerners" that swept through my hometown. Sometimes they would get so bad you couldn't see three feet in front of you. Heck, you could get lost trying to walk home. The worst part of these storms was the disorientation I felt—even inside my house—from the constant whirling winds and the ceaseless roars throughout the night. It got so bad it was almost impossible to think clearly.

Stress storms throw us into the same state of confusion. In fact, as a result of technological advances, we can now literally "see" this happening on a brain scan. For example, some scans look like two cyclones churning on each side of the brain. That phenomenon is seen when someone is having difficulty letting go of an idea that has no workable solution—similar to that obsessive-compulsive behavior of returning to the house twenty times to make sure the door was locked.

TAKING CONTROL

Management skills and well-planned solutions for stress are at the very heart of preventing downward spirals. Without flexible, adaptable reactions, you're left vulnerable to the danger of plummeting from your platform of stability. Even seemingly minimal stress has the potential to overwhelm your emotional center, thereby devastating your psychological composure.

Chronic stress can magnify (and even create) some of the most powerful and far-reaching causes of pain, suffering, and disease imaginable. However, with the right rerouting tools, stress can also serve as a constructive motivator to not only improve your productivity, but also increase your self-esteem.

When the mind loses its sense of stability, there's the dangerous possibility of creating a cascade of life-damaging choices that may lead to a profoundly deteriorated life (as was the case for Maria, prior to slaying her dragon). These types of debilitating brain storms come from excruciating levels of fear and confusion. In this type of situation, the person is literally not thinking straight. In extreme cases, I've seen people enduring these types of stress storms go from being successful executives to homeless in a matter of months. One minute everything seems great, and the next, you discover your spouse is having an affair; that leads to family turmoil, and then friendships are crushed, job performance tanks, the mortgage can't be met, you get arrested for DUI . . . you get the idea. Without a workable method of coping, the results can be devastating. And it can happen to anyone.

Miles

Even the smartest people can have stress storms. I met a very enthusiastic doctor named Miles, who wanted to come to work for me in a postdoctoral fellowship. Miles was from one of the most prestigious Ivy League schools in the country and his references were superb. He was unquestionably a brilliant and gifted researcher whose contribution to the field was exceptional. I was very excited to work with him.

On the way from Boston to Texas, he spiraled downward. The moving company temporarily lost his belongings. While others might have experienced this mishap as a very annoying inconvenience, for Miles, it was devastating. He became despondent. Why? He had an unusually strong identification with his "things," and felt literally lost without them. He then met with a loss of a more intimate nature: his wife filed for divorce. Devoid of those familiar support systems, Miles began to lose his previously solid sense of self-confidence, and instead felt anxious, fearing he was losing all control.

In an attempt to mute his fears and psychological pain, he began to abuse alcohol, and the toxicity that builds from substance abuse made it even harder to function. With his thinking abilities compromised, he went into a robotic state. As his brain went into a storm, the stress began to weaken his body defenses and he got a bad virus. Of note, scientific research has demonstrated that negative, stress-inducing life events can indeed compromise your immune system, making you more susceptible to infections and diseases. And to add insult to injury, through some universal law yet to be defined, when you start giving up on yourself, the world becomes even more confusing than ever. It seems that everything you know starts crashing down on you until your whole life is imploding. Been there? I know I have.

To his credit (as it's particularly difficult to get motivated when you feel everything you try will fail), Miles agreed to go through the 45-day program (the same one I'm about to outline in this book) to gain back his personal set of keys to the doors of happiness. And find the keys he did.

Miles began his healing journey by having the luxury of gaining access to a QEEG (quantitative electroencephalogram) brain scan, which clearly suggested what type of stress storm he was experiencing. These scans may not be available to many readers and therefore are not included in the 45-day program for this book. To help his body detoxify, he needed to lower his stress levels, and increase endorphin production—which naturally helps reduce stress levels, relieves pain, and increases one's sense of well-being. Not surprisingly in fact, the word *endorphin* is Greek for "the morphine within."

Miles's detoxifying process consisted of exercising an hour a day, soaking in the sauna (which studies show also increases endorphin production), and drinking lots of lemon juice. Not only is lemon juice a powerful antioxidant that reduces oxidative stress, but evidence-based studies show that consuming foods and beverages high in vitamin C (about 250 mg/day) can significantly lower your bad (LDL) cholesterol; which, in turn, lowers your blood pressure. You see how all this is fitting together?

GETTING GROUNDED

Miles's story is similar to a million others. Stress can swallow people whole as a consequence of many events: you lose someone you love to death or a misunderstanding; you lose your job or even your identity through theft or a simple mistake in the administration office; you enter into a marriage, but all too quickly discover you're married to an abuser, and you lose faith in yourself. The list goes on. But the critical issue is not the stressful event that sets off the stress storm, but rather, the inability of one's mind to get past the storm and become stronger.

The majority of stress storms we experience last only a few minutes. However, if you don't have a healthy grounding in stress management, the effect can be very similar to the way a tornado sweeps through an area—an isolated storm can result in major physical and psychological damage.

Physical pain can also create brain storms, and if chronic, may lead to a devastating depression. And unfortunately, it's also not unusual for storms to be so subtle that you never knew one happened. Your life just suddenly appears to hit a wall, with no foreseeable way out.

When stress storms happen, the brain shifts into a state of disassociation for its own protection from pain or disorientation. And without a plan of restoration, the *synapses* (junctions or connecting points in your brain where messages—in the form of chemical signals— are passed along) begin to reform into negative circles of thinking. That makes getting your world into perspective a Herculean task, without the critically important benefit of having clarity. You may become paranoid concerning your friends and family or feel isolated from support; you may even feel hopeless and resign yourself to a barren life. Further, your brain may stop processing new information and regress into survivor mode, which increases your isolation and erodes your self-esteem and confidence. Of particular note, drug and alcohol abuse make brain storms far worse, as they chemically disrupt and distort both your brain's outgoing and incoming messages.

THE THREE-POUND WONDER

Before chaos of the brain can be fully understood, it's important to define what "normalcy" is. What is optimal brain functioning? Let's start with brain geography. A look at the geography of the brain's outermost layer, the cerebral cortex—which is in charge of voluntary actions, thinking, memory, feelings, and conscious experience—will help you to understand this three-pound wonder, otherwise known as our brain.

The brain's cerebral cortex has several regions. These are essentially the organizational divisions, each of which is responsible for different physical and intellectual skills (see figure 2.1 for a map of the brain). For example, when people are injured or have lesions in the parietal lobe (the voluntary movement/motor and sensory region), there's a direct correlation to a function in the body. More specifically, if you suffered a certain type of stroke in the left parietal area, you'd experience paralysis in your right arm or leg. Why? Nearly all the nerve signals from the brain to the body cross over both coming and going. So, your left cerebral hemisphere controls the right side of your body, and vice versa. (But contrary to popular belief, whether you're left- or right-handed doesn't signify which side of your brain is "dominant.")

The good news is that, as we discussed earlier, your brain can and does adapt to injuries and traumas. For those who have suffered a stroke—depending on the nature, extent, and brain location— state-of-the-art physical therapists are successfully using a new technology, called *transcutaneous electrical nerve stimulation* (TENS), which actually encourages brain reorganization and recovery of function! This is possible because, while each part of the brain has its own special functions and properties, each part also has the capacity to influence other parts.

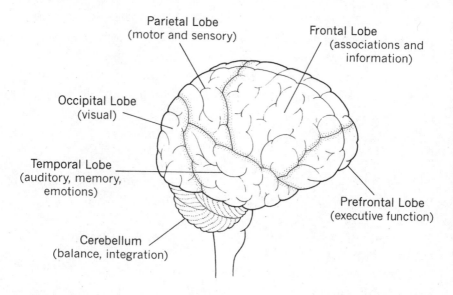

FIGURE 2.1
A TOPOGRAPHICAL MAP OF THE BRAIN

Brain Processes, In Brief

- Prefrontal lobe: Primarily responsible for integrating information and organizing our perceptions into meaningful concepts. People with prefrontal lobe injuries often have difficulty organizing new information and appear to be in a daze. The prefrontal lobe plays a critical role in memory retrieval.

- Frontal lobe: Primarily responsible for planning, reasoning, judgment, and impulse control, as well as some aspects of speech. People who have problems in this lobe frequently are impulsive and have very poor planning.

- Temporal lobe: Primarily responsible for auditory processing (hearing), comprehension of words, and emotional affect in context with language. People with low-functioning temporal lobes also exhibit memory problems.

- Parietal lobe: Primarily responsible for processing sensations such as touch, pressure, cold, heat, and pain, as it gets its data from the skin. It's also strongly involved with primary motor functions (voluntary movements). People with limitations in this area often have trouble controlling their body and may lose sensations (touch, smell, etc.), perhaps because of strokes and traumatic head injuries.

- Occipital lobe (visual cortex): Primarily responsible for processing data provided by the eyes and translating it into meaningful symbols. People with damaged occipital lobes may become blind, even when their eyes are functioning well.

- Cerebellum: Primarily responsible for balance, posture, and coordination as well as learned physical skills, such as riding a bike. *Cerebellum* is also Latin for "little brain," which refers to its ability to coordinate millions of impulses instantaneously.

Technology Extraordinaire

The quantitative electroencephalograph is a type of brain-mapping diagnostic tool that displays how the brain's regions are performing in terms of frequency ranges, and thus can gauge emotional imbalances (see table 2.1). For example, in Miles's case, the QEEG brain scan showed too much high beta frequency in the frontal lobe, and an overall imbalance in the rest of his brain regions—which ideally should be on par with each other. This is an indicator of anxiety, similar to a machine that is running too fast, and it meant that the rest of the body was unable to to catch up with his racing beta waves. The signature of high anxiety and stress storms was reliable and treatment protocol was clear: the treatment phase would include techniques that would moderate the abnormally high frequencies in the frontal lobe to more efficient ones in concert with the rest of the brain. As discussed earlier, this course ultimately resulted in a successful outcome for Miles.

TABLE 2.1
BRAIN FREQUENCY MEASUREMENTS

Range (Hz.)	Wave	State of Consciousness
0.5–4	Delta	Sleep, subconscious, not awake
4–8	Theta	Twilight, dreamy, semiconscious
8–12	Alpha	Very relaxed, little information being processed, tranquil, high memory
12–15	Low Beta	Focused, studying, processing
15 +	High Beta	Anxious, stressed, overwhelmed with data, little concentration

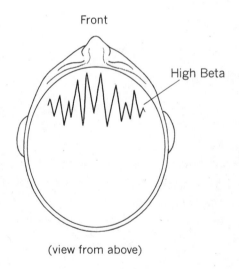

(view from above)

FIGURE 2.2

The SPECT scan (single photon emission computed tomography) is a type of nuclear imaging test that can show how blood flows through arteries and veins in the brain, as well as where blockages or reduced blood flow are occurring. This is particularly helpful because we know that highly active regions usually produce more blood flow and less active areas receive less blood flow.

For example, in the case of ADHD (attention deficit/hyperactivity disorder), the frontal lobes would show less blood flow than normal. Likewise, overly high blood flow might suggest that the areas are overactive or inflamed, which would be cause for a treatment plan to reduce blood flow.

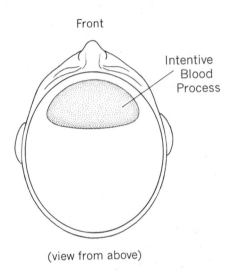

Front

Intentive
Blood
Process

(view from above)

FIGURE 2.3

Now that you have a basic understanding of these concepts, I hope you can see how truly remarkable brain scans can be as tools for identifying the stress dynamics in the brain. And more important, I hope you're beginning to see that you absolutely have the power to improve how you function, feel, and live from day to day.

BIOLOGICAL CAUSES AND CONDITIONS OF STRESS

As we watch the weatherman explain to us the reasons for his weather predictions, we perceive that there is a science to how storms are formed and triggered. The concepts in weather generally have to do with low- and high-pressure systems that tangle with each other to produce shifts in wind velocities and subsequent changes in storm conditions. But have you ever noticed weather forecasters often point out that they can only interpret the "conditions" for predicting weather? That's because they can only look at the potential for storms.

This metaphor can be transferred to the world of stress, where conditions based upon our metabolic or environmental vulnerabilities can result in the "forecasting" of a storm. For example, we may have a weakened coping response, which forces our brains to struggle with stressful situations with less than adequate control.

I've found four metabolic factors that are definite underlying threats to lead to ineffective coping behaviors. These factors have been discovered through a combination of research and clinical interviewing. Many of these storms can be caused by basic biological factors that serve as unconscious stressors and operate beneath our radar. However, some are lifestyle behaviors motivated at a subconscious level and having a negative impact on our lives.

Hormonal Stress

Hormonal stress can be as devastating to the brain's harmony as a vicious divorce. Excessive adrenal hormone activity (which increases the heart rate and raises blood pressure) can be related to mood swings, anxiety and panic attacks, insomnia, and poor concentration. Melatonin is a major modulator of annual and daily cycles of activity: it helps you sleep and be alert at the right times. Abnormal melatonin production intensifies high levels of worry storms and is related to depression, insomnia, and seasonal affective disorder.

The hormonal stresses that I always get interested in investigating are those produced by the thyroid, because mine has played a whopping—and sometimes mean-spirited—game with my brain. The thyroid is located in the neck, and its function, broadly stated, is to be in charge of our metabolism, regulating our body temperature and "secreting hormones necessary for our development." The unscientific explanation is that it controls a zillion extremely important functions, especially in the brain. People with an overactive thyroid may exhibit marked anxiety and tension, emotional instability, and irritability. They may be very uncomfortable in the world around them, and easily distracted. In extreme cases, they may appear schizophrenic, losing touch with reality.

My particular problem was the opposite—hypothyroidism. People with low thyroid activity tend to lose interest and initiative, suffer from poor memory, depression, and eventually, if the condition is left unchecked, can potentially even experience dementia. You could say I was not the most interesting guy to have at your party.

The problem of hormonal stress is of special concern to women, because women who suffer from hormone fluctuations are particularly vulnerable to stress storms. Because of various feedback mechanisms in the body, fluctuations in sex hormone levels (such as estrogen and progesterone) influence the secretion of important stress hormones. When this interplay becomes chronically imbalanced (during puberty, menstruation, pregnancy, and menopause), behavior and mood disorders often increase dramatically. Depression, eating disorders, alcoholism, or other addictions may also occur.

As with many of the body's physiological responses, balance is the key. Overproduction of estrogen is associated with melancholia (anxiety, insomnia, loss of libido), while underproduction is linked to atypical depression (fatigue, lethargy, indifference). Women are also twice as likely as men to experience unipolar depression, a major depressive disorder with symptoms such as extreme difficulty concentrating, dramatic change in appetite, feelings of worthlessness, self-hatred, and withdrawal from previously enjoyed activities. But men can experience hormonal stress, too (especially with testosterone surges). The sex hormone testosterone can create brain storms, and fatigue and irritability may be signs of testosterone imbalance.

Malnutrition Stress

Malnutrition stress can seriously clog your brain's ability to function as it should. In fact, eating right is absolutely essential to healthy mental function. For example, a recent study of twenty thousand people found that eating plenty of fruits and vegetables, getting regular exercise, drinking alcohol only in moderation, and not smoking adds fourteen years of life! Additionally, studies also found that eating a nutritionally poor diet is significantly associated with depression, sleep disorders, and poor quality of life. Have you noticed that ever since we started regularly eating calorie-dense, nutritionally void fast food products, our nation has been on a downward health spiral? Eat right. Your brain will thank you.

Toxic Stress

Toxicity in the brain is more common than you think. We live in a polluted environment and there are few places remaining in which we can breathe clean air, drink pure water, or walk on unadulterated soil. There are between fifty thousand and one hundred thousand synthetic chemicals in commercial production, and new synthetics are introduced at the average rate of three per day. We don't know how this chemical stew is impacting each of us, but the data strongly suggests that we're all vulnerable to neurological damage and even autoimmune reactions. Even something as innocuous as a new house frequently contains paints or carpets that give off invisible toxic gases. Many people develop sensitivities and their immune systems are compromised by histamine overreactions in the brain, resulting in a hyperresponsiveness to the environment—better known as allergies. Three fourths of the homes that are lived in today still have lead-based paint or lead pipes, which are well known to be a source of toxic poisoning.

We have also had an explosion of heavy metals such as lead, mercury, cadmium, and PCB-like flame-retardants in our environment as the result of people continuing to discard their old computer equipment irresponsibly. Texas alone will discard over fifty million TVs and PCs by 2009; and 70 percent of heavy metals in landfills come from this waste—which can lead to ground water contamination. Too many of these toxins can cause havoc in our brains.

Sleeplessness Stress

Sleeplessness stress is perhaps one of the biggest problems we have in our nation. We could probably blame Thomas Edison for inventing the light bulb and giving us more hours in the day to use for work and play. Today we have late-night television and twenty-four-hour access to the Internet—not to mention cell phones, so we never miss a call. Call them conveniences, but the fact remains that our brains were not engineered for this 24/7 schedule. Our brains need sleep time for very important reasons, one of which is to help store and organize the experiences of the day in such a way as to keep the processes running smoothly.

SUMMARIZING THE IMPLICATIONS

I can't tell you how valuable the new technologies are in identifying emotional problems. As I discussed earlier, diagnoses until recently have been based primarily on the art of therapy. This takes years of skill and training, as there can be a multitude of causes contributing to a problem. Further, not only is data reliability an issue, but the diagnostic categories can be confusing. These categories are defined (and redefined) periodically by a committee of known experts and published for the field as *Diagnostic and Statistical Manual of Mental Disorders* (DSM).

But with the technological advancement of brain mapping, scientists and laymen alike can finally get a leg up. Professionals and patients can now talk to each other in real terms, on a more level playing field, and reliability can be attained and a scientific foundation established for all.

This is an amazing feat. No longer are we left with only our best guess about what's going on in the brain. We can begin the process of changing the functioning of our brains and modifying the organizational abilities (brain plasticity). For example, the military has been studying the effects of post-traumatic stress disorder for years, and now we can evaluate it over time and determine the best treatment protocols for it. We can teach individuals better prevention practices as we understand the disease components better, and we can develop protocols for efficient evaluation as well as for modifying brain dynamics.

3

Brain Plasticity:
The Key to Your Best Future

The brain is truly the last frontier in understanding human nature—a grand and glorious mystery. With its amazing array of over one hundred billion intricate fibers and endless connections, this marvel still reduces even the most brilliant scientists to the humble admission that we haven't a clue how to replicate even its simplest functions. That being said, the brain is beginning to relinquish some of its secrets. Did you know the brain can *simultaneously* calculate 10^{24} bits of information? That gargantuan number (which is called both septillion and quadrillion) is a 1 with 24 zeros after it! Pretty impressive, to say the least.

Anyway, suffice it to say that we're still rather primitive when it comes to understanding how exactly the brain equips us to do the incredibly complex things we do as a matter of course. For example, our brain coordinates everything from walking and sitting down for breakfast to solving complex problems, enjoying a sunset, and bike riding. We're able to talk and listen (well, some better than others) to hundreds of thousands of sound vibrations; we perceive and understand millions of light waves coming into our retinas; we interpret the world around us; and we have a sense of justice and fairness that helps us live together.

So, somewhere along the line, one would think we'd come to the realization that we have a mind that goes beyond the mere confines of predetermined brain chemistry. Well, we have, and that time is now: we *do* have the ability to not only discover, but also invent who we are and who we become. We simply need to bring together the will and the way. If you're willing to commit to the former, I can supply you the tools for the latter.

It helps to take a quick look at the journey of brain plasticity from its rudimentary beginnings to appreciate how far we've come.

PIONEERING IDEAS

Born in 1891, a brilliant, pioneering brain surgeon and researcher named Dr. Wilder Penfield created the "brain maps" that we still use (virtually unaltered) today. He used simple electrical probes to gently stimulate different parts of the brain to see what would happen. For example, he would stimulate the motor strip at the top of a subject's head and an arm would fly up. He'd probe another area, and a leg would turn. His subjects were fully conscious during these procedures—that way, they could tell him what they were experiencing. For example, he'd touch a certain part of the temporal lobe, and the subject would start to cry or laugh. Another spot might stimulate the visions of various symbols or sounds. Fortunately (as I imagine you're curious), there are no pain receptors in the brain . . . so the subjects felt nothing.

Although Dr. Penfield never stipulated that brain maps were identical for every human being, some experts insisted this was the case. But they turned out to have been mistaken. For example, we now know that while the language region is located in the brain's left hemisphere in about 95 percent of right-handed people, 30 to 40 percent of left-handers' language region is located in the right hemisphere.

Brain plasticity is now recognized as scientific, evidence-based fact. Indeed, the brain has an amazing capacity for creating backup systems that can renew lost functions. And, if the brain comes to an impasse, *it can literally grow alternate routes.*

For those of us with weakened or damaged functions, being able to capitalize on our brain's flexibility opens up a whole new world of possibilities. For example, the brain of a person who has suffered a stroke damaging the language and speech regions—called Broca's area, located in the left frontal lobe—might compensate by rerouting language through an adjacent region, called the Ross area of the brain, usually located in the right hemisphere. This is an area that gets more activity when the Broca's center becomes less active, and it is considered to be the backup or compensating region for speech development. We have discovered the hidden treasures of what our minds can do if allowed to relearn. And since we are always remodeling our brain throughout life, these are within our reach.

From a neurochemical perspective, there is no difference between good and bad habits. Both result from the interplay of our neural networks—and that's good news. Why? That means we can fix things. This "fixin'" ability works through a two-part process: one, retrain or replace the networks we don't like; and two, reshelve that information in a different part of the brain. Bottom line? We need some regrouping and focused shaping expertise.

CAUTION: WRONG WAY

In reviewing the multitude of theories and applications in brain function rehabilitation, our profession had tried many wrong methods. Many of these practices are still being carried out today, and not surprisingly, they're rarely successful. Let me briefly summarize the worst of the worst, so that you'll know how to recognize them—and more important, know to steer clear of them:

Making the Worst of a Situation

Whenever you make a conscious decision that progress will not or cannot be made, you will always be proven right. You see, the brain acts upon whatever goals or intentions are placed there. Consider this exchange from *Alice's Adventures in Wonderland*:

ALICE: Would you tell me, please, which way I ought to go from here?

THE CAT: That depends a good deal on where you want to get to.

ALICE: I don't much care where—

THE CAT: Then it doesn't much matter which way you go.

ALICE: —so long as I get somewhere.

THE CAT: Oh, you're sure to do that, if only you walk long enough.

In the absence of any real goals or intentions, there will not be any progress in the brain function or—subsequently—any changes in behavior. This is sometimes referred to as a self-fulfilling prophecy. Conversely, as any successful athlete will tell you, positive intention and focus are essential to creating positive outcomes.

Hare Today, Gone Tomorrow

For real change with long-lasting success, the brain has to compile, rewire, and reshelve a plethora of new neural connections. To achieve this, the process must be done consistently over time, and at an even, unhurried, deliberate pace. Thus one of the secrets to learning a new language is to pronounce each word s-l-o-w-l-y enough so your brain can comprehend and appropriately process the meaning by the time you finish saying the word. For example, if you're trying to learn the Spanish word *corazon* (which means "heart"), you need to be sure you're consciously focused on both the word *and* meaning of "heart" by the time you finish enunciating "kor-ah-zaun." Over time, your brain's new language processes will quicken, stabilize, and stick. However, if you try to cram everything in as fast as you can, the processing is corrupted, and your brain won't hold on to the new information over the long haul. So be the tortoise, not the hare.

One Size Does Not Fit All

Different people learn differently. I learn best visually (as most men do). For me, writing down my lessons and drawing images works best. Women tend to learn best verbally. They can rapidly comprehend information and concepts by simply listening to the words (imagine that!). And still others learn best through color associations or stories. Brains vary as much as individuals do. So don't get discouraged by rigid theories about how you should learn; one size does *not* fit all. Different strokes for different folks, as the saying goes.

Structural Deficits Diminish Success

Many (many) years ago, when I was a mathematics teacher at a public school, my fellow teachers and I were very excited about the "new math." We thought that our students weren't interested in math because it was boring (too much memorizing and too repetitious). So instead we decided to emphasize the thinking behind the system, and deprioritize the routine memory effort. Well, while no one would outwardly admit this . . . it was a disaster. Most of the kids were unable to get the number system firmly seated in their brains with enough neurological framework for it to be useful. The hard-learned lesson was this: memory work needs to be done for developing the structural integrity of any system.

RANGE OF EMOTION: SUPPORT MATTERS

Working with the right coach is the most efficient way for the brain to learn. How so? A coach can optimize the brain's plasticity through continuous support and encouragement. It takes an extraordinary amount of effort to break through the bonds of old habits. Think of old habits as built-up scar tissue—thick, inflexible, and rigid—which limits your range of motion. Your job is to slowly, carefully, and deliberately break those bonds, so that you can create new, more fluid and desirable connections. This takes enormous motivation because it often hurts. A strong (but also caring) coach can provide the support you deserve to get through the ordeal of pain and frustration.

MEDICATION LIMITATIONS

Now that you're beginning to understand the concept that stress storms are caused mostly by a lack of balance in the levels of brain activity (and not the whole brain), it's probably easier to understand why psychotropic medications have their limitations. Research indicates that these drugs work by influencing the lower levels of the limbic system, which controls many of our emotions and motivations. Using medication alone is a lot like slowing down the traffic to unwind the chaos of a traffic jam. The tension may diminish for the time you use it, but the problem with the traffic pattern still persists.

That isn't to say that medication can't play a valuable role. It may indeed be both wise and prudent to slow the traffic in order to slow down the chaos and build new pathways in the brain. Medications are tremendous tools that should be used as building blocks—just not necessarily as solutions in and of themselves.

BRAIN PLASTICITY PRINCIPLES

Don't think you can understand brain plasticity methodology? You absolutely can. I've studied it extensively, read the scientific literature, and applied the methodological principles with my own patients. And you know what? As is often the case with things that are undeniably true, once the premise and concepts are broken down, they make perfect sense. These principles are important to understand because when we can comprehend the potential power available to us, it provides a strong motivation to begin applying their truths to our everyday lives. As you read the following, I'd like you to begin thinking about how you might embark on your own personal challenges in brain plasticity, especially in regard to alleviating stress storms. Perhaps you'll see a specific plan for modifying your own neurological network you hadn't considered before—one that can help you to conquer the unique set of problems you face.

Principle I: Neurons that learn together become attached.

In certain savvy scientific circles, they have a saying: neurons that fire together, wire together. Indeed, as the latest technological advances have clearly shown, the more often two or more neural conduits share common frequency patterns, the more they can combine into common activities, including thinking patterns. This is the very basis for habit formation—both good habits and bad ones. (It's also the basis for coordination of body components such as muscles and organs.) Remembering that the brain produces electromagnetic frequencies in one of four general ranges (delta, theta, alpha, beta), and since they produce energy in the form of waveforms (depending on the intensity of the amplitudes), there is a way of measuring how the neuron firing is either building up or losing power collectively across the collective grouping. When you measure two or more neurological frequencies at the same time, you can actually see how the waves are similar to each other, which is measured as "coherence" to each other. (See figure 3.1.) The more coherence, the more collective power to create a mutual thought or habit. Now, in EEG terms, when we see similarities in frequency waveforms, we call them *coherence patterns*. In figure 3.1 below, the two neural patterns are correlated at 0.99—which is an impressively high coherence number!

As the neurological pathways merge, they also collect other neurons, which build and refine as they develop the most efficient pathway that can be generated. This process will continue to build neurological strength as long as it is appropriately reinforced. And let's hope the habit being reinforced isn't destructive, because as we discussed earlier, breaking those bonds can be a difficult and painful process.

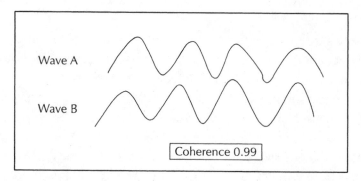

FIGURE 3.1

Coaching Is Fundamental to the Process

There's a system that all great coaches utilize when developing fundamental skills in their team members. When I was coaching basketball, I studied the great basketball coaches—which I define as those coaches who had good teams consistently throughout the years, regardless of the talent they started with at the beginning of each season. Their methods were consistent with Principle I. The three steps of developing excellent basketball skills (as well as other types of skills) are as follows:

1. Demonstrate and create a visual image of the desired skill.
2. Practice, practice, practice.
3. Celebrate success with positive feedback (and then repeat steps 1, 2, and 3).

In practical terms, I would show the student what I wanted him or her to do; and whenever I wasn't the best example (which was often the case when it came to basketball) I would ask another athlete who excelled at this skill to demonstrate, and/or show films of superstars performing this skill. I wanted them to see the whole-body motion and have solid imagery seated in their minds before they attempted to develop this new ability. Why? This is the initial stage that gets the nerves primed to start actively communicating with each other.

A multitude of sports psychology research studies have found that when students see techniques demonstrated before attempting them, those who grasp a clear image of the technique excel at it. The same principle holds true for training airplane pilots and automobile drivers. Even greater rewards are achieved if your initial success results in your receiving consistent, positive reinforcement. This further confirms (and begins to embed) the desired new behavior pattern, which, with consistent practice and ongoing positive reinforcement, develops into a natural reflex—and that's the goal.

Imagine That

The implementation of this type of imagery has also been used successfully in helping alcohol addicts. For example, I've worked with groups of individuals who'd been diagnosed with substance abuse. I had them imagine situations in which they were more apt to abuse alcohol, such as being frustrated with authority, interpersonal conflicts, and periods of low self-esteem. I encouraged them to consider the specifics of each potentially vulnerable situation and imagine what constructive steps they might take that would help foster a positive outcome. They were asked to do this mental exercise for no less than three scenarios.

Next, each of these individuals verbally walked through his (or her) imagined scenarios with the group members; and it was the group's responsibility to ensure that no details, no matter how small, were left out. For example, if a person imagined calling a friend or sponsor, he or she would be asked what the number was, the person's name, whose phone, what type of phone, what would be said, what the expected response would be, and so on. The individual would continue to retell the scenario until all details were rehearsed and complete clarity was achieved.

At the conclusion of each session, everyone would have written down his or her own three options in response to the scenarios and committed those plans to memory. This approach was a success with over 90 percent of the participants in the recovery process. If you suffer from substance abuse, this is a technique you may want to try.

Clearly, the principle of brain plasticity has profound implications for effectively dealing with problems or potential issues. I call this process *making a plan*. It may sound simple, but that's the point. We all need clear, simple plans to better handle chaos and unexpected situations. Now you have one.

Principle II: Experience and need can change neurological bundles.

There are three processes that are basic to all brain plasticities, and as simple as they are, an understanding of them can prove revolutionary. The first is the process of dispersion or disruption, which must occur in our nerve patterns prior to assimilating new information. As you now know, it's exceedingly difficult to break habits that are neurologically or behaviorally motivated merely by announcing a desire to do so. Smokers will attest to the experience of consistently meeting failure when attempting to break the smoking habit. Similarly, it's difficult to stop overreacting to your spouse when in conflict, or to stop obsessively worrying about your children when you've had so many reinforcing years of practice. As a psychotherapist for over forty years, I can also assure you that simply asking people to change their ways is rarely if ever successful. As the old psychology joke goes, "How many psychologists does it take to change a light bulb?" The answer: The light bulb has to *want* to change.

Disrupting Behaviors

Over the years, psychiatrists have used a number of disruptive techniques, such as electroshock therapy and insulin-induced coma—the latter being discontinued because of unacceptable medical complications. In other cultures, disruptive techniques included drowning or choking a person to induce a coma. For example, in Egypt and Ireland, something known as a "purposeful ritual" was observed, in which a person would be placed underwater until his "transformation" into a more spiritually minded individual was complete—which seems more than a little risky, if you ask me. Dr. August Reader, an expert in the field, has theorized as to why this seemingly barbaric process is actually quite effective at promoting change.

To summarize what happens: in reaction to the shock of possible drowning, the brain shunts blood into different parts of the brain, based on a priority system of immediate needs. The first area is the need for survival, in which the person experiences a barrage of information from the past, including a life review. Once the brain believes that death is inevitable, it reserves its remaining energy for relaxing and preparing for a transition, including such experiences as hearing or seeing angels.

The next step is particularly fascinating. In the final phase of the physical response to the ritual (the one we hear most reports about) is a message—since you're probably not going to survive—of what you might have done to benefit the world and those you love. If you are then brought back to this reality and somehow escape death, this last phase of philosophy appears to have a lasting effect. For example, this frequently leads to spiritual enlightenment, which compels some to dramatically reinvent their lives as missionaries or messengers of spiritual truths regarding death and beyond. This step also explains why some people choose to devote the rest of their lives to humanitarian causes and selfless behavior. I have no idea why or when these stages occur, or what an EKG machine would show, but despite the intriguing results, I don't recommend this disruptive process at all. The risks are too great. Nevertheless, the changes in brain activities have been noted for centuries.

Altered States

A related (but enormously safer) process for disrupting brain activity is the practice of *altered states of consciousness,* in which your conscious awareness of reality is changed subjectively or psychologically. The most comprehensive—and most complicated—definition is a pattern of physiological and subjective responses (cortical and autonomic), which shift with changes in imagery, ideation, and fantasies. These disruptions are generally anticipated and embraced in an effort to find preferable thinking habits.

Historically, altered states of consciousness have been orchestrated by some of the following means:

- Sensory deprivation (solitary experiences, such as vision quests and confinement, extreme boredom, sensory deprivation chambers)
- Overstimulation (hyperventilation, firewalker's trance, shamanistic trances, free association in confrontation with fear)
- Profound relaxation (hypnosis, mystical inductions, sonic rhythms)
- Direct commands and sudden distractions (crisis, sudden commands, direction to different activities and duties)

The direct consequences of disruption are essentially short time-outs between points of powering up again. During the brief suspension of activity, many of the following states have been reported:

- Alterations of thinking
- Disturbed time sense

- Loss of control
- Shift in emotional expression
- Changing perceptions of self and reality
- Feelings of rejuvenation
- Hypersuggestibility

You know how sometimes you "can't stop thinking" or feel like you "can't shut your brain off"? Well, now you understand the futility of depending on your will alone to disrupt immediately the neurological patterns underlying your thinking, as in the case of stress storms. However, you now have some new resources and techniques (although the drowning ploy is off the table). But really, you can begin the process, even though at first it only works for a short period. You can stop drinking for a day. You can stop gambling and searching for porn. You can even stop obsessively washing your hands. You can engage your brain in new and better habits and behaviors.

Principle III: Suspension of thoughts or elimination of specific experience can allow neurological changes to happen immediately.

Based on the tremendous contributions of Dr. Michael Merzenich, who in my opinion has championed brain plasticity with his foundational research, we now know that when you eliminate or diminish a function, even a thought pattern, the neurological networks of other functions will grab the newly available space and incorporate the extra storage into their areas. Think of a glass filled with water that has one ice cube. The moment you remove the ice cube, the water fills in the available space. Brain neurons compete for space (and attention) as well.

Although this is a less than pleasant example (warning: it's gross), one of the outstanding experiments that Dr. Merzenich conducted was to assess the cluster of neurons that activated a monkey's right-hand middle finger. He amputated this finger, and waited a month to see what would happen. To his surprise, when he evaluated the brain neurons, he found that although the middle finger was missing, the neuron clusters relating to that finger had been taken over by the two adjoining fingers. In the case of the monkey, he developed compensating abilities in those fingers that remained. Similarly, people who go blind develop higher abilities in hearing, smell, and touch.

The implications are huge. For example, if you had a stroke and could no longer use your preferred hand, practicing with the other hand long enough would result in your being able to "transfer the intelligence" to learn to write or throw with the other hand. There are many examples of people who relearn to talk and listen from completely different parts of the original neural clusters.

Changing behavior can work this way, too. For example, if a person has always used aggressive behavior to express his rage, you can teach him to express it with words and alternative behavior that resolve his emotional conflicts more successfully. This shift in behavior stimulates different nerve patterns. A mother can learn not to scream at her children in a futile attempt to gain control of their behavior. The change in reflexive behaviors, like screaming and rages, shifts the brain wiring. A boss can learn there are far better ways of "motivating" his workers than by using harsh words and fear tactics. In spite of the myth, old dogs can learn new tricks—if you know how to change the brain patterns. Learning how to redirect them (which I'll show you how to do through the exercises) is the key to taking any other therapies or self-help to a new level.

Principle IV: Times of growth and change are opportunities for learning and relearning.

Learning in the brain, whether for motor skills or emotions, is not a continuous process. It starts and stops rather abruptly with the biochemical dispersion of brain growth factors (thank you, Nobel Prize recipients Rita Levi-Montalcini and Stanley Cohen). Brain growth factors turn on the nucleus basalis and coat each neuron with a rich, fatty substance that "lubricates" it and speeds up the learning process exponentially. As I just said, it doesn't stay turned on forever: when it shuts down, the whole system slows back to a stable pace. The question of why it slows down abruptly has to do with lack of attention and positive reinforcement.

Intention and Attention

Our concern is how to turn this process on. In the plasticity of the brain, the experts agree that attention and intention are vital to the critical stages of learning or relearning. Unfortunately, you can't learn much without trying. And no, listening to CDs that claim you can learn foreign languages while you're asleep won't actually work. (Wish it would.) The truth is, although technically your brain is always awake, that process neither has your intention nor your attention to create the necessary neural networks.

Plus, not only do you have to have clear intention, you have to be excited about what you are doing. This emotional edge is what provides you the vitality to open up the door. Being emotionally invested (in a jazzed, positive way) helps get your brain prepped, too. (No wonder I never made a grade above a C in History— I hated that class.)

Many foods have been implicated in increasing learning curves, and I have found this approach to have high impact, whether it is for better control or actual growth factor influence. High protein (as in eggs and meat), omega-3 and omega-6 (as in fish), and some complex carbohydrates have some pretty meaningful research supporting their usefulness in this regard.

Another very powerful stimulation is rhythmic stimulation, such as music and drumming. The brain is sensitive to external rhythmic vibrations of any kind, and as we will learn, the frequencies of the brain can be driven with such intention. This is the stuff of neurological training, and it requires finding the right personal sonic stimulation for your brain.

Principle V: New pathways can be changed and improved.

Frustration often rears its ugly head when you observe a new behavior (such as showing respect or making good, positive choices in stressful situations) and a month later you see the old stuff come flooding back again. This is a problem in therapy. You see a patient once a week—which is just enough time for the person to go back to the old habits you were trying to change in the first place. So, once you stop your old destructive response and create a better one, how do you learn to live it?

Practice. It takes practice and time for your brain to reorganize itself around your newfound insights. All the insight in the world can't help you create and sustain a new life in the absence of practice. I remember a famous golfer who was asked how it felt to get paid for playing a hobby. He replied, "You see me today, swinging my club maybe a total of three hundred times. What you *didn't* see is me practicing each shot over a hundred thousand times during my early training years." The incredible basketball great Michael Jordan would practice shooting the same shot from the same place ten thousand times. Potential is one attribute, persistence is another.

Here's the thing: everyone has the potential to change his or her brain plasticity—and that's amazing! You have to follow a plan, and to make it last, you have to practice. But it works! You have the real ability to reorganize your neural networks. This process of birthing new connections even has a cool name: it's called neurogenesis.

Positive Reinforcement and Attention

When I was a resident at the New York Medical Center, Friday mornings meant seminars with guest speakers. I remember this guy named Neal Miller walking in and telling us how he could change the blood flow in one ear of a rat while keeping the flow in the other ear constant by electrically stimulating the enjoyment center of the rat's brain. He called this process *biofeedback*. And although the professional application has changed for humans since, the approach has been validated in brain plasticity. This is simply the rule that *you need to enjoy what you're doing in order to establish a brain shift, and that enjoyment can be defined psychologically as a positive reinforcement.*

The brain needs to experience positive reinforcement in making these changes in order for them to be fully integrated into the system. Dr. Miller discussed how he electrically stimulated the "happiness center" whenever the rat behaved in the desired way. (I'd like to know where that place might be in my old brain so I can get to it.) Giving treats as rewards stimulates the "happy place" with dogs. And I can teach myself new approaches to life's problems by enjoying social acceptance from my family—or I could use tasty treats on myself (yes, that would work!).

The problem is that we often forget this important—and very real—cycle. We cram for an exam at the last minute, and in short order, forget everything we learned because we didn't add the zing of positive reinforcement necessary for sustainability. Think about it. We make our children learn the multiplication tables without so much as a smile, only fear of failure. And then we wonder why they can't learn them quicker. The brain opens up to new learning when we use this powerful approach.

Relaxation Cycles

Just as we have forgotten the value of joy in the process of new learning and brain plasticity, we've also lost the value of relaxation. We try to shove information and belief systems down the throats of our children. Real behavioral changes and new ways of thinking don't stick that way. It takes thirty-six hours of restoration, on the average, for a concept to be integrated into the whole system—and that's only if you've taken restorative breaks along the way. Certainly you can learn a concept in a few minutes. But it takes far longer for it to become fully integrated.

When I was coaching basketball, I knew that the most vulnerable time for establishing a failure in athletic skills was in the practice and restorative time. This is when self-evaluation happens, and if you're not successful as quickly as you want to be, that's a potential problem. This is also the critical time for emotional states such as depression and anxiety, for the same reason. When you fail to make a shot with a basketball, the first response from most people is: "I must be doing it wrong." The next failure results in "I am so stupid—why can't I do this?" and the kicker is, "I am not good at this and am giving up."

When you take away the positive response and invite the demon of self-criticism, you will incorporate that message into your imagery and into your life. The same process happens with changing fear and addictions. If you deem yourself a failure, you practice being a failure. This is the time to step it up and reroute the whole process. Otherwise, your brain pathways will be sealing negative patterns (which you'll need to break), instead of sealing positive ones, which make you happy and assure long-term success.

I can't urge you strongly enough to embrace and implement this last step in redefining your brain pattern. As the saying goes in bathroom etiquette, you ain't through until the paperwork is done.

DIRECTING YOUR OWN INTERVENTION

The purpose of this chapter was to introduce the enormous potential that brain plasticity holds for you as you take an active role in developing the brain bundles you need to support the life you want to live. You don't have to resign yourself to your stress storms—you can choose a different way. I've mentioned just a few of the metabolic factors that you can decide (at this very moment) to avoid or change. You can protect yourself against toxicity, addictions, and bad food for your brain. If you want to, you can build a safety region for how you live, so your brain can function at top speed.

This is a self-paced program, so if you have special traps and want to spend more time in any stress profile, I've provided extra steps to give you more in-depth skills and abilities to turn it around. I will show you how. Be honest with yourself, and assess your problems as you see them. Through direct interventions in your life, you can resolve stress and create new paths for personal growth—leading you out of the storm and into a better future.

4

The Anxiety Patterns of Confusion and Fear

Charles was a very nervous man. He came to my clinic at the age of twenty-five, seeking help with his ambivalence about possibly returning to college to study law. Charles worried about everything from global warming to what he should eat for breakfast. I don't believe he knew (at least not consciously) how nervous he was; he'd simply always felt that way. Charles's parents were highly educated, ambitious people who were greatly enamored of politics. His father, George, was a successful small-town physician, who aspired to become governor of the state. His mother, Mary, was a middle school principal, who invested a considerable amount of her time in various town organizations, often functioning as president.

Charles was a middle child with an older sister, Fran (a *full* three years older, as she often reminded him), who prided herself on having the highest grades in her class, as well as being the most beautiful girl in the school. She thought of Charles as bad baggage for her social life, and although she would on occasion (when it suited her) try to help him with his studies, she usually gave up quickly, labeling him a "waste of her time."

Charles's younger sister, Crystal (two years younger), was far kinder. She played with him endlessly and encouraged him to keep plugging away at his studies. However, Crystal had a rebellious streak and a mischievous nature, which often led her to unfairly pin blame on Charles when she got caught.

Charles had difficulties in school, and was pronounced as

having attention deficit/hyperactivity disorder by age eight. He was placed on the stimulant Adderall (a commonly prescribed ADHD medication) because he couldn't concentrate on school assignments. As Charles began his regimen on the brain-stimulating drug, he felt better about himself, and his school grades improved. But along with the increased energy came the complications of high blood pressure. Soon he was on three drugs: a brain stimulant for his ADHD, a antihypertensive medication for his blood pressure, and an antidepressant because he often experienced sadness and cried about being lonely for extended periods of time.

CHARLES'S QUIET DESPERATION

As time passed, Charles sank into an attitude of quiet desperation. He eventually stopped taking his medication at the age of thirteen, because it no longer seemed to be helpful and it made him feel numb. He found some friends who accepted him for who he apparently was: a slow, shy kid who knew a lot about cars and engines.

In terms of his family interactions, the more his father advanced his political career, the less time he spent with Charles; and the other members of the family seemed to be on another planet. Charles would usually choose to stay at home while the rest of the family went to various campaign events—maintaining that the events bored him. Truth be told, he felt he wasn't exactly a poster child for a successful potential governor. He also felt his parents were ashamed of him. And, frankly, on some levels, they were.

Charles did get his high school diploma, but there was little (if any) joy in his accomplishment. His grades were low. He advanced no farther than third-chair baritone in the band; but he did belong to the hot rod club. Fully aware his family saw him as a disappointment, he decided to join the armed services instead of attending college. This may have been the best choice he could have made for himself.

BE ALL THAT YOU CAN BE . . . FOR A WHILE, ANYWAY

Charles was accepted into the Army. He'd lied about having ADHD because he'd heard that might prevent his acceptance. (As a brief aside, the armed services do currently allow people with ADHD to serve; however, they cannot be on ADHD medication.) Becoming a soldier proved to be an enormously wise and valuable decision for Charles, as he experienced true pride in his ongoing military accomplishments. He excelled in the challenges they put him through, and he found himself becoming a leader. His self-esteem grew every day, and he finally saw new possibilities for his life . . . possibilities that he actually liked!

Then, he got shot in the leg during the Iraq War, which abruptly ended his service career. He was offered a discharge upon his (physical) recovery. I suspect his discharge was hastened because of the way Charles had been acting: he was exhibiting strong symptoms of post-traumatic stress disorder (PTSD).

Without his sense of accomplishment from military service to prop him up, Charles began to feel anxiety in a pronounced way, suffering with vivid nightmares about his combat experiences. Although he didn't have the usual flashbacks of PTSD, he was very nervous and was hyperaware of his surroundings. He constantly scrutinized the environment around him, as if some threat was waiting just around the corner. It wasn't so much that he was fearful per se, but rather, he'd been well trained to survey all situations in detail. Regardless of how well the PTSD diagnosis may have fit, the experience heightened the stress storm pattern already residing in his mind; and he again began to find it difficult to maintain his focus and concentration, just as he had when he was a boy.

CHARLES TAKES CONTROL

Despite the trauma of his injury and the disappointment of his discharge, Charles was still able to access—albeit not consistently—some of the self-confidence he'd gained in the service, which undoubtedly helped him embrace his desire to set new goals. He chose law school possibly in an attempt to make some kind of a connection with and/or gain the approval of his father. This question remains unanswered; but regardless, he felt this was something at which he could excel. It was at this particular juncture that Charles appeared at our clinic door, asking for help with "the storms in his brain."

Charles did have storms, but not ADHD or PTSD. He was having *anxiety*—which is my clinic's terminology for the constant barrage of chaotic noise the brain makes when it's in a highly stressful and fearful state. To put it plainly, overstimulation of the nervous system makes it hard for the brain to pay attention and maintain focus. It's like trying to listen to an orchestra play while someone is shooting guns next door, while at the same time, someone else is whispering in your ear demanding your full attention.

Charles's brain displayed classic anxiety activity, which happens when the brain's beta waves are way too high too often. In other words, his brain showed the random, chaotic, persistent waves that are typical of waveforms conducting small bits of information. In essence, Charles was in a constant state of anxiety that grew from fears dating back to his childhood.

CHARLES IN CHARGE

Charles learned several ways to battle his anxiety. We taught him how to use biofeedback as a way of learning how to breathe more effectively. He learned that he was breathing at twice the rate of most healthy people. In fact, that accelerated breathing pattern alone is enough to deleteriously impact a person's brain, as it can erroneously activate surges of chaotic fear. Fortunately, by learning how to modify his breathing, Charles discovered he could think more clearly and reduce his sense of anxiety, not to mention increase his attention span as he gave his brain more oxygen and better pacing.

One of the tools Charles used to help modify his breathing patterns is a device called an *emWave*. This device showed him how to regulate his breathing to stay within the range necessary for maximum efficiency in brain activity. Another key benefit of staying within this optimal range is that it also helps lower depression. Another device, called the *BAUD* (Bio-Acoustical Utilization Device)—which enhances one's ability to master biofeedback— enabled him to train his brain to convert his overly high beta waves into low beta waves with increased efficiency. In Charles's case, his biofeedback self-regulation capabilities increased by 300 percent.

Charles also successfully embraced a type of therapy called *cognitive psychotherapy,* which focused on his perceptions and interpretations, and utilized techniques such as imagery and self-guided instruction (which I'll introduce you to later in this chapter) to help him become aware of what role he played in undermining himself. He was able to address his self-esteem issues and his internal dialogue, as well as the mixed feelings he harbored about his family. His hard work paid off, as he found a place in his heart to forgive his family; he also gained a newfound appreciation for why his family believed they were giving him what they thought he needed. And in so doing, Charles grew emotionally stronger, and his new brain waves confirmed as much.

So how did it ultimately turn out for Charles? He did extremely well in his law school endeavors, passing the bar with the third-highest score in his class. He continues to be a remarkable young man with a very fine mind, who now knows how to quiet the lightning strikes in his head, so that he can better listen to his heart and soul.

ANXIETY DEFINED

Anxiety is defined in the *Diagnostic and Statistical Manual* of the American Psychiatric Association as a state of consciousness in which a person worries excessively—without having the ability to control it. Restlessness, being easily fatigued, difficulty breathing and concentrating, irritability, muscle tension, and disturbed sleep patterns often accompany this state. Anxiety can also be the basis for other syndromes, such as inordinate concern with health issues (hypochondriasis), phobias, and obsessive-compulsive disorders.

Anxiety is considered to be a human condition. Why? Because 70 percent of adults say they experience it daily, and 30 percent report their anxiety levels are constant. Anxiety is crucial to our survival (you've probably heard of "fight or flight") as well as to our socialization. So clearly, not all anxiety is bad. In fact, many people successfully use anxiety as a form of motivation to achieve higher goals, e.g., they look forward to experiencing a profound sense of relief once they've accomplished their goal. Anxiety, then, can serve you well—or it can seriously get in your way.

Anxiety has been associated with several psychological diagnoses. It can be the underlying denominator of obsessive-compulsive disorder, post-traumatic stress disorder, panic, phobias, and multiple personality disorder. Anxiety can also trigger various other personality disorders, such as borderline personality and dependency disorders. The storms that trigger borderline personality disorders can become dangerous and have resulted in violent crimes, domestic abuse, homicide, and suicide. So while this disorder has a benign-sounding name, it's anything but.

That being said, anxiety doesn't have to become a threat to your identity, your progress, or to anyone else for that matter. You *absolutely can* get past the anxiety brain storm. Here's what's going on in the anxiety-filled brain: Fears and stress trigger an anxiety storm in your brain—which in turn creates chaos that your brain tries to resolve, but can't. Instead, it just lingers there, endlessly spinning, with surges of raw shocks. In psychological terms, that means you're in a chronic (which means constant) state of anxiety. Also, there don't have to be any obvious external sources of stress in your life for your brain to be on "spin." In fact, anxiety brain patterns can be generated by merely worrying or stewing about what might have happened in the past, or what you think might happen in the future. Fear begets fear.

Can't Keep a Thought in Your Head?

Do you ever feel when you're stressed out that you just can't keep a thought in your head? You'll probably be relieved to learn that when someone is in that state, it's *very common* to feel like you just can't stay focused (loss of concentration), as well as to experience diminished memory capacity. That's cortisol making you feel stupid—a hormone that your adrenal gland produces under stress. So, you're not losing your mind, you're not alone . . . and you *can* do something about it. Good to know, yes?

Trick Question

When I'm giving a talk on stress storms, there's a trick question I sometime use to illustrate a point: holding a small glass of water in my hand, I ask the group, "How much do you think this weighs?" Some people make guesses such as two ounces, one hundred milliliters, and so forth, and others try to calculate the volume using mathematical equations. But they're all mistaken. The answer is, it's a matter of time. The longer I hold it, the heavier it will feel. It's the same with anxiety and stress.

RAGE AND ANXIETY PATTERNS

Much the same way that anxiety triggers your brain circuitry to get stuck on a fear and stress treadmill, rage and violence trigger an immediate action without rational processing. When a person's brain is smoldering with hot high beta waves, it only takes a tiny spark of heightened arousal (like misplacing a pencil, or seeing someone we dislike) to set off an illogical, full-blown rage.

This counterproductive brain pattern can get so tightly locked, it becomes very difficult for the person to justify his behavior to himself (or to anyone else). Plus, the person becomes unable to gain control or glean any insight as to why he's reacting this way—which of course increases his level of agitation (and everyone else's, too). In my experience, as long as your brain storm is dictating how you think, all of the insight, education, and psychotherapy in the world will only get you so far. To truly get off the treadmill, you need to unlock the brain storm door. But first, you have to see the door. And that's the first step.

When using a QEEG brain map, patterns are very easy to see. Figure 4.1A shows a frontal lobe brain wave pattern. See how it's raging with high and chaotic beta activity. That's a high beta anxiety storm. Figure 4.1B is what a low beta wave pattern looks like.

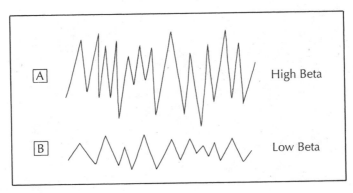

FIGURE 4.1

Figure 4.2 illustrates what a brain in a chaotic state looks like, when measured as electromagnetic frequencies. It doesn't take a rocket scientist to see that this person's brain isn't functioning at optimal levels. And the longer and more stress this brain has to endure, the more often the lightning will strike.

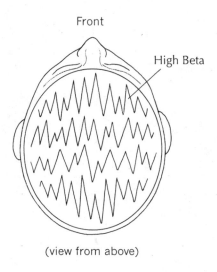

Front

High Beta

(view from above)

FIGURE 4.2

BRAIN SELF-AUDIT

While having a professional electroencephalogram performed is ideal, you can conduct a fairly good assessment on yourself based on certain behavior patterns (if you're honest with yourself). Below is a list of symptoms. Using a pencil, please indicate to what extent each symptom *currently exists at this time* in your life by circling the appropriate letter: (A) always present, (S) sometimes present, or (R) rarely present.

BEHAVIORAL SYMPTOMS OF THE ANXIETY BRAIN PATTERN

Symptom	Always	Sometimes	Rarely
1. I get frustrated easily with others.	(A)	(S)	(R)
2. I can't concentrate because I am anxious.	(A)	(S)	(R)
3. I feel as if I am going to explode from fear.	(A)	(S)	(R)
4. I don't sleep well.	(A)	(S)	(R)
5. I don't express my feelings clearly.	(A)	(S)	(R)
6. I worry a lot, even when there is no cause to.	(A)	(S)	(R)
7. I fly into a rage with very little reason.	(A)	(S)	(R)
8. I feel that I am on the brink of panic.	(A)	(S)	(R)
9. I feel fatigued so much that I can't work.	(A)	(S)	(R)
10. I can't shake the feeling that something will happen that I will not be prepared for.	(A)	(S)	(R)
11. I am too tense to enjoy things and activities.	(A)	(S)	(R)
12. No matter how hard I try to stop dealing with my life in destructive ways such as blowing up or withdrawing, I never feel that I cope well.	(A)	(S)	(R)
13. I keep reacting to the same obstacles in ways that do not get me what I want.	(A)	(S)	(R)
14. I think that I am a very mixed-up person.	(A)	(S)	(R)
15. I think I am always reacting instead of making conscious choices in my behavior.	(A)	(S)	(R)
Totals	_____	_____	_____

Scoring: Total up each column to determine how many A's, S's, and R's you had. If you circled (A) Always for seven or more of the items above, you probably have an anxiety pattern in your brain. If you circled three of the items as (A) Always, and eight as (S) Sometimes, you may not have the entire pattern locked in, but you probably have long periods when your brain is in anxiety mode.

OKAY, NOW WHAT?

If you want to prevent (or at least minimize) your anxiety brain patterns so that you can make better choices and live a happier life, then the next steps are for you. First, I'll explain each principle, and then I'll give you exercises you can do right now. You can also teach someone else how to identify his or her storms (depending upon the person's receptivity) and help them practice the following exercises, too. For optimal benefit, having your child(ren), spouse, or other loved ones participate in these exercises with you is even better.

The following are the DSM designated names of emotional problems and mental disorders that exhibit anxiety brain storm patterns.

Phobias

Compulsive thoughts

General anxiety

Post-traumatic stress disorder (PTSD)

Panic attacks

Acute stress disorder

Attention deficit/hyperactivity disorder (ADD/ADHD)

UNCHAIN YOUR BRAIN: LEARNING TO COPE WITH ANXIETY

Just as Charles did, you can restore your brain's capacity to engage in healthy thinking patterns. In fact, not only can the following exercises dramatically help to diminish your anxiety, but some of the positive effects are immediate. Is there a catch? Absolutely. As I already shared with you in chapter three, time, pacing, practice, and long-term commitment must occur if any of the changes are going to stick. Bearing in mind that patient repetition is the key to learning, we are going to keep revisiting our principles of brain plasticity as we examine strategies for coping with the many varieties of stress.

Principle I: Neurons that learn together become attached.

Listen to the Music

The best way to stop my brain from getting stuck in anxiety is to turn on some music, preferably selected songs in my iPod, but in a pinch, the radio will do (it just requires some station surfing). The tempo and melody of my favorite songs can dial my stress levels down to manageable emotions in about fifteen minutes. Some of my personal favorites (if you're curious) are Mozart, Cher, and Simon and Garfunkel. What type of music will help you relax depends on your personality. Whatever your musical preference, research clearly shows that self-selected relaxing music significantly reduces anxiety and nervous system arousal. For me, I can almost see the neurons begin to join a chorus in the alpha zone. Also, if you can play an instrument in a way that you find soothing, the research shows that's a great stress/anxiety reducer too.

I can't tell you how many patients have jump-started their brains by listening to "When the Saints Come Marching In" and "Amazing Grace." I used to work with patients who were diagnosed with cancer, and there was always a depression and anxiety that naturally (and very understandably) halted them in their tracks. Just the thought of having cancer became a massive roadblock to their plans and dreams. Plus, the dreaded treatments could be excruciatingly exhausting, wearing them down to the point where they became stuck in their anxiety and were unable to think beyond their fears. All of these walls could be transcended with a rousing jazz anthem or powerful spiritual, leading to transforming attitudes and healthy responses.

Move to the Beat

The body likes rhythmic, soothing movement. Yoga and tai chi are particularly effective in getting your motor neurons "hooked up" with feeling soothed. And of course, dancing is great (. . . if you have rhythm).

As a required part of therapy, I always have my anxious patients dance with my drumming CD, which I call *Life Rhythms,* as part of their homework. This requirement has also been especially effective for medical students who are so anxiety-filled that they start failing their classes, even when they understand the topics being taught. Without exception, they report that moving to the beat helps them to feel "different and better" and clearly not as fearful the first week; by the second week, they turn the corner and find new directions for their lives. Incidentally, this CD is a basic home-made recording of some continuous conga drums and a few other acoustical instruments I have around the house, but unsophisticated as it is, it works. If you're so inclined, try making your own tape! Otherwise, finding a rhythmic tape is a snap these days: just go online and search.

BAUD-Assisted Neurotherapy

The Bio-Acoustical Utilization Device (BAUD) can be calibrated to emit sonic frequencies that can shift your brain levels. As you listen to the frequencies emitted by the BAUD, you can measure wave levels taken from the EEG readings and find those sound waves that stimulate the brain to shift to the desired levels and to calmer waveforms, such as alpha or low beta. These changes can be very notable in cases where the brain is producing high, unusable frequencies, as in a stress storm. As the participant learns to control the sonic output of the BAUD, he also gains control of his brain levels and in so doing learns to control the anxiety produced by the brain activities. The advantage of using the BAUD is the speed with which a person can learn to control these functions and discern the differences. Even children can usually accomplish this control in thirty minutes. The experience can be very rewarding.

Take Deep, Cleansing Breaths

There are over two thousand organs and hormones that can be affected positively or negatively in a matter of minutes by shifting your breathing patterns. Taking quick, shallow breaths usually signals to the brain that a threat exists, which stimulates a stress response, and therefore establishes destructive thinking patterns. Conversely, taking slow, deep breaths usually signals to your brain that the coast is clear and all is well.

Of course, we rarely (if ever) want to inflict destructive thinking patterns on ourselves—they are created involuntarily. The best model I've found to calm the storms is a technique I call *circle breath*. The name comes from the idea of keeping a steady exchange of air inhaling and exhaling, thereby creating a circle of airflow through the lungs. This is done in a relaxed manner utilizing imagery, such as inhaling while visualizing good nurturing air coming into your body and mind . . . and then exhaling while thinking about releasing your inner toxins and unhealthy mental habits out into the ether. Poof! They're gone.

Until you master this technique (which I'll walk you through below), you may find it beneficial to have someone coach you through this breathing pattern. Why? It can be difficult (at first) to maintain concentration and focus while you're experiencing an anxiety stress storm. Another really good method is to record yourself reading the transcript I'm about to share with you, so that you can listen to your own voice soothing yourself. For optimal benefits, do the following exercise in twenty-minute intervals, ideally twice a day, thus totaling forty minutes.

TRANSCRIPT FOR BREATHING TECHNIQUE TO DEAL WITH ANXIETY BRAIN PATTERNS

Choose a place where you can be comfortable and won't be disturbed. The best places may even be in your closet or bathroom. Turn off your cell phone, and be nowhere near a computer or a television. Get into a position that requires as little gravity resistance as possible—you need all of your attention focused on your breathing, so you don't want to have to do any shifting around. This usually means a prone position, but you can also achieve the pattern by sitting in a very comfortable chair or lying on your back.

As you begin the breathing exercises, I want you to slowly close your eyes. This helps you to concentrate better and note the differences in your body and brain. Take a deep breath and hold it for a second, and let it out now in a very even flow of air as I count to seven. 1–2–3–4–5–6–7. Good, now, breathe in to the same count. 1–2–3–4–5–6–7. Now out, 1–2–3–4–5–6–7, now in, 1–2–3–4–5–6–7. Now out, 1–2–3–4–5–6–7, now in, 1–2–3–4–5–6–7, out. While you are breathing out, let yourself feel more relaxed and let go of any stress with your breath. Now in, breathing in the good things that heal you and make you stronger. Now out, 1–2–3–4–5–6–7, now in, 1–2–3–4–5–6–7. Now out, you may feel yourself getting dizzy, and that is OK, as you are changing brain patterns. Now, in, learn to accept yourself as perfect. Now out, letting yourself release and relax, 5–6–7. Now, in and becoming very relaxed, letting your brain relax. Now out, feeling relaxed, very relaxed and safe, nothing to worry about, now in, 1–2–3–4–5–6–7, now out, 1–2–3–4–5–6–7, in, 1–2–3–4–5–6–7, out, 1–2–3–4–5–6–7. Continue breathing in that pattern in your own silent count from 1 to 7.

Catch the emWave

The emWave is a device I described earlier in outlining Charles's treatment. It uses breathing patterns to regulate your brain patterns, and has a computer that gives you a personal breathing pace to co-ordinate with your heart pace. The idea is that when you have anxiety, your brain is out of sync with the rest of your body. So, if you can learn to appropriately pace your breathing, you will be doing your heart and the rest of your body a double service.

What Charles learned (and you can, too) is that the rhythmic breathing not only tends to balance the relationship between the brain and heart, it also balances other systems within the body, especially the hormones. Research has shown that a centering effect happens when a person is regulating his or her breathing in step with the heart rate. More important, the brain finds a peaceful pace within itself. The lightning ceases. You feel a sense of calm.

Principle II: Experience and need can change neurological bundles.

Turn the Other Cheek

Instead of meeting aggression with aggression, you can make a different choice. For example, I have a great friend, Sonny, who stands six foot five, weighs 325 pounds, and has a body composition that's about 10 percent body fat. For sure, he's a rather imposing-looking fellow. He's also a target in any bar he walks into for any fool who's fixin' for a fight. But whenever someone tries to pick a fight with him, Sonny just laughs. Even when they try to hit him (which is hard to do), he just laughs harder. Befuddled and frustrated, the would-be aggressor invariably gives up.

I asked Sonny why he laughed so much, and he told me that no one could really hurt someone if he kept his cool . . . and knew how to handle the blows correctly (old martial arts rule). Those are words to live by, if you ask me.

Laughter is also a good way to distract yourself from fear-based anxiety. From my years of extensive study in pain, I have learned that the body is programmed to tolerate a maximum of pain. You won't die from it, although you may wish to at times. The real threat to pain is chronic pain that you have to endure—but keep in mind that you can battle that if you laugh at it, so that you can handle it for short periods. Biologically there is nothing that can defeat you, and the mental side has the major advantage of your input. As an aside, even fear of death can be diminished (i.e., you can laugh in the face of death) if you embrace the belief that life on the other side is a wonderful thing; there are credible reports of people who've had near-death experiences who corroborate this belief.

Distraction Action

Knee-jerk response habits really can be changed. How? You need to learn the art of self-distraction from your worries, such as changing the subject, or taking away a worry's power over you by moving it from the high-priority filing cabinet in your head to the "no big deal" drawer. Your brain really will catch on and shift its priorities. For example, when Janis reached her limit of frustration in trying to meet the unrealistic goals set by her boss, she would shift her focus to thinking about how blessed she was to have her children, and would feel sorry for her boss, who clearly had his life priorities in a jumble.

One of my patients, whom we'll call "Sue," suffered horribly with anxiety and was actually documented in the scientific literature as having dissociative identity disorder, or DID ("multiple personalities"), which—contrary to popular Hollywood and soap opera belief—is extraordinarily rare. This disorder results from traumatizing fears and events too overwhelming to handle; it's believed the victims "remove" these memories and emotions (i.e., dissociate themselves) from their consciousness, and in effect give their horrid history to someone else . . . in their own mind.

Why does this happen? Essentially, there's a failure to integrate their anxieties into a tolerable coping method. Instead, they separate themselves into different personalities (ranging from highly aggressive to meek) that can tolerate the pain. Successfully helping individuals such as Sue who have DID is excruciatingly difficult because even the slightest hint of anxiety can trigger the other personalities to take over.

I had Sue commit to keeping a daily journal, so that she could actively document and review her day-to-day experiences. I also had her listen to the rhythmic drumming CD. By the second week, she was experiencing some moments—albeit intermittent—of real peace, which soothed her immeasurably. She says she continues to faithfully listen to the drumming CD every day for her sanity. That being said, and to be perfectly clear, Sue is far from cured. But her life is improving and continues to do so, slowly but surely. That, in and of itself, is amazing.

Principle III: Suspension of thoughts or elimination of specific experience can allow neurological changes to happen immediately.

The immediate application of this principle can help you learn how to stop the stress storms. Here are a few recommendations that work on the basis of brain science.

Medication Consideration

Many individuals find that taking medications (especially early in the treatment process) profoundly helps them ease their stress levels and improves their focus—and therefore increases their brain's receptivity, which can be a great help when trying to learn and integrate new skills. Of note, there's a plethora of scientific research that supports these individuals' experience.

Anxiety Medications

Psychotropic medication has long been the gold standard, dating back to the days of sanitariums. Some of the most highly valued medicines for anxiety used today include:

ATIVAN (Lorazepam)
KLONOPIN (Clonazepam)
LIBRIUM (Chlordiazepoxide)
VALIUM (Diazepam)
XANAX (Alprazolam)
XANAX XR

Possible Adverse Effects: clumsiness, weakness, fatigue, dry mouth, blurry vision, sexual dysfunction, headache, palpitations, tachycardia, nausea, vomiting, diarrhea, hypotension. Can manifest paradoxical effects with usage: irritability, increased anxiety, aggression, euphoria.

Discontinuation/withdrawal symptoms may range from restlessness, headaches, insomnia to (rarely) severe depression, myoclonus, involuntary movements, seizures. Likelihood of withdrawal reaction related to duration of use and daily dosage. Triazolo-Bz (Xanax) may be especially hard to discontinue.

Although the disorders these psychotropic medications are used to treat are considered chronic, they are not stable. They are triggered in episodes, and yet the medications are not reactive enough to respond to changes in mood and brain chemistry. For these applications to work best, a consistent mood and brain state are needed. Without that it is best to use them as short-term treatment options rather than as permanent solutions for stress.

Using the BAUD to Desensitize Triggering Mechanisms

A special application of the BAUD can be used for neutralizing powerful emotional triggers. For Charles, the memory of people criticizing him was a major trigger. So, he imagined a past emotionally charged situation of his father being critical of his actions. The goal here is to find the frequency that actually stimulates the anxiety response and then, in a second step, to find a secondary frequency that neutralizes the high-anxiety frequency and the emotional response as well. In Charles's case, as he kept the image of his father in his mind, he slowly moved the frequency knob on the BAUD until he felt the surge in his emotions. He became increasingly angry and upset. This was the frequency he found for the setting that best correlated to his lightning stress. That's the first step.

The next step is to use the knob that creates a separation in the two tones and find a setting that neutralizes the emotion. As Charles moved the knob—while still holding the highly charged image in his mind—he suddenly stopped with a smile on his face. The two frequencies had cancelled the emotion . . . and he felt a sense of calm. What the BAUD is accomplishing is neutralization. In essence, it's a method that uses contrasting frequencies to cancel out the emotional brain response.

What I find particularly fascinating is that in most cases when we monitor the sympathetic (arousal) and parasympathetic (relaxation and restoration) measures (such as heart rate variability and muscle tension), the patient has an immediate shift when the neutralizer frequency emerges: the heart rate variability becomes steady and the muscle tension releases! In Charles's situation, he felt immediate relief from the anxiety.

As you can tell, I have a fondness for the BAUD because of the success we have had, but chances are you don't have one and may never get one—and that's okay. Instead, I would suggest you try some basic methods of desensitization which have been known to work well with music; Native American flute and classical guitar are good choices—but whatever soothes *you* is best. Here's the basic protocol: Cue up the music you chose. Then, in a safe environment, try to imagine your worst fears, even if it makes you very uncomfortable. Take the anxiety to the highest level you can manage. Then as you recognize the maximum, turn on the soothing music and begin to breathe in a relaxing way. It might be helpful to have a relaxing massage and/or to fill the room with some wonderful scent, such as vanilla, rose, or sandalwood. Surrounded in this calming environment, continue to imagine the triggering events until you've changed your brain reactions. You may also find it helpful to have someone you trust with you as you go through this process, so you are assured that your anxiety doesn't get the best of you.

Principle IV: Times of growth and change are opportunities for learning and relearning.

When the conditions are set for learning and relearning with the suspension of old learning and responses, the ideal opportunity to change the lightning stress is put into motion. Here are a few excellent ways to capture that opportunity with behaviors to change brain patterns.

Cognitive Psychotherapy

The forms of cognitive therapy are very helpful in shifting behavioral patterns. Think of this process as ditching the old recorded messages that play in your head, and replacing them with far better, infinitely more accurate, brand-new ones. As you note the beliefs that cause your anxiety, consider the following criteria to help you decide which beliefs are keepers and which need to be ditched:

THE FIVE YAHOO QUESTIONS:
YOU ALWAYS HAVE OTHER OPTIONS (IN THINKING)

1. Is the belief absolutely true?
2. Even if the belief might have some validity, does refusing to let it go best serve my spirit?
3. Even if the belief might have some validity, does refusing to let it go best serve my emotional and physical health?
4. What possible payoff am I getting by holding on to this negative belief?
   a. Do I crave any form of attention—even negative attention?
   b. Does this belief give me an excuse not to succeed?
   c. Does focusing on this belief distract me from taking responsibility for my current situation?
5. Can I name one way that I would feel better (physically or emotionally) if I chose to let this belief go? (If yes, that's reason enough.)

Now that you've given some serious thought to these beliefs, the next time you begin to think them I want you to challenge those self-destructing, limiting thoughts with the five questions above.

Charles's YAHOO journey: Charlie maintained some very irrational ideas that governed much of his perception of the world and caused a great deal of anxiety. For example, he could express three very powerful concepts that he maintained all of his life:

> Everyone should like him.
> Others could make him upset.
> Compared to the achievements of his family, he was a
>   failure.

Considering his history, it would be easy to understand why he held these beliefs, and why he felt so stressed much of the time. He was walking around as a potential victim. Someone could upset his whole day if he or she mentioned any limitation he might show. This anxiety would quickly grow to spark the low self-esteem he harbored. Reacting by becoming defensive or withdrawing is not unusual. But it's also not productive.

His first irrational belief (*everyone should like him*) was untrue. Being liked by everyone is both an unrealistic and an unhealthy expectation. For Charles (or any of us) to be liked by *everyone* he'd have to be claylike, molding and contorting himself to everyone's expectations, to the point where he would hardly exist as an individual.

His second belief (*others could make him upset*) was also a myth. Others don't have the power to "make you" feel anything. How you *choose to respond* is entirely within your power. Charles had the power to decide how he would respond, and consequently he had the power either to be upset or not. He could decide how he wanted to think, which was a very critical concept for him to master.

His third belief (*compared to the achievements of his family, he was a failure*) was obviously an outgrowth of the first two, but served to remind him of his low self-worth. Over the course of his therapy, Charles learned that he deserved to make his own path and enjoy his own life; and that measuring his life against anyone else's not only was counterproductive, it was shortchanging his own possibilities!

Discover More Effective Behaviors

My father taught me very early in my life that if I wanted to get the things I desired, or accomplish anything of value, it was up to me to make it happen. Such things would rarely, if ever, just appear at my front door. Over the course of his life my father had learned (and then taught me) that the first step to success was to listen carefully to what was required and determine if you could meet the conditions . . . but that sometimes the conditions would not be what they seemed. For example, when I was struggling through school with a serious case of ADD (yes, I had attention deficit disorder), he taught me to carefully listen to my teachers to figure out what they really wanted. Yes, they wanted good performance on tests, but they also wanted something more: usually it was to see that you were trying hard and making a real, concerted effort. Fortunately, more times than not, my teachers would give me the benefit of the doubt on close calls, and would offer opportunities to improve my poor grades. What they didn't want (and had no toleration for) was a bad attitude and snotty responses. This is an invaluable lesson for anyone: having dreams is essential, but without a plan to get what you want, they'll just remain dreams. So, adjust your behavior and brain patterns with these goals in mind. Your brain doesn't judge your choices, it merely responds accordingly. Set goals clearly in your mind, and your brain will recalibrate to help those goals become a reality. Imagine in your mind's eye going through and achieving each of the steps necessary not only to make your plan feel possible, but also to determine if your goal is a realistic one. If not, recalibrate your goal to require smaller steps, and then revisit the imagining process. Rehearse your steps mentally, all the way through successfully achieving your goal. This is the secret of champions.

Principle V: New pathways can be changed and improved.

This principle is essential to solidifying your new and improved brain pathways. It may be a new golf swing or a new pathway to improved communication. This is also the step that helps you keep your gains, instead of reverting back to old brain patterns.

Celebrate

The importance of this recommendation cannot be overstated. Celebrating is extremely important to your brain patterns. Too few people know how to celebrate themselves. They wrongly think of it as tooting your own horn. Nothing could be further from the truth—especially when it comes to your brain patterns! Your brain needs to learn that it feels good to do good! Plus, experiencing joy (not to mention fun and laughter) has genuine therapeutic value. In fact, in the past I used to hold conferences on fun and humor and the turnout was always huge. So clearly, a lot of people are in need of learning how to celebrate.

Have a party for yourself and allow yourself to enjoy a time that's about what life has been for you, mistakes be damned. Mark a day to stop and really think about all the good things in your life. Allow yourself to experience the joy of coming across a piece of paper dancing in the wind, or a child's smile. Heck, you can even find joy in realizing you're speeding and then slowing down . . . and then moments later, safely passing a speed trap.

Relax, Relax

Give yourself at least thirty minutes *every day* to relax. You deserve it, and it will make you healthier. Listen to a relaxation CD, do yoga, play a relaxing game, or sing a song. This is the time to restore your brain pattern to normal.

This bears repeating: the value of relaxing is not just a once-in-a-while thing, and is definitely not something you do only when you can scrounge up the time. Relaxation is essential to your emotional and physical health. It needs to become a process as basic as brushing your teeth. And before you know it, you will feel its profoundly rewarding benefits. Your brain loves rewards and responds by filling you with a sense of pleasure and peace.

Meditate in Action

Practitioners of the form of meditation known as *mindfulness* learn to achieve stability and peace by focusing on their own thought processes at a calm and deliberate pace, and consciously releasing any negative thoughts. This approach has been adapted by psychologists for treating stress and depression, and it really helps formulate excellent prevention for anxiety. The main theme is to focus on the present only, not the past or future: just be where you are and think about what you are doing. This form of meditation may sound too easy to work, but in fact it's a very powerful tool, and one I strongly recommend you make a habit.

Many of us were raised with the work ethic that we must be "productive" to be worthy. We need to understand it doesn't work that way. First we must understand how we can work in the present. If we look at the end of the task as our goal, our brains think in two undesirable phases. We place all the value on the completion of the task and not on how well we are accomplishing the task. This is "quantity instead of quality" evaluation for the brain. Many athletes face this problem. They think about the final score and winning instead of the next play.

The principle of living in the present is that you can focus on the here and now, making the best decisions at each second. You begin to enjoy the immediate challenge. If you only focus your attention on the future, you will miss a big part of life and lose huge sources of pleasure. When I played football, I was surprised when the final score was announced because I was so grounded in every play and thoroughly enjoying it. It can be the same way with manual labor. When I was a teenager I used to dig ditches for utility companies and when I focused on each shovelful of dirt, time lost its power over me and I looked forward to every task I faced. My brain was focused on what I was doing right, not what I was lacking.

The gift of any opportunity is to embrace each and every second of your investment in it. Too often parents miss out on the enjoyment of watching their children grow up because they are looking at the time they leave. We lose the pleasure of our work because we can't wait to finish. We age quicker and miss most of our lives until it is too late.

The only thing that can possibly get in the way of achieving your goals . . . is you. It is your own responsibility to gain what you want to accomplish in life. If you're willing to embrace a new approach to thought processes, you can reinvent your life.

SUMMARIZING THE IMPLICATIONS

The anxiety patterns of the brain can be as debilitating to your quality of life as a hole in your brain, creating obstacles to effective, rational thinking, and seriously diminishing your ability to access joyfulness.

The possibility that you will be successful is reasonably good, but it's not like a magic pill that you swallow and suddenly the world melts into a beautiful sunrise. You have to commit to a lifestyle of peace and harmony, starting with how you breathe and feed yourself. You have to retrain your brain so that it can unwind and feel safe with the idea of being relaxed. This requires courage because it's not easy to change. Not because it's hard, but because it's uncharted territory, and that scares most people. But you can't discover new lands if you're afraid to lose sight of the shore. So go ahead, jump in. The water's fine.

A word of caution: success will not be achieved if you are partaking of recreational drugs like marijuana or alcohol. Granted, these substances may have a calming effect and will temporarily slow down your brain, but they'll always come around and bite you in the butt. I promise you that this is not the way. These substances damage your neural (brain) connections, fill your body with toxins, and asphyxiate your spirit. So if you're serious about improving your life, they've got to go. Have I made myself clear? Good.

5

The Attention Deficit Stress Storm

A thick fog can make it really difficult to see which way is up and which way is down. To compensate, a person's brain often struggles to make some sense out of the mass of apparent nothingness: sounds, smells, and tactile sensations become your clues, as does your intuition. Imagine hearing the drip . . . drip . . . drip of a leaky faucet, feeling a puff of cool, damp air rushing across your face, and sensing that somewhere off in the distance, a person is standing . . . before vanishing into the fog, leaving you feeling vulnerable and isolated.

Indeed, sometimes our imaginations get the best of us, as we allow emptiness and fear to become squatters in our head. We think wild, fearful thoughts and imagine the worst. But if you can relax and realize the fears are unfounded, or if you are able to find the humor in the absurdity of the situation, that can go a long way toward getting you through most foggy situations.

If you're suffering from an attention deficit stress storm in your brain, then chances are you feel lost and isolated most of the time. Adding insult to injury, when you do reach out to others in an attempt to explain why you feel the way you do, I bet people usually respond dismissively. Having someone tell you "it's all in your head" is cold comfort, at best—and only serves to further validate your sense of isolation and aloneness. You feel your only option is to accept the notion that you're alone in the world, and the only person's perceptions you can trust are your own. And in so doing, you separate yourself even further from other people in your life, who then may erroneously label you as socially odd, self-absorbed, or perhaps eccentric.

CYNTHIA: APPEARANCES CAN BE DECEIVING

Whenever anyone looked at Cynthia, what they saw was a very pretty thirteen-year-old strawberry-blond girl, with an exceptionally beautiful smile and a slight weight problem. But appearances and first impressions can be deceiving—and that was certainly the case with Cynthia. She appeared in conversation as though she was deeply engaged in every word. But in reality, her mind was a thousand miles away. Her retreat had nothing to do with being bored, nor with her like or dislike of her companion. Indeed, it was possible to occasionally bring her "back" for a few minutes (for those who caught on to her obliviousness), but all too soon her eyes would glaze over again.

Cynthia's fog resulted in her failing seventh grade. For her this was particularly devastating because her friends would be moving on to another school, and she would be left behind. She became indifferent with regard to school in general, and her demeanor became sullen and withdrawn. Soon she had labeled herself as "beyond stupid."

When Cynthia first came to our clinic, we asked her how she dealt with her challenges. She said, "My mind never seems to stop. It's like trying to watch a dozen TV shows at once—and I can't follow the story line of any of them! It's not like I'm not trying to prioritize and stay focused on one thing at a time. But I never can. I just go from one thing to another, trying to understand as much as I can. I'm such a loser."

Cynthia also shared that she felt very sad because she knew she was letting her family down. Her two older sisters (three and five years older, respectively) were honor students, and her parents had the same expectations of her. Knowing this added to her feelings of anxiousness, which frankly only made her struggle worse: the harder she tried, the more distractible she became. When she told us this, her eyes welled up with tears. It was heartbreaking.

Cynthia's parents weren't mean-spirited or overbearing—but they weren't as helpful as they could have been. The two elder daughters were sources of great pride for them. The eldest, Judy, was sure to graduate as valedictorian, and had already won a music scholarship. Knowing their firstborn was about to leave the nest for college, her parents were consciously savoring every moment they had with Judy. Kay, the middle child, was into cheerleading and played volleyball competitively. Kay's schedule required that her parents spend a lot of time on the road with her. So, when it came to Cynthia, her parents ran out of (or chose not to make?) time . . . except when the principal called to discuss Cynthia's academic failings. That they made time for.

WAKE-UP CALL

Cynthia's symptoms presented a lot like attention deficit disorder (ADD), but ADD is misdiagnosed almost two thirds of the time and we are very suspicious of any label based only on a brief set of questions, usually answered by the teacher, so we conducted a QEEG brain scan. The brain scan confirmed what I suspected: Cynthia's brain dynamics were in a signature related to ADD patterns—which refers to the brain's diminished capacity to organize the information presented to it. Remember, fog storms can be very disorienting; and the brain's attempt to sort through the confusion without the proper tools generally makes things worse, not better.

The QEEG scan revealed that Cynthia's stress storms were displaying low-intensity brain waves in areas that are supposed to organize and store information. It was as if those areas in her brain were sleeping . . . which in a way, they were: we saw on her QEEG scan that her low-intensity areas were located in the same areas that primarily produce delta (sleep) and theta (drowsiness) frequencies. So in essence, we had to teach her how to wake up her brain.

And wake up she did. Using a variety of treatment techniques, we helped Cynthia begin to reclaim her place in the world. We jump-started her treatment with medication for a short period of time, along with BAUD-assisted neurotherapy, music therapy with rhythmic exercise, and a high-protein diet. In just two months she had improved significantly, and a few months after that, her school saw fit to promote her to the next grade, reuniting her with her friends—and that meant the world to Cynthia.

One could argue, of course, that the most profound success Cynthia achieved was to create a brand-new, fully engaged life for herself: one in which she had a sense of pride and joy. Her grades soared, she began to write stories (her favorite theme would be heroism) for which she won awards, and eventually she won a college scholarship. She was even able to stop comparing herself to her sisters.

As you can see on the brain map of the attention deficit storm pattern below, the problem appears to lie in the frontal and prefrontal lobes. These areas of the brain are responsible for organizing and executing information from the rest of the brain into meaningful, actionable plans. This is the similar signature pattern for ADD and ADHD, i.e., it shows that this part of the brain is drowsy and asleep, as the major frequencies are in the delta (sleep) and theta (hypnagogic) state.

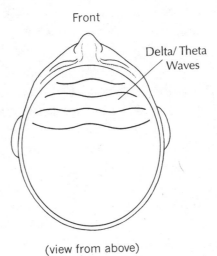

(view from above)

FIGURE 5.1

INFANTS AND CHILDREN AND TEENAGERS, OH MY

Attention deficit stress storms are an equal opportunity challenge. Infants, children, and teens (along with adults, of course) can all suffer with them. Imagine a toddler who—presumably out of nowhere—starts flailing his arms and running all over the place. He then gets *really* cranky and irritable (to put it kindly), and nothing you do or say will appease him. Then it dawns on you: he's a very sleepy boy who's fighting like mad not to go to sleep; he wants to stay up and play with the people around him, but he can't. He's too overwhelmed and frustrated to sort out (or even comprehend) why he's in a spin.

You may have witnessed this dynamic of a child struggling to keep his brain awake by seeking novel situations (like trying to jump off the bed and land on a skateboard) and/or allowing his brain to wander into other thoughts that are especially stimulating to think about (how mad would my sister get if I hid her favorite sweater?). He may also become very physically active—another classic ADD characteristic—in an attempt to keep his brain thoroughly engaged. ADD teenagers are also at increased risk for engaging in dangerous behaviors, such as driving recklessly, becoming hypersexual, drinking (alcohol) excessively, and using drugs. As an aside, in terms of juvenile delinquency, studies suggest that individuals with ADD are more likely to be incarcerated at an earlier age than those juveniles who do not have ADD.

NO CLOWNING AROUND

Having fog stress storms can be particularly deleterious in highly regimented situations, such as most school environments. Candidly speaking, identifying fog-filled students is usually a snap . . . well, if they're boys, that is: the boys constantly tapping their toes, or bouncing their legs and feet about. They're chewing gum (if they're allowed) at a furious pace, and their eyes will be darting around the room. They're also likely to be the class clown or wisecracker, and thus they're also least likely to be the teacher's pet.

Girls display their symptoms far more subtly—which personally causes me great consternation, as it's too easy to miss their plight. They are far more likely to quietly gaze around in their own inner world, without calling attention to themselves. Girls also are more likely to simply doodle on a piece of paper or in the margins of a book—and know to do so at the very back of the room, where no one will notice. If you call on one of these girls for an answer, they get anxious and withdraw further. Consequently, they do all they can to become invisible, which results in their getting even less attention, and none of the help they truly need.

The hard truth is, having fog stress storms can significantly interfere with your achieving successes in your life, however you define success. Without the brain serving you with clarity and focus, the information overload is too intense. People in attention deficit storms frankly have a harder time in the beginning of life:

- 35 percent never finish high school
- Over 50 percent turn to drug abuse
- 43 percent of male ADHD students are arrested for a felony before the age of sixteen.

Clinical diagnoses commonly correlated to the fog stress brain pattern include:

Attention deficit/hyperactivity disorder
Conduct disorder
Oppositional defiant disorder
Generalized anxiety disorder
Reactive attachment disorder
Bipolar disorder
Extended grief disorder

ATTENTION DEFICIT STRESS STORM AUDIT

The attention deficit brain storm is very difficult to diagnose based on symptoms alone. Why? A multitude of other disorders have the same (or nearly the same) impact on a person's attention and concentration. For example, consider the list below. Any one of these difficulties can negatively impact our attention and concentration capabilities:

1. Grief
2. Depression
3. Being stimulated by the love bug
4. Poor sleep
5. Fatigue
6. Post-traumatic stress
7. Psychosis
8. Aftermath of conflicts and arguments
9. Addictions
10. Hypoglycemia (low blood sugar)
11. Boredom and very high intelligence
12. Hormonal imbalances

One clue that can help differentiate attention deficit storms from other maladies is time. Attention deficit storms tend to be with you for a long time. Take grief for example: regardless of how overwhelmingly intense the experience of grief may be, it nonetheless tends to lessen over time. However, if you've had fog storms since you were a child, you'll likely have them when you are twenty-six or forty-six—in the absence of learning how to master them.

The first thing you should do if you think you might be in the fog storm pattern is to get a thorough evaluation, including a brain scan. However, if the cost of doing so is prohibitive, the following questionnaire may be helpful:

THE ATTENTION DEFICIT STRESS STORM QUESTIONNAIRE

Place one check mark in the space provided if the following apply to you. For those that you've experienced for a year or more, place two check marks.

1. You are bored with life and nothing interests you. _____
2. Trying as hard as you can, you can't pay close attention to details, so you don't get sufficient information to appropriately perform a task. _____
3. You make careless mistakes by not reading the instructions as carefully as you could. _____
4. You avoid engagement in tasks that require sustained concentration. _____
5. You tend not to finish projects that you start, because you get interested in or distracted by something else. _____
6. You easily forget to complete your routine chores and responsibilities, probably because you get distracted by other events and lose time. _____
7. You have trouble organizing or prioritizing concepts when they're offered all at once.
8. You fantasize a lot, and enjoy your images and flights of the imagination so much that you often lose track of your "real" world. _____
9. It's difficult for you to focus on one topic and ignore other distractions going on at the same time. _____
10. It's hard for others to keep your attention. _____
11. When you fall asleep, it is difficult to wake you up. _____
12. You often fidget with your arms, legs, or hands. _____
13. You feel you have to move your body at times or you'll burst with frustration. _____
14. You crave excitement, even if it brings the disapproval of others. _____
15. You are impulsive, often jumping ahead of others in events that require patience. _____
16. You have difficulty when you have to wait to take your turn with others. _____
17. You often interrupt others, especially when you feel their input isn't as important as yours. _____
18. You often withdraw into your fantasy world when you're too frustrated. _____
19. You usually feel a sense of urgency in sharing what you have to say, because you know you'll forget it if you have to wait. _____
20. You are very creative in many forms of expression. _____

Scoring: If any of the behavioral items were checked twice (meaning they've existed for a period of at least a year or perhaps more of your life) and/or you checked more than twelve items, then there's a reasonable chance you have fog brain storms. If that is indeed the case, it's essential that you decide (ideally right now) that you need to resolve to learn novel ways to manage your attention deficit brain storms—and you really can.

Interestingly, many high-level executive training programs are geared to help people find solutions "outside the box." The nature of these exercises actually relies on the tendency of our attention to stray as a way of discovering creative detours. In other words, the attention deficit state is not necessarily always a bad or destructive way of processing information, since it facilitates people's openness to considering alternative ways of approaching issues and problem solving. It's only bad if you can't shift into other productive states when it's appropriate.

TRAINING THE BRAIN TO COPE WITH THE
ATTENTION DEFICIT STRESS STORM

If you have the symptoms or pattern of the attention deficit stress storm, you're probably anxious to figure out how to deal with it. Using the brain plasticity model, here are some basic steps to help you achieve that goal. Which of the following will work best for you is very personal, so you'll have to embrace trial and error. But again, you can do this . . . if you resolve to do so.

Principle I: Neurons that learn together become attached.

The most powerful approach is to learn to stimulate the brain directly and raise the frequencies from delta/theta to low beta and put you directly into organization mode for focus and concentration. Experts at neurotherapy are specifically trained to help you accomplish this through a process whereby you visually see the four frequencies and their relative amplitudes (strengths). You are then coached on how to change your brain waves at will. Excellent studies have demonstrated this method.

Bio-Acoustical Utilization Device (BAUD)

We've made this process quicker (and more accessible) through the Bio-Acoustical Utilization Device (BAUD)—which is easier to use with the monitoring EEG tracking process. In essence, this process increases the low beta amplitudes and lowers the delta/theta in order to accomplish the correct sonic level. Once you have the correct personal sonic frequencies, it takes about four minutes for your brain to change.

In Cynthia's case, we wanted to change the high beta frequency to low beta, so we handed the device to Cynthia and began an exploration to see what could be accomplished. Her graph of the EEG readings looked like this:

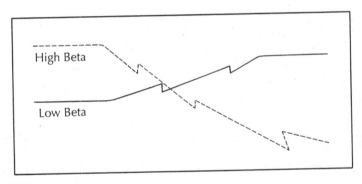

FIGURE 5.2

Cynthia started off by humming a tone that she perceived as relaxing; and if she hummed it long enough, she liked the emotional result. This is nothing new to researchers like Dr. Don Campbell, author of *The Mozart Effect,* who makes use of tones in a similar way. Cynthia used this tone to adjust the sound frequencies on her BAUD, and the EEG monitor supported this experience. Now she could consciously engage her brain waves to her advantage.

Once it was calibrated, Cynthia used the BAUD only when she needed it to assist her in calming herself down. Having this tool readily accessible whenever she began to feel anxious or on the edge was also a stress reducer, in and of itself, as she now knew a way to effectively manage her fog storms. The EEG showed that the response she wanted could be achieved in three minutes, so she could expect shifts in storms to subside in a short time.

Hum Drum

Actually, if you could hum consistently for fifteen or twenty minutes, your brain would react similarly to the way it reacts to the BAUD. In academic research conducted by Don Campbell, this is termed *toning*. He's done extensive research on this method in learning disabilities and attention deficits. I've observed toning effects firsthand in workers whose professions demand extreme focus for long periods of time. Using one's voice in this way helps the brain become and stay more focused—which improves concentration capabilities for the task at hand. For example, when I was a lot younger I used to pick cotton, and our group of workers would just hum along the rows. I found it very calming, and it allowed me not to become impatient with my pace.

I also used toning at a different level to train students how to concentrate on what we call "vigilant" tasks, similar to what air traffic controllers have to do for their jobs. The tasks were to detect objects on a radar screen that were different from other signals. When students hummed a high tonal pitch, their performances improved significantly.

The advantage to using a scientific device like the BAUD is the objective measurement and feedback it provides. However, an arguably greater advantage to the humming or toning is that it's free and always available to you, wherever and whenever. Plus, when you add a tune of significance, it adds to the power of your intention.

Rhythmic Physical Exercise

Just as the brain reacts to the sonic stimulation of the BAUD, it also responds to the physical beats in dancing and rhythmic movements. We use a CD (MindbodySeries.com) and require at least thirty minutes (two sessions of fifteen minutes each) of movement by the individual.

Rhythmic movement can also be done nearly anywhere at any time. I've had people move their bodies—well, at least parts of their bodies—lying in bed, sitting in chairs, and in swimming pools. The more body parts you can move, the more your brain will be required to incorporate the stimulating activity. It helps to have some rhythmic music or drumming available to set the beat, and it's super powerful to create the music in a group. For example, I've been caught conducting a workshop demonstrating these ideas only to discover that there was no access to an electrical outlet. So, we'd choose a tune that the individuals knew, such as "When the Saints Come Marching In," or "She'll Be Coming 'Round the Mountain When She Comes," with great success.

And sometimes, we'd simply make a chant. For example, once I was conducting a workshop with a group of people in a public relations department who had problems with high frustration. Each and every day, all day long, all they heard were complaints, and they got zero gratitude for their hard work. We created a song that repeated the lyrics: "One more call to go, one more grin to make, getting stronger, stronger, stronger." As we sang these lyrics, we would use our bodies to accent the movements. It was wonderful. After ten years, I can still hear that song and my body reacts. What we were doing was converting the negative energy that the brain perceived into positive energy throughout the body. By the end of the day, they reported higher energy than when they started.

Blue Light and Chewing Gum—Cynthia Style

Cynthia became a good researcher in her own right. She discovered that chewing sugarless gum gave her an additional concentration level. Her experience is backed up by some impressive research that shows that the temporal and frontal lobes of the brain are stimulated by the action of chewing—which (for whatever reason) improves concentration and memory and reduces stress. Plus, chewing sugarless gum has the added benefit of decreasing the incidence of dental caries (which lead to cavities).

Cynthia also purchased a 25-watt blue light (from a local hardware store) and started using it upon awakening each morning. This was recommended to her based upon research suggesting that exposure to blue light increased alertness. She added the blue light to her dancing routine as well, which she felt gave it additional value. I'd certainly say this is worth a try.

Principle II: Experience and need can change neurological bundles.

In this principle, the concept is to shift the brain to higher levels of concentration and focus. Listed below are some successful methods we have used to give individuals better control.

Breathing

One of the most typical symptoms seen with individuals in attention deficit stress storms is the tendency to breathe in extreme patterns. If you're breathing in a very fast rhythm (faster than ten to twelve respirations per minute), this pattern does not allow the proper absorption rate of oxygen from the air brought in by the lungs. Consequently, your brain becomes depleted of oxygen fairly quickly. If you're breathing too slowly, the same problem happens. Either way, your brain is running sluggishly, because it's not getting enough air fuel.

The solution is deceptively simple: you need to moderate your breathing cycle to the best rate, which for most people is usually in the twelve-plus or -minus range. It takes practice to get it right, but you can do this.

The hardest thing to accomplish is to maintain this breathing pattern, because, frankly, it gets boring. If you have a brain that has trouble concentrating, counting breathing is going to get old fast— like in about thirty seconds. For that reason you're going to have to plan for accountability, regardless of where your mind goes. In other words, yes, it'll initially be a drag, but make yourself do it anyway; real change is rarely easy—but it's more than worth it.

I'd recommend focusing on your breathing for five-minute intervals at a time. Count aloud as you exhale and inhale, repeating as 1–2–3–4–5–6–7, 1–2–3–4–5–6–7, etc., or just counting complete cycles, such as breath 1, breath 2, breath 3. Figure that you would complete about five or six cycles per minute, and when you reach breath 35 you can let go. Then check how you feel and count another 35 complete breaths.

The brain gets adjusted to the higher frequencies in about five to six minutes, so completing about ten minutes of the breathing exercise should suffice for a while. The effects don't last forever, so when you find yourself drifting again, charge your brain up with another set of breathing exercises. It will get easier (and far less monotonous) as you practice—primarily because your brain will know the reward is imminent.

Listening to High-Energy Music

I know that parents around the world will want to hang me for this recommendation, but loud music works pretty well with kids and teens to get their brains in higher gears. Hey, the Harlem Globetrotters work out to "Sweet Georgia Brown"!

You may have some special music that you can put on your iPod or some other device, or you may just turn your radio dial to the hottest spot you can find. Unless you're located somewhere close to the North Pole, it won't be hard to find a station with a variety of songs that you'll find helpful. Or better yet, you could make your own music: get out some wooden spoons, cooking pots, steel pipes, or whatever you can find to make noise and beat out a rhythm. Who knows? You might have some musical genius lying dormant inside you, just itching to get out.

Principle III: Suspension of thoughts or elimination of specific experience can allow neurological changes to happen immediately.

Simply put, this principle focuses on the suspension of negative brain patterns in order for new ones to form. For the foggy brain, this is a bit awkward because that is exactly what the individual normally tries to do to change his pattern in destructive ways.

Medication Issues

ADD and ADHD medications are designed to increase the brain's activity and wake it up. They do so in different ways, meaning that some may work better for you than others.

Stimulant Medications

Medications for ADD and ADHD work indirectly on the central nervous system and peripheral nervous system. The medications often prescribed include:

ADDERALL (dextroamphetamine-amphetamine)
CONCERTA, METADATE, METHYLIN (methylphenidate-ER)
DEXEDRINE (dextroamphetamine)
RITALIN, RITALIN-SR (methylphenidate)

Possible Adverse Effects: Depression, dizziness, headache, insomnia, tachycardia, nervousness, hair loss, anorexia.

Medications definitely have their place as a tool in the therapeutic process (especially early on), and they can help individuals who need brain stimulation. That being said, if the person feels better, it's not necessarily a confirmation of ADD or ADHD. These medications are stimulants, and thus will probably make any one of us feel more alert. In fact, some ADHD/ADD medications have morphed

into becoming street drugs and are very popular on college cam-
puses for students wanting to pull all-nighters during exam time.

Nutrition

As with every other organ in your body, you have to nurture your
brain with food (and oxygen of course). Low-fat, complex carbohydrates are the key, since glucose (which is a type of sugar) is the
only food your brain can use. And research clearly indicates that
the more you use your brain (such as to solve cognitive tasks), the
quicker your glucose burn rate. Now, to keep the flow of energy
steady and even in your bloodstream (instead of having dangerous
spikes and crashes), this is what you should do:

When you eat complex carbs (which naturally break down into
glucose your brain can use), add a little bit of protein, such as a
handful of nuts or some fish, because by doing so, you can significantly steady the flow and even out the glucose delivery system to
your brain. As an aside, this way of eating (to keep the sugar supply
in the blood slow and steady) is also recommended for people with
type 2 diabetes. Examples of low-fat complex carbs include most
vegetables, brown rice, beans, lentils, skin-on potatoes, and whole
grains (swirling some peanut butter into hot oatmeal is my friend
Wendy's favorite). Eating whole foods (versus processed, prepackaged foods) in their most natural state is also the best way to get
the full benefit of vitamins, minerals, and antioxidants.

Water

Keep a bottle of water handy at all times, and set goals for consumption on a consistent basis. This isn't new information . . . it's
just often ignored. Proper hydration is absolutely essential for brain
health. Period. Now, it doesn't have to be water, per se. But caffein-
ated fluids, such as most colas, coffee, and tea, are definite no-no's,
because caffeine acts as a diuretic (meaning it does the opposite of
hydrating you). Alcoholic beverages are diuretics as well (that's the
reason they make you have to pee so much, by the way). If you're
craving something different, try adding a squeeze of lemon or lime,

or a splash of grape, pomegranate, blueberry, or orange juice to your water. That's a great way to add some refreshing flavor and give you a nutritional boost.

Omega-3s

Technically called omega-3 essential fatty acids, omega-3s are one of the "good fats." The term *omega* refers to the classification of the kind of fat, and this kind of fat is what the brain and the neurons use for their insulation. Basically, we're talking about increasing the speed of nerve impulses and connections. Omega-3s combat depression, enhance learning and memory, and are major aids in brain plasticity, since they help recreate brain structures for efficient neuron transmission.

The best way to get your omega-3s is by eating flaxseeds, salmon, winter squash, and walnuts. Other good sources include soy foods (such as edamame), quinoa, bell peppers, and spinach. Incidentally, in food, omega-3 fats come in three forms: alpha-linolenic acid (ALA), eicosapentaenoic acid (EPA), and docosahexaenoic acid (DHA). ALA is found mostly in plant foods. EPA and DHA are found in fish. You can also buy omega-3 oils in health food stores. My personal preference is krill oil, which is made from shrimplike sea creatures.

One of Cynthia's many talents was cooking. Could it be that there's magic in all people who love to make good food? But I digress. Cynthia found success by increasing her consumption of these foods:

Salmon	Shiitake mushrooms	Sweet potatoes
Cherries	Peanut butter	Irish potatoes
Grapes	Almond butter	Walnuts and other nuts
Eggs	Avocados	Berries
Bluefin tuna	Low-fat yogurt	Dark chocolate
Lake trout	Edamame	Turkey

Principle IV: Times of growth and change are opportunities for learning and relearning.

This concept is basic to all brain relearning: you gotta practice. The more you practice keeping your brain alert, the easier it gets. I've personally learned how to juice up my frontal lobe, and I've pretty much mastered it . . . except for when I'm extremely tired. Then it takes a far greater effort on my part. Here are some recommendations that have really worked for me:

Practice Focus Techniques

I learned a great deal about focusing through martial arts: you have to start off slowly and deliberately, and you really need to learn how to focus your attention on one thing, such as a mark on the wall or someone talking. Try this: For the next thirty seconds (after you finish reading this section), put everything out of your mind except one point of focus/concept (suggestions follow). Once you've successfully maintained focus for thirty seconds, try to increase your focus time to one minute. Then tomorrow, begin again at thirty seconds, but then try to reach two minutes, three minutes, and so on. Take breaks and relax between focus sessions. Your goal is to maintain concentration for twenty minutes, as this is a nonfoggy brain's average concentration period.

Focus Suggestions

Friendly competition in focusing techniques—I find it easy and fun to practice focusing techniques by playing games that require my complete attention (especially if I want to win . . . or at least not embarrass myself). Some of my favorites include:

Scrabble	Chess
Double Solitaire	Checkers
Bridge	Charades
Clue	Poker

3 Stones	10 Days in Africa
Basari	Jigsaw puzzles
Sudoku	Brainstrain
Curses!	The Bridges of Shangri-La
Rubik's Cube	DAO
Doubles Wild	

Personal competition (games you play against yourself) include:

Mensa Think Smart Book	*Great Word Search Puzzles for Kids*
Mensa Book of Words,	Crossword puzzles
Word Games, Puzzles &	
Oddities	
Solitaire	

Additional self-focusing suggestions include:

Spelling words	Memorizing vocabulary of another language
Recalling names of people	Reciting multiplication tables
Reading a book	Memorizing poetry
Lipreading	Observing an athlete or dancer

Principle V: New pathways can be changed and improved.

This principle is extremely important for maintaining the shift in your desired brain pattern. Please don't forget this essential step. Starting over is a drag. Get it and keep it. You deserve nothing less than your hard-earned success.

Brain Excitement and Learning

There are periods of time during each day when the brain has a higher learning capacity than during other times of the day. This window of opportunity is related to the influx of biochemicals, called *brain growth factors*. These biochemicals coat each brain neuron with a rich, fatty substance that speeds up the learning process exponentially. How do you turn these factors on?

The most direct route is by stimulating your imagination. The more excited you become, the better your brain can learn and concentrate. Positive reinforcement also has a tremendous impact on this process. In fact, your brain enjoys getting some serious traction toward that end simply by hearing the words "great job," "atta' boy," "I'm so proud of you," and even getting a gold star. So, if you're a parent, don't forget that even if your child should want to be an A student on his own, positive reinforcement from you really does improve your child's initiative, not to mention that his brain will develop positive associations with you, school, hard work, and success. Unless your child is one of those exceptionally rare self-directed kids (the kind that read themselves bedtime stories before they were potty-trained), trying to motivate your child with truisms like "hard work pays off" will quickly lose its punch, and at best provide a payoff of diminishing returns. Emotional rewards are essential to your child's lifelong success.

But back to you: you need to build in your own emotional rewards and incentives. Here's a terrific one: make a big deal of accomplishing those tasks where focus usually eludes you. I remember when I had to wash and dry the dishes, I used to talk like I was a major radio sports announcer, announcing my own actions in a play-by-play format and giving myself crowd cheers. My spiel went something like this: "It is all up to Frank now to win the game . . . there he goes, starting to engage his famous super quick and incredibly agile hands! He grabs one, then another . . . Sure, he's fast—but will he be fast enough? And can he maintain that momentum?? Wait for it . . . wait for it . . . YES! He makes the final buzzer. The crowd goes wild! Take a bow, Frank. You won the game!"

Laugh if you like (laughing is good too), but being your own play-by-play announcer really works. Whether you want to win at finishing homework, writing a paper, fixing the car, organizing the garage—really any task you need to finish—give it the winning spin! Heck, I've even completed my taxes in record time because I can hear the cheers in my head . . . which thrills my wife, too!

Sleep on It

As you prepare for bedtime, take a few moments to review the successes you've had during the day when you're focused. Then, gently ask your mind to allow you to dream about your times of successful focus. You may or may not remember the dreams that follow once you awaken, but that's fine. That's the business of the unconscious, and that is exactly what we're shooting for—the transformation of brain patterns.

Celebrate in the Conscious Hours

Get your circle of friends and practice your concentration skills, perhaps using some of the games discussed in Principle IV. Have some celebration times in which you can demonstrate your abilities and gain rewards such as applause and pats on the back. These small choices of reinforcement only take a few seconds, but the positive impact they have on the brain is amazing! These mini-celebrations are especially valuable in improving the self-confidence of those of us who suffer problems associated with failure or disparaging remarks from friends and peers.

Make It a Big Deal

When you see any significant improvement in a performance review, such as grades or work assessments, make a big deal out of it. You know better than anyone that it takes an enormous amount of effort to concentrate and focus your brain. Whether or not your success was assisted by way of sonic stimulation, dancing, breathing, or medication, you've achieved something terrific! Remember, your brain loves reinforcement, so don't hesitate.

THE ATTENTION DEFICIT PATTERN AND CAUSES

No one has the definitive answer as to why some people have this brain anomaly. My story was that it was caused when I was born with oxygen deprivation, but this event usually causes retardation.

Some reports have shown that lack of breast milk is associated with ADD because of high levels of substances a baby cannot metabolize, such as soy milk and large amounts of manganese. That could fit for me as well.

High exposure to television and video games has also been implicated, and research has shown that after the age of seven, for every hour of television time daily you gain 10 percent probability of having an ADD diagnosis. The waveforms of the tube output have been blamed for the reprogramming of the brain, which may disrupt the higher-functioning beta frequencies for learning new material. The dust that comes from the heat shields and sound-proofing in the back of color television sets has been shown to have very negative effects on hormone levels and disruption of cognitive abilities. Anyway, we didn't have television or video games when I grew up. We barely had telephones.

The fact that there's a weak but significant genetic link might also suggest that the fog brain pattern has a DNA component. Many of the fathers admit to similar foggy challenges when they were growing up, which creates a deep empathy and tolerance for their children's problems. Of course, we also tend to mirror many of the coping behaviors of our parents, too.

The search will continue for years to come. Being an optimist, I think that like other disabilities, any limitation can be developed into an asset, which was obviously what Einstein and Edison achieved.

6

The Obsessive Stress Storm

Arguably the most mysterious of the stress storms, the obsessive brain storm is usually the easiest to understand. A circle of forces keeps turning you around and around, so you keep finding yourself back where you started. You can fight it, but you quickly "learn" that it's easier to just go with it . . . because your self-confidence has been broken. You feel like a victim, yet in the obsessive stress storm, you actually know those feelings aren't based in reality.

BERNICE'S STORY

Bernice was a very productive individual both at work and at home. If anyone needed a detail-oriented person, they came running for her. She appeared to the world as a cheery, kind-hearted woman who was always dressed immaculately, right down to her perfectly applied makeup. A young thirty-eight years old, Bernice was a slender woman who stood five feet seven inches tall, and had a no-nonsense business attitude. Every detail was carefully considered and reconsidered.

Bernice also had a secret life . . . a dangerously obsessive one. Her husband and children had helplessly watched her for years as she repeated her behavior over and over. For example, in the morning, she would go back and turn off the coffeepot twenty or thirty times, usually making the kids late for school. She would check (and recheck) the door to see if it was locked; she'd do the same with the storm door. After her children went to bed, she'd repeatedly check to make sure they were breathing. Doing so often wakened the kids, which resulted in their being sleep deprived much of the time.

Although Bernice's work was impeccable, her obsessive need to make sure her work was "perfect" repeatedly resulted in her turning in her work late, which often led to her being fired. Other times, she'd pull all-nighters for projects she'd already completed days earlier—as she would be compelled to double- and triple-check that there were absolutely no errors. And sad to say, she took zero pride in her herculean efforts and never felt satisfied with her work, in part because she wrongly believed that her superiors were so desperate to get the final product, they'd accept anything, no matter how dreadful. Of course, she was entirely mistaken.

The Filth Element

Bernice's worst fears were filth and germ infestation—especially in the meals she prepared and in the clothes her family wore. She was also compelled to scrub her hands "clean" until they bled, and would rewash clothes to the point of wearing them out before anyone got any decent wear out of them. And if you were up after midnight, it wasn't unusual to see that the bathroom light was on . . . as she'd be disinfecting it until she ran out Lysol.

These problematic behaviors of Bernice's didn't pop up out of nowhere, and they didn't just suddenly present themselves. No, these behaviors had begun building up when she was just a young girl, who unfortunately had a mom with obsessive compulsions. When Bernice was only five years old, her mother made her clean the family bathroom every Saturday. Bernice clearly remembers (and can even "smell" this memory) how she wasn't allowed to leave the bathroom until her mom had literally inspected every inch of it. If something was found, such as a hair left in the bathtub or even a discoloration on a doorjamb, Bernice was forced to start the cleaning process all over, until the bathroom had absolutely no signs of potential "germ-houses." Her mother instilled in Bernice a horrible sense of shame associated with any lack of duty toward the health of the family. Of course, Bernice's mother was clearly ill, so I'm not casting blame—but these are the circumstances that were Bernice's reality.

A Mixed Sense

What Bernice remembered most of all was the disappointment in her father's eyes when she was humiliated in front of him. Personally, I suspect what her dad was actually feeling was a deep sense of powerlessness and pity for his young daughter's suffering. Maybe that's because I'm a dad. Regardless, Bernice's childhood perception was that she was a terrible disappointment to her dad; and ever since then, she still imagines her father's displeasure. Stress storms can do that: alter reality and then intensify the misplaced pain.

No stranger to psychotherapy, Bernice had no trouble explaining her childhood in great detail and the dynamics that contributed to her perfectionist compulsions. She also harbored fears that one day she'd end up in a mental institution—doomed to endlessly cleaning the halls, like some twisted eternal Sisyphean curse. Bernice had suffered for so many years (sometimes to the point of both mental and physical exhaustion) that she prayed for relief. Over time, the therapy helped her insight, but it didn't stop her compulsions. She was out of control, she knew it, and it sickened her.

To experience even a modicum of relief, Bernice was open to exploring the possibility of trying some medications. She tried the antidepressive drug Zoloft (sertraline), which has solid evidence of efficaciousness for obsessive-compulsive disorder (OCD). But for Bernice, it didn't work; she only "felt numb," and her drive for perfection persisted. Another therapist diagnosed Bernice with having a bipolar disorder, and thus prescribed her Lithobid (lithium)—another drug that has a fine success rate with this disorder. However, Bernice again didn't experience any relief.

The Breakthrough

Bernice saw me on the *Dr. Phil* show and contacted me through my clinic. Clearly displaying signs of depression, she was pessimistic (to say the least) about the possibility of ever getting better. (I was frankly more worried about her despondent attitude than I was about her behavior.) I committed myself to helping this woman experience some measure of relief, no matter how small. I reviewed countless pages of literature, and began investigating anything she hadn't tried. Heck, I'd have slain a dragon to get dragon blood if I thought it'd work.

The breakthrough came as a result of a SPECT scan. SPECT scans help us to make brain maps, which are created by administering a radioactive chemical intravenously to the patient. The chemical remains in the bloodstream and doesn't cross the blood-brain barrier. As a result, the SPECT scan can safely map the brain's vascular system (blood supply). Because damaged or dead brain tissue (usually) ceases to receive a blood supply, this allows us to see focal vascular defects (lack of normal blood flow in important areas)—which can be very helpful when investigating brain functioning. Oh, in case you're curious, the advantage of conducting the SPECT scan assessment in addition to the QEEG assessment is that we can see deeper structural functioning (versus the brain's electromagnetic outputs).

Spin Cycle

The discovery was made that Bernice was suffering from the obsessive brain stress pattern. This pattern is highly correlated to the diagnosis of OCD. It's also associated with a form of depression in which the person cannot stop recalling bad experiences and/or errors in judgment. In many ways, this pattern resembles two simultaneous cyclones in which the brain is capable of only limited cross-referencing. Think of it this way: each cyclone keeps spinning into itself, having no end or beginning, no understandable point of reference, and just keeps seeing the same things over and over again . . . so it can't get new (valid) information.

Having a visual understanding of what was going on in her brain wasn't just useful for us diagnostically speaking, it was also profoundly helpful for Bernice herself. She now clearly understood why we needed to identify a method that would help the two sides of her brain start communicating with each other. She now dared to consider the possibility that there might be a light at the end of the tunnel for her. Fully embracing this new journey as her mission, she gave it a name: Bernice's Integration and Resolution.

Mission: Not Impossible

There were some additional medications (with encouraging profiles) we wanted her to consider trying, but understandably, she was reluctant to do so. What she was interested in pursuing was utilizing imagery. She liked the idea of thinking of different parts of her brain as a community filled with various cultures living in distinct and separate neighborhoods—which she wanted not only to introduce to each other, but also to seamlessly integrate. She learned that a successful method for bringing ostensibly disparate communities together was through music and dance. So she found some folk music she liked, and as she danced, she imagined all of the brain parts dancing together. As you now know, the research supports this type of integrated neurological firing (i.e., neurons that fire together, wire together). But more important, Bernice began to experience a sense of calm, and better resolutions to her obsessions.

A special method of breathing—the alternate-nostril method discussed on page 111—was also integrated into her daily routine. The idea behind this concept was to assist her brain in breaking old pathways so that she could forge new ones. The idea that she could "breathe new life into herself" thoroughly intrigued her. She had faith that if she could successfully change her breathing style, her hormones (such as adrenaline and cortisol) would respond the way they're supposed to, which would result in positive change. How did it work for her? She reported immediate beneficial results. For example, now whenever she started to obsess about cleaning the bathroom, she breathed in the alternate-nostril pattern, and in very short order, she experienced comfort and relief.

As Bernice advanced through the process of decreasing her stress storms, she embarked on first identifying and then managing her triggers—which were primarily found in her internal dialogue (the things we tell ourselves, which "define" who we are, what we believe we deserve, etc.). Her internal dialogue was largely based on her memory of her mother's harsh words, which would get stuck in an endlessly looping tape in her head; then would come her father's look of disparagement. So, whenever she began spontaneously to feel bad about herself, or whenever some authority figure would presumably chastise her for her performance, her self-destructive mom/dad warped belief system would get triggered. Fortunately, she finally "got" that unless she could begin to detour these thought patterns to a new and improved highway (neuropathway) and break the cycle, her struggles with obsessive stress storms would continue.

A cognitive therapy program proved very successful for Bernice as she confronted this childhood baggage. One of the techniques we taught her was to imagine her parents in front of her, and with their full attention, she forgave them, as she understood they did the best they could. Dear reader, forgiveness frees the person wronged, not the wrongdoer. It's easier to do if you remember that just because something is forgivable doesn't mean it's acceptable. So please, for your own sake, think about this important distinction.

In her mind, Bernice conducted a wonderful ritual in which she offered her parents joy and peace for themselves. Bernice then imagined herself unknotting a very old cord that had ensnared her and them. She then imagined they all celebrated together and exchanged small, thoughtful gifts. It should be noted that Bernice's parents are still alive and the ongoing challenges she has with them did not just magically disappear. However, that wasn't the goal. The goal was to release Bernice from her own compulsive mental trap, which she successfully accomplished. And for Bernice, that was incredibly freeing.

Of course, Bernice's success didn't happen overnight either, and her obsessive tendencies weren't entirely eradicated. But instead of allowing these tendencies to work against her, she had them work for her. How? Using her obsessive tendencies to channel her discipline into *achieving wellness* within her daily routine, she now was able to feel good about her professional competence and attention to details, without the unnerving sense of compulsion. Perhaps her greatest accomplishment was her realizing that joy and peace did indeed reside within her. . . . And her last brain scan confirmed her amazing progress.

SPECT SCAN IMAGE

A representative drawing of the SPECT scan pattern is presented below*. A fascinating aspect of this picture is that the image of the post anterior segment of the cingulated gyrus (the rounded ridges on the brain's outer layer) is clearly visible as having a very high activity level.

Note: a "real" image is significantly more complicated.

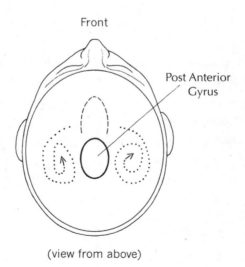

Front

Post Anterior
Gyrus

(view from above)

FIGURE 6.1

Psychiatric Diagnostic Categories Associated with the Obsessive Brain Pattern

Psychothenia depression
Obsessive-compulsive disorder
Bipolar II disorder
Schizophrenia NOS
Dysthymic disorder
Post-traumatic stress disorder
Acute stress disorder

OBSESSIVE PATTERN SELF-ASSESSMENT

The most direct method of determining whether you have an obsessive brain pattern is to get a brain scan. However, there are alternative methods, such as exploring whether you might have some of the symptoms associated with the obsessive brain pattern. To follow are a list of symptoms. Place a check mark next to all those that apply to you, not occasionally, but on most days:

1. You have intrusive, persistent thoughts and images that interfere with your day-to-day functioning, including interfering with your emotional access to positive feelings, such as joy and peace. _____

2. You have intrusive, persistent images that often trigger anxiety and stress. _____

3. You attempt to control these intrusive thoughts by excessive behaviors to reduce stress. _____

4. You attempt unsuccessfully to ignore the intrusive images with some distracting thoughts or actions._____

5. Although you may recognize the thoughts or images as irrational, you feel driven to reduce the resulting anxiety and frustration at all costs. _____

6. Often you feel the irrational compulsion to perform certain activities, such as washing your hands, counting, etc., as a means to reduce your anxiety._____

7. The time it takes to deal with these intrusive thoughts and images takes up at least an hour of every day, and interferes with your daily routine. _____

8. You often feel depressed because of the persistent memories of regret and disillusionment. _____

9. At times images or thoughts are triggered by external events and you can't control them or find ways to diminish their intensity. _____

10. In an attempt to control the onset of anxiety and frustration, you behave in a perfectionistic manner in your work, in the hope that by doing so, you won't be criticized, which you know would trigger ruminating images and thoughts. _____

11. In order to maintain control over the intrusion of ruminating thoughts and images, you cling tightly to your daily routines or to a specific set of rules, so much so that any deviation from that routine can trigger anxiety. _____

12. Your thoughts and worries keep spinning in your head without resolution, causing you constant and extreme stress. _____

Scoring: If you checked off more than eight of these symptoms, there's a reasonable chance your brain is vulnerable to obsessive brain patterns. Perpetual conflict isn't good—not for your brain, your body, or your spirit. Training your brain to overcome these conflicts is essential. So please read on.

BRAIN-WISE WHYS

The question that is often asked of me is: why did this happen to me? To date, nobody fully understands exactly why anyone suffers from stress storms. But there are a number of theories: the psycho-analytic/Freudian perspective generally says that we become fix-ated (stuck) at one of the developmental stages (i.e., oral, anal, phallic, latent, and genital), which frame how we grow up. For ex-ample, if you became developmentally stuck in the anal stage (typi-cally occurring between eighteen months and 3 ½ years of age, i.e., the potty-training years) this theory suggest you'd have issues with self-control, and be overly rigid and compulsively organized.

In the cognitive-behavior perspective, the focus is on anxiety-reduction responses. For example, a person feels insecure and threatened, which makes him anxious. With his limited coping re-sources, the only road to relief he feels is available to him is through attaining perfection, as defined by some authority figure, be that a parent, a boss, etc. Hence, as a person grows up, he projects inter-nalized fears on others (especially in authority), thereby creating (and empowering) his own critics—oftentimes with the "authority" figure being completely unaware he's participating in this process.

In the spirit of full disclosure, I believe cognitive psychotherapy is the most useful and successful approach, and I am a supporter of using relaxation and desensitization combined with rational internal dialogue. In my clinic, we use cognitive therapy as a primary therapeutic approach—after we get the storm under control, because nothing works when the cyclone is still erasing any message you try to offer to the patient.

Both one's genetic predisposition and environmental factors can certainly influence the development of this stress storm, but to what extent remains unclear. That said, it's SOP (standard operating procedure) for us to test for toxicity and metabolic factors, as invariably we discover one or both occurring at some level. Thus, this brain storm is probably the result of a combination of factors, rather than a singular, primary problem, and that means the solutions will also operate at multiple levels. In order to create harmony in a chaotic system, you have to apply multifaceted approaches that reinforce each other for a foundation of stability.

My impression as to the cause of this brain storm is based on themes that we can identify in the problem areas we see. The first is the emergence of the repetitive thought process common to obsessive-compulsive disorder, post-traumatic stress disorder, and ruminating depression. The instigating stages of this process are usually relatively easy to trace back to the anxiety formation of early childhood learning experiences—a basic tenet of the cognitive perspective. For example, cases of OCD are invariably strongly linked with past experiences of acerbic criticism for not being perfect. The second theme that emerges is a traumatic insult that can create a deregulation of the cingulate gyrus. The high stress of violence, particularly in military combat and combined with fatigue, can often cause such a disruption. And third, a maladaptive behavior response to anxiety is initiated. Being an irrational response, this may also be the result of a brain dysfunction. But no matter how you slice it, people stuck in the obsessive stress storm experience profound anxiety, which needs to be understood and then conquered if they are going to live their best life.

PROTOCOLS FOR SHIFTING OBSESSIVE STRESS STORM PATTERNS

Mental health protocols are not a one-size-fits-all thing. Anyone who suggests otherwise is either sorely misinformed . . . or has a less than honorable agenda. (Some want to sell you "secret cures" the government doesn't want you to know about. That's a bunch of bunk.) By the simple and honest process of trial and error, each of us must find the unique combination of techniques that will help us to best manage our personal obsessive stress patterns. I have witnessed great successes, and I am sharing my knowledge and insights with you for your careful consideration.

For example, I've seen prayer have an incredibly positive impact, but whether or not you'd be a good candidate for this method is not up to me. I've also witnessed Navajo healing and forgiveness rituals that have helped both individuals and entire communities. Again, how this works is far beyond my understanding. Of course, there are those who will wonder, do they "really" work? Personally, I don't cast judgment upon these methods—and I have no objective models to understand or evaluate them. But if these rituals work (and they certainly do for some people), who am I to deny their success?

I am, however, a scientist at heart. So, for the most part, claims of cures from isolated incidents don't wash with me. Whenever possible, I believe it is incumbent upon us to understand the strategy and test to see if those results can be replicated. That said, it wasn't until the 1970s that we learned some of the mechanisms as to *how* aspirin works (for which pharmacologist John Robert Vane won a Nobel Prize) and yet we've been taking aspirin since the days of Hippocrates, since, as you probably know, it's an extract (salicin) from the bark of the willow tree. (If you want to see for yourself, go look at an aspirin bottle—it'll say, main ingredient: salicylic acid.)

The following are some methods and protocols that have worked for a lot of people who suffer from obsessive brain storms. These are not the only approaches that work, mind you, but they are approaches that I have followed up with, and have found to be relatively easy for people to perform.

Principle I: Neurons that learn together become attached.

Neurotherapy

Although Bernice didn't opt for this therapeutic intervention, neurotherapy is probably the most direct method for learning how to change the stress storms. If we find that a part of the brain, such as the cingulate gyrus, is overactive with high beta frequencies or is abnormally low with delta frequencies and causing disruption, the process of neurotherapy would be to hook up an EEG monitor and attach electrodes to the skin surface to measure the electromagnetic energy of that region, which would likely show the same extra-high levels as found on the QEEG brain scan.

The therapeutic process would involve the patient being educated as to the significance of the graphs generated on the computer monitor, including becoming knowledgeable as to what the dysfunctional ranges are and utilizing the auditory and visual feedback. The EEG monitor is like an emotional mirror; and, with the help of a trained therapist, the patient can learn ways of balancing the discordant frequencies.

Imagery

One of our other patients, Fran, displayed brain waves in the cingulate gyrus region that were extremely high, and her emotional state was as if she was on a roller coaster of ever-repeating images, much like post-traumatic stress disorder. As she watched the monitor and heard some auditory feedback in the form of high and low tones, she discovered that the imagery of water created a positive change in the measurements. Later she learned that breathing patterns also helped in her control. Finally, she was able to lower these destructive frequencies and replace them with slower but higher-quality waveforms by imagining the waveforms themselves. Her concentration abilities improved almost immediately, and her feelings of panic soon subsided.

Using symbolic imagery—configurations of multiple meanings that are partially unconscious—offers you another excellent route to altering your brain patterns. One of the most intriguing findings made by Dr. Penfield when he was conducting brain mapping (see chapter three) was that all of his patients shared a common set of symbols, including webs, lattices, spirals, and circles. If you're as curious as I am, you will wonder if these apparently universal symbols might hold some particular power in rewiring the brain. Incorporating symbols of geometric figures in sand paintings and other art forms was a mainstay for ancient medicine healers. Dynamic images, such as the disposition of animals (their temperament and natural tendencies) and the special spirits within nature, have been utilized to shift brain focus for aeons.

This type of imagery has been shown to have very promising benefits for chronic pain, especially back pain, and has also been found to have some measurable, positive therapeutic effects for autoimmune diseases such as arthritis and even for cancer. Fran's symbolic use of water as a source of emotional cleansing (not unlike the concept behind baptism) enabled her to calm her obsessive brain storm. I've also personally observed the incorporation of some particularly powerful symbols such as fire (to figuratively burn away brain tension) and smells (to breathe in the calmness of pure love). Below is a brief list of symbols that individuals have successfully used to shift their obsessive brain storms:

> Spiritual figures (such as the calming voice of Jesus
>   Christ)
> A cyclone becoming calmer and smaller
> Hot colors becoming cooler
> The smells of Mother
> The smells of baking bread
> The companionship of a wolf or bear or dog

The touch of fur or silk
Unwinding a rope

I teach three basic steps to using imagery as a brain-altering tool. One, isolate the image of the problem; two, use a symbol for therapeutic change; and three, embrace external symbols for enhancement of your goal.

The first step in any challenge is to acknowledge what the problem is in specific terms. In this case, you will use an image or symbol of the problem, although it can be based on a physiological process. For example, let's assume that you have an obsessive storm problem and you visualize your brain's cingulate gyrus as the culprit—which it probably is. For the best results, keep your image of the problem symbol (the bad guy) very simple and unthreatening. You don't want your brain struggling to "get" a symbol that's too abstract, and you want something you know you can outsmart. One of my patients successfully imagined his problem as an errant ballpark hot dog that was in charge of coordinating his brain processes, but was failing miserably because it was too hot, and the mustard was short-circuiting his neuropathways. I loved that.

Now, choose a very complex and multilayered symbol for therapeutic change (the good guy). Let's choose a very wily and clever animal, such as a fox; and let's have his sole purpose in life being his unwavering, unconditional dedication to you and your well-being. Okay, now imagine your fox sneaking up behind the hot dog and dousing it with a bucket of cold water . . . or eating the hot dog, if you prefer! Or maybe you prefer to have the fox show the hot dog the error of its ways, and teach it how to do a great job, instead. Whether you choose any of these ideas, or have an idea that better suits your sensibilities, part of this process is the very personal quest for specific symbols that have meaning for you. As long as it works for you, it's all good.

Lastly, once you've created the imagery for healing that works for you, imagine how you can enhance the process and make it stick. For example, you might find that going through steps one and two are enhanced if you do so while listening to certain music, or doing some gentle breathing patterns. Many people have found that certain scents, such as vanilla, cinnamon, or rose, enhance the process too. Then, just thinking about some of these wonderful smells (or actually smelling them, of course) may have the potential to calm your storms. Be sure you practice and redefine your imagery until it feels effective.

Here's what's going on: you will actually be using your brain's own internal mechanisms for help. Instead of only seeing your brain as weak and in chaos, you will see your brain as having the power to heal you as well. It takes about twenty-one days of consistent imagery to stabilize the association. Thus, if you can stick with this imagery process for a mere twenty-one days—and there's no reason you can't—your brain will incorporate the imagery within the storm neural network and have an internal key to conflict resolution. In other words, your path to positive healing may only be twenty-one days away.

As an aside, embracing imagery as a tool for success isn't some wild, newfangled idea: even a superstar like Tony Dorsett of the Dallas Cowboys (now retired) has shared that he imagined himself like a running tornado—and few would argue that his spinning motion didn't have a great impact on his successful avoidance of being tackled. And of course you know that Olympic athletes are taught to visualize their events with success before their participation. There has even been research that suggests that imagery can improve not only coordination, but also strength.

Rhythmic Exercise

Bernice's daily regimen of dance and rhythmic music played an important role in her effort to calm her obsessive stress storms, and I can justify this application based on years of research into the effects of rhythmic exercise on the brain. When you start moving the body in a consistent movement, you will affect every organ and muscle in the body, and if you do this consistently, you'll build an integration of muscular coordination. This is what happens when you learn to play golf, tennis, or any other sport. Some call it "muscle memory." You keep doing the same motion over and over again, and your body will default to that movement. So, you want to be sure you're practicing the right moves.

The basic reason we have that ability to reshape our bodies is because our brains are plastic enough to change nerve pathways very efficiently. Although this process affects the whole brain, I give a lot of credit to the cerebellum because it's responsible for the bundling of nerves and for coordinating them. It achieves this process by interacting with all of the brain, much the way the cingulate gyrus does. It makes sense that if you stimulate the brain overall into rhythmic and harmonious connections, and the cingulate gyrus in particular, the deregulation will be helped back to normal, naturally.

Principle II: Experience and need can change neurological bundles.

The obsessive stress pattern is thought to be more of a learned pattern (in reaction to anxiety and fear) than a genetic one, which is actually good news for brain reeducation. However, the pattern is seen in the lower brain regions—where logic and rational processing have no grip. This is a challenge for protocols in psychology, since we deal primarily with thought processes. So here are new patterns that work on positive experience.

Rehearsal

The idea of rehearsals is to prepare for a performance. We've found success with the imagining of alternate methods for dealing with anxiety or fear. For example, I had a patient who could never leave her house for fear that she'd left the iron or stove on, and that it would shortly set the house on fire. So, we initiated rehearsals by which we'd go through the process in her imagination, but with the addition of methods of reassurance. She started the rehearsal by imagining herself leaving the house, using an itemized check-off system that she imagined she thoroughly could trust and believe in. During her imagery she was given relaxation techniques for her anxieties whenever they came up, and was forbidden to continue on her checking. In terms of practical changes, she exchanged her appliances for those that had automatic shutoffs. These improvements made her feel good. And feeling good makes the brain happy . . . and compliant. Basically, she learned to use more attractive alternative methods to deal with her ruminations.

Thought-Stopping Techniques

Another approach that I find interesting is prohibition of anxiety-related behaviors. The patient is told to stop the behaviors the instant they start. This is similar to the "thought-stopping" techniques in which the disruptions can be as simple as yelling, "STOP!" or creating a negative reinforcement, such as an electric shock. I've rarely used this method because it requires a lot of skill. If it works, it works quickly, but that doesn't mean the game is over. I have witnessed the process, however, and have seen how effective it can be.

Principle III: Suspension of thoughts or elimination of specific experience can allow neurological changes to happen immediately.

Breathing

I know some may scoff at the idea of this breathing method, called *alternate nostril breathing*. But I have some impressive brain scans to support my conclusion that this breathing tool has therapeutic value. Perhaps it's a placebo effect, but if the patient has faith, and it works, then we've achieved our goal. Besides, what's wrong with mind over matter—especially when the process is free? Here's how you do it: it's simple, really. Just gently press your index finger against your right nostril, so that the passage of air is blocked. Cycle through slowly, purposefully, inhaling and exhaling through your left nostril; then, switch nostrils. Continue until you feel a sense of calm. Then, do it for six more minutes; three minutes per side. Brain scans confirm a rapid change in frequency intensity.

Patients of mine have successfully used this breathing technique to halt intrusive, obsessive thoughts in their tracks; and it's a fine method even for the comforting aspect alone. Plus, new associations can be formed for a new inventory of anxiety-reducing practices.

Nutrition

One need not have a Ph.D. in diet and nutrition to know that the brain functions best when fed whole, natural (unprocessed, unbleached) foods, including citrus fruits, vegetables, oily fish (such as salmon), whole grains (like oats), berries, and dark chocolate.

Individuals who've found nutritional plans that work for them have usually focused on foods that stimulate them—which would be consistent with the results achieved through regular exercise and BAUD-assisted neurotherapy.

By simply eliminating junk food from your diet and replacing it with real foods, you'll be amazed how quickly your brain can make the shift to improved focus and emotional stability (go rent *Super Size Me*). So walk down the fresh fruit aisle or go check out a local farmers' market and try some real foods from God's rainbow.

Chanting

As we've seen, the brain responds to music and rhythm, and the impact is magnified when it responds to the internal vibrations made by our own vocal chords. Chanting in repetition has been shown to shift the overall frequency toward alpha (which is the relaxation range), and tends to create a harmonious level across the brain. The psychological impact is one of feeling peaceful and confident.

If we look at current theories on quantum physics, we see additional support for a cellular or even molecular model for the impact of chanting. All particles including atoms, electrons, and subatomic particles are energy in a state of oscillation. Since sound is a vibration, we can assume that any sound generator will cause other particles to act as resonators, picking up the sound from the source. This change in the vibration of subatomic particles can affect how larger entities such as atoms and cells are structured. If this associative process is generated from cell to cell, neurological changes would be consistent with those manufactured frequencies, especially if they come from within the body.

I'm compelled to share with you a study done with houseplants. (Yes, it's a stretch, but I think it's cool, and I'm betting you'll think so, too.) One group of houseplants was exposed to acid rock every day, one group was exposed to classical music every day, and another group was exposed to "inspirational" music every day. The plants exposed to acid rock actually began to grow away from the sound source (speakers) and began to turn yellow and sickly. The classical group grew and flourished. The inspirational group had accelerated growth and grew toward the sound source. Though some might find acid rock inspirational, most people find it energizing (at best) and irritating (at worst) . . . except for teenagers.

In addition to the sound influences, the words you use as mantras or inspirational sentences can have a big influence as well. It's well accepted that telling yourself destructive things (like "I'm a total idiot; I don't deserve good things; I'm a bad person; I'm sinful") can create negative brain patterns. Likewise, positive phrases can create positive brain patterns, but you must practice them consistently. I usually require those with this obsessive stress storm to repeat a positive phrase a thousand times a day in order to entwine the brain patterns to combat their negative ones. Remember, neurons that fire together, wire together.

I would start by choosing one phrase, such as "I can do this" or "I am enough" to use as your chanting phrase. Spiritual ones like "God loves me, I am forgiven, God walks with me" have shown excellent results as well. In my therapeutic interactions, I've chosen specific phrases that pertain to a person's unique needs and brain function. I recommend you do the same. Choose what's right for you.

Principle IV: Times of growth and change are opportunities for learning and relearning.

As we've discussed, this principle has the change agent in the brain as its basis. For me, this is the critical turning point in the effort to shift the obsessive brain pattern.

Psychotherapy and Counseling

Unless you identify and resolve the psychological triggers, using protocols alone won't stop the obsessive brain storms. Whether we're talking about OCD or PTSD, there are events that triggered the cycle in the first place, such as a trauma or childhood stress or another tragic event.

A person can be triggered into having a cyclonic episode by a seemingly benign cue from the environment that they somehow associate with the original trauma. The response can be so immediate that the person may already be in a full-fledged storm before management can be attempted. By addressing the surface stresses of the events and situations, a person can gain insight and find ways to prevent or avoid being overcome by the unconscious response.

Just as Bernice discovered how her stress response was related to her mother's intensive drive for cleanliness, anyone can learn to change his destructive psychological responses to more constructive ones. Bernice realized that as a child she was a victim of extreme stress, and had little or no control to alter her environment—or her responses to it. Her choices at that time were limited, but as adults, we can to choose to take appropriate control both internally and externally. Whether one chooses to leave a toxic environment behind, or to resolve it, is a personal decision. But it is also one that can be helpfully shaped by working with a caring therapist.

Psychotherapy and counseling that focus on making mature choices about anxiety management appear to be the best avenues for psychological growth. Having encouragement to grow and take responsibility for our feelings and emotions can be extraordinarily helpful in overcoming a variety of the traps we find ourselves in.

Practice, Slowly and Deliberately

When you want to formulate a new brain pattern, you have to work to establish the pattern you want to achieve. I once talked to a piano master about how he reached the heights he has, and he voiced this principle as his "secret" of success. He explained that if you want to be a piano player, you have to start with one note and understand the feeling and frequency of that note. Then, add another note and compare them. As you add the full complement of notes, you pay close attention and set your brain to each tone. He also made a point of emphasizing that this doesn't just happen over the course of one day or even in a year. His investment of thirty years attests to the necessity of discipline. As the old joke goes: a tourist exploring the wonders of New York City asks a local, "How do I get to Carnegie Hall?" To which the local replies, "Practice, practice, practice."

Principle V: New pathways can be changed and improved.

Celebrate Success

I realize that I often repeat my requirement that you learn to celebrate whatever success you've made toward your goals of thinking differently . . . and I'm going to continue to do so. Celebration is almost entirely a brain sensation. Our joy is personally interpreted in the brain cells. As you practice alternative thinking patterns in calming your fears, give yourself due credit. Even a brief period of peace is to be prized. Take time to give yourself compliments.

Reach for Support

Bring your support group and have a party with your brain at the center. The group energy can enhance your new brain shift by means of collective support. Friends' encouragement is invaluable. However, here's a warning concerning toxic relationships: a single negative attitude can block three positives, especially if the (toxic) person has been part of the fear response to begin with. Even if circumstances make it difficult, to the best of your ability, stay away from all people who will do more damage than good—at least early on in the process.

OVERALL THOUGHTS

The ruminating, obsessive brain storm is perhaps the most destructive of all stress storms because it's so incapacitating to the individual. You feel trapped in your own private hell from which you feel there is no escape. You realize you're behaving in bizarre and strange ways and indulging in ritualistic behavior, but you feel powerless, and frankly, too afraid to change. The fear is unbearable, although in your mind you know it's not reality. You can't make sense of why you behave as if someone else were controlling you.

The exciting thing is that there is hope. There are some medications that can stabilize you; controls you can find in rhythmic movement, neurotherapy, and nutrition; and a host of personal changes you can incorporate into your daily life to banish hell from your reality and step into a better and joyous life. Most important, you are not condemned to a lifetime of anxiety and fear. The brain can be reset with the right tools. Your free will and true sense of self will come back to you.

7

The Depressive Stress Storm

Paul walked into the clinic looking more like a robot than a man. He was tall and slender, with shoulders that slumped forward, as if in a feeble attempt to hide his heart. While he was only fifty-one years old, he looked more like ninety. His face was expressionless, except for an overall look of pessimism. Visibly uncomfortable in his own skin, he moved awkwardly, as though he were using another person's body—a person he didn't like. The only thing that suggested he wasn't one of the walking dead was his saucerlike eyes, which were those of the proverbial scared deer in headlights.

Paul's voice was so soft you could barely hear his question: "Can you help me with my depression?" During our initial evaluation, he had great difficulty finding the words to explain his emotional history and the trials and tribulations he had endured. In fact, his evaluation required twice the time usually necessary (two hours instead of one). He clearly wanted to be heard, but was unpracticed in expressing himself.

Paul came to our clinic because he was very depressed, yet when we asked him what his feelings were, either good or bad, he looked confused and answered, "I really don't know. All I know is that I am unhappy." For someone who is suffering with depression, such a response is rather common: one of the hallmarks of depression is a basic lack of joy and a vapid emptiness. Paul had tried many things to feel better, but nothing had helped. Peace and happiness had morphed into a vague, unattainable concept only available to others to enjoy.

Paul's attempts to bring himself out of his doldrums included going on trips, attending bridge parties, taking cruises, and joining others to watch football games on television. Odd as it may sound, he didn't describe himself at these events as a loner or wallflower. He interacted appropriately and even had some dates along the way, but despite his concerted use of energy he remained depressed.

SOME BACKSTORY

Paul's depression had begun four years before, shortly after his wife had succumbed to cancer. Throughout the mourning process, Paul received substantive support from his family, and he really didn't think his wife's death was the cause of his depression. He explained that she had been suffering with terminal cancer for years, which had given her and Paul sufficient time to make plans, forgive each other for past issues, and say their goodbyes.

Although Paul described his early family experiences as normal, he recalled many incidents in which his father was particularly hard on him when he was (ostensibly) responsible for losing a basketball game. He also remembered a time in which he'd cheated on a test, but never told anyone. Racked with guilt, he went to the teacher fifteen years later and apologized for his act, but the teacher barely remembered him and had no recollection of the test. Nevertheless, he still carried the self-criticism in his head.

Psychological testing revealed principally what we'd thought: he was suffering with some form of depression; and, his brain scan (QEEG) confirmed he was indeed in a depressive stress storm. This is a pattern in which the part of the brain that experiences moods and feelings (especially positive feelings) is stuck in a delta state, or perhaps closer to a coma.

EASE ON DOWN THE ROAD

With a diagnosis in hand, a program was defined. The first goal was to get that sleeping part of the brain stimulated so Paul could begin to have some feelings, even if they weren't going to be good ones. He believed in exercise, but was uncomfortable with the "dancing alone" idea. So, he began a treadmill-jogging program that he did while listening to rhythmic music. Soon thereafter, he also enrolled in a dance class (rumba and waltz) for people without partners. His assigned dance partner was apparently a godsend, as Paul kept telling us how "energizing she was."

TALK TO MY DOG

While Paul was no stranger to psychotherapy (he had seen a therapist after his wife's death), he was reluctant to give it another try. "In my past therapy situations," Paul revealed, "all I did was talk, and the therapists would say almost nothing. I felt like I was doing all the work. And frankly, I get more feedback when I talk to my dog." He promised, however, to reserve judgment and give it another shot.

He was pleasantly surprised to find that this time the therapy was actively engaging. It downright intrigued him. He learned quite a bit about himself when he was administered several tests about his interests, and he was very impressed that he had a high intelligence score and a solid self-concept. In essence, he got to know himself more objectively.

Paul also learned that he had self-imposed rules that were emotionally destructive. For example, he discovered that he had a habit of shutting down his feelings whenever he was overcome by negative thoughts. I suspect that this happened when he was faced with his wife's dying. When he felt grief, or even joy, he interpreted these feelings as weak or improper and shut them down, essentially flipping off the switch to his feelings. Unfortunately, he didn't know how to flip the switch back on . . . But now he does.

Within six weeks, Paul was a different man. He still had trouble acknowledging some of his negative feelings, but he kept up with therapy, which proved exceptionally helpful, as well as with his jogging and dancing. On our last follow-up, Paul shared that he just received a first-place trophy in a golf tournament and had a steady girlfriend. He had a suntan anyone would give good money to get, and was working at a job he liked very much. I watched him drive away on his motorcycle and wondered if he could teach me a thing or two. Ladies and gentlemen, the robot has left the building.

THE DEPRESSIVE BRAIN STORM PATTERN

As I shared with you earlier, I grew up in West Texas, where I sometimes had to deal with 50 to 60 mph winds that were so thick with dust you couldn't see ten feet in front of you. Plus, those storms made everything rattle and clang—which only added to the sense of unsettling creepiness. Did I mention that those storms would last for weeks? Sometimes they seemed like they were never going to end. That's as near as I can describe what it's like to have a depressive brain storm whipping inside your head. Although, if you learn to embrace it, you can, at times, make it work to your advantage: when faced with such a powerful force, you have to lean against it, which can give you a sense of resistance that you can count on for support. You begin to feel this force teasing you and welcoming your intention to work with it. That being said, when you do have a calm day, it can almost feel like you're missing something, the companion who pushes against you in order to support both of you.

FLYING IN THE FACE OF THE WIND

Possibly because of my kinship with the wind, I enjoyed learning to pilot my own plane, mastering the art of gliding through the updrafts and slipping through the thermals like a hawk. For the same reason, I love boating—especially harnessing the wind in my sails to speed me along. For most of us, however, the depressive wind pattern in our brains is not a constructive force, especially as the emotions whip up paralyzing fears and underlying insecurities. In fact, according to a recent study, depression is described as being the disease most destructive to humankind, largely because of the devastation it wreaks on our lives and how it exacerbates disease. Yes, we could set up our minds to ignore our feelings and barricade ourselves from the winds and dust of the brain pattern. And we could become like robots, refusing to consider the passion and joys that could be ours. But then, we also might as well be dead.

The high correlation between the depressive brain pattern and the vacuous depths of depression is so consistent that I believe there's some link at the neurological level. The classic brain pattern we see as part of the depressive emotions (and which correlates very nicely with clinical analysis of melancholia) is one in which there's very low activity in the left frontal area and the nearby temporal lobes, indicating very little capacity to experience pleasure by the slow amount of neuron firing. The relatively higher activity in the right lobe creates a dominant left frontal lobe function, which then blurs focus.

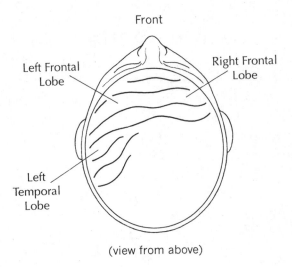

(view from above)

FIGURE 7.1

When you think about these parts of the brain, it makes sense that a person with a low-functioning left frontal lobe with slow activity to the temporal lobe would feel empty. As explained in chapter two, the frontal lobe is assigned the role of processing and organizing information, often prioritizing it as important or not. The temporal lobes are related to memory and emotional management. When the activities are high in these regions, you will likely experience high levels of excitement. In this case, you may be trapped into very low activities of emotions if the frequencies indicate chronic low energy. I would predict that people who have lost the joy and meaning in life might have the same or similar patterns. In my experience, men are especially vulnerable to shutting down their emotional life in order to succeed in objective pursuits, such as in business. Men's sexual interests also go by the wayside, because they feel dead inside. If Ebenezer Scrooge were a real person, I'm betting his brain pattern (pre-ghosts, of course) would have shown his "joy centers" to be numb as well.

Scores of people who have this brain pattern (along with the accompanying psychological profile of emptiness) have reported that sometime in their history they've felt entirely unable to handle life's barrage of stresses and emotional demands. Some of these difficulties were connected to professional problems, but most of them related to an incomplete grieving process, whether it was the loss of a loved one, a relationship, or a job. These people had all in one way or another shut themselves down. And in the absence of a major inspirational experience or epiphany, they couldn't break away from the self-defeating, destructive pattern.

ASSESSING THE DEPRESSIVE STRESS STORM PATTERN

In order to determine if you or someone you love may be having a depressive stress storm, some of the primary symptoms are described below. Please place a check mark indicating how long you've been experiencing each of the following:

1. You feel empty inside and are totally unable to feel anything, good or bad.
   All the time _____ Most of the time _____ Sometimes _____ Never _____

2. You no longer enjoy doing the things that used to bring you happiness and joy.
   All the time _____ Most of the time _____ Sometimes _____ Never _____

3. You use irritability to cover up your feelings of depression.
   All the time _____ Most of the time _____ Sometimes _____ Never _____

4. You have a marked decrease in any kind of interest or pleasure.
   All the time _____ Most of the time _____ Sometimes _____ Never _____

5. You have had a significant weight loss, lost your appetite, and/or food no longer gives you pleasure.
   All the time _____ Most of the time _____ Sometimes _____ Never _____

6. Your sleep patterns are disrupted.
   All the time _____ Most of the time _____ Sometimes _____ Never _____

7. Although you may expend energy in carrying out tasks, you enjoy no sense of accomplishment or pride.
   All the time _____ Most of the time _____ Sometimes _____ Never _____

8. Your abilities to concentrate and focus have diminished.
   All the time _____ Most of the time _____ Sometimes _____ Never _____

9. There is a noticeable sluggishness in your usual behaviors that is not merely a sign of fatigue or a purposeful slowing down.
   All the time _____ Most of the time _____ Sometimes _____ Never _____

10. When it comes to making choices, you're indecisive or simply don't care what happens.

    All the time _____ Most of the time _____ Sometimes _____ Never _____

11. You discover that regardless of what you do, you cannot feel a sense of joy or embrace any perspective other than a negative one.

    All the time _____ Most of the time _____ Sometimes _____ Never _____

12. Although medications, food, or encouragement may help you become more active, there remains a sense of emotional emptiness.

    All the time _____ Most of the time _____ Sometimes _____ Never _____

13. You have an underlying attitude of pessimism.

    All the time _____ Most of the time _____ Sometimes _____ Never _____

14. You feel as though you're mourning the emotional loss of yourself.

    All the time _____ Most of the time _____ Sometimes _____ Never _____

15. You no longer feel any passion about your direction in life, and can't remember if you ever did.

    All the time _____ Most of the time _____ Sometimes _____ Never _____

Scoring: If you marked at least eight descriptions as "All the time" or "Most of the time," there is a high probability you may be experiencing the depressive storm pattern. If you have marked three to seven descriptions as "All the time" or "Most of the time," then you are likely entering into a vortex of attitudes and behaviors that may shut down your feelings and emotions.

Some of the diagnoses correlated with the depressive stress storm pattern include:

Depression disorder
Catatonic schizophrenia
Dysthymic disorder
Bipolar disorder
Cyclothymic disorder
Histrionic personality disorder
Adjustment disorder
Hypochondriasis

Even if you're experiencing a major brain storm marked by these characteristics, or if you've consciously avoided fear and anxiety at the expense of experiencing any pleasure or happiness, it doesn't have to stay that way. I'm here to help you understand your options and give you the tools so that you can make your life better.

WHEN BAD BECOMES WORSE

When you have the right tools and generous guidance, the process of emerging from the darkness is obviously less cumbersome and, frankly, easier. But most people don't have these resources at their disposal. Plus, when you're depressed, you don't really want to do anything—even a guarantee of a 100 percent improvement (which no ethical person can make) wouldn't be enough to get a lot of depressed people motivated. Depression can even make you lack the energy to so much as change the channel on your remote. You may prefer to sit in total darkness rather than deal with the disturbing sights and the sounds of unwanted chatter. You may have the feeling that it would be simpler to just die. You may also have a gnawing feeling that suicide would be more trouble than it's worth. *Important note: If you suffer from any form of suicidal thoughts, please seek immediate professional attention. Call 1-800-273-TALK (8255), 1-800-SUICIDE (784-2433), or go to: http://suicidehotlines.com/.*

A DAILY GRIND

The flip side to these thoughts of dropping out is the realization that you owe it to your family (if not yourself) not to abandon or embarrass them or cause them emotional harm. So, you resign yourself to accepting this bleakness as your lot in life; and you wish that each day that passes wouldn't drag on so slowly. Depression begins to define who you are, and may tragically become the primary focus of your life.

You probably do recognize that your friends and loved ones really are worried about you. You might even eke out a smile, attempt to act as if everything is fine, and make the occasional effort to join them for a meal, a movie, or a shopping trip. It's also likely that you experience participating in these sorts of activities (and maintaining the "things are great" façade for any length of time) as totally exhausting. You probably feel a sense of relief moments after returning home, getting back to your chair or bed, and sitting in front of your television set, not caring if it's on or off.

As you meet this situation day after day, there are many things you can do . . . to make it even worse and completely destroy the dignity you have left. Not where you thought I was going, right? Well, I'm here to help you help yourself, and sugarcoating the reality of the situation won't help you one iota. That would be like my not warning you (at the top of my lungs) that medicating yourself with drugs like alcohol and cocaine is a recipe for disaster. Recovering alcoholics have told me thousands of stories in which they started drinking because they were depressed. That drives me nuts.

As the old saying goes, "troubles don't sink, they float." Drugs and alcohol can do worse than damaging your attitude for a short period of time. They become toxic to your brain, they wreak havoc on your nervous system, and your whole metabolism can be disrupted. Psychological addiction becomes a biological disease and one from which you may never totally recover—especially when it is coupled with depression. If you try (or persist in using) these horribly destructive approaches, you might as well make friends with the devil, because you're going to stay with him the rest of your life. I'm not kidding. This is very serious business.

The dangers I've discussed thus far are certainly not new information for most of us, and will be too familiar to all of us at some time in our lives. You can bet on it. Depression, sadness, and grief are part of life. We all suffer loss, pain, disappointments, and dishonest relationships, and meet our worst nightmares as part of living. However, when we reach the lowest depths of despair, when we feel that last gasp of self-respect dissolve, we will have reached the pivotal point that defines what we recognize as "hell."

COMMUNITY DEPRESSION: A DARK FORCE

Just as a depressive crisis can create transformation, it can also destroy the entire body. And sometimes, a crisis may feel like a cosmic test, one in which a person has never been taught the skills necessary to meet its challenges. If so, the root of the problem can often be found in our society. In today's world, we seem to teach ourselves how to be depressed. Do we not create the greatest amount of anxiety over grades and competitions in which there is only one winner and many losers? Do we not define our achievements as compared to others, rather than within ourselves? Do we not sometimes gloat over another's miseries and feel shame when we ourselves lose? Do we not create an unfair society, replete with health-care disparities, and become stressed when we are treated inequitably? How often do we give our controls over to others just because we do not want to take responsibility for the outcome? These are not the hallmarks of an evolved, educated society.

This of course begs the question: *What causes depression?* The answer is profoundly complex, because there are many ways in which we're vulnerable to it. For example, sometimes a family history of abuse and neglect is involved. The research is full of accounts of depression relating to family histories, especially when violence, drugs, and alcoholic parents are factors. Depression might also stem from environmental contamination, such as exposure to pesticide, lead, mercury, benzene, or a whole bevy of toxic elements. Our veterans certainly can testify to the detrimental effects of exposure to various toxic compounds of war. It can come from an overzealous attitude, or a misplaced sense of entitlement, from how you think the world should treat you and the disappointments from the "unfairness" you experience.

We still don't know if people are predisposed to depression, or whether it's caused by one specific event or by a combination of factors. What we do know for certain is that 1) You shouldn't count on depression resolving on its own, 2) Finding ways to merely live with your hellish existence is not acceptable, and 3) If you feel otherwise (like you deserve to be in hell) that's your depression talking. To put it another way, if you think you aren't worthy of joy and happiness—no matter what you've done, think you've done, or believe you deserve—then your brain is betraying you. You must somehow find it within yourself to take the steps necessary to whip your brain into shape. This will take hard work and commitment on your part, but your brain will thank you. Promise.

NO MAGIC PILL

The medical quest of the twentieth century (which has sadly spilled over into the twenty-first) was to find that magic pill to eradicate the suffering of depression. To some extent, this makes sense: prescription antidepressive medications absolutely have their place. Indeed, when combined with psychotherapy, particularly the cognitive style, antidepressants can have a pronounced positive effect and have been shown to yield longer-lasting, powerful results. I've had patients who had reached the point of mental paralysis, and medication clearly helped them to free up some of their emotional resources, which in turn allowed them to be able to learn new pathways toward success. It was as if the antidepressive medication gave them a desperately needed jump start. But in my opinion, taking medication without discovering new pathways for conflict resolution isn't just an ineffective Band-Aid to depression, it's irresponsible, and can lead to dire consequences. Resolution of depression almost always includes a change in lifestyle, learning and mastering new sets of abilities, retooling your coping skills, and learning how to identify and accept a brand-new life path you never thought possible.

I remember the first time a friend of mine shared the following truth: *If you always do what you've always done, you'll always get what you've always got.* Many people want an instant "add water and stir" cure to expedite their return to their old life. But that's the life that led to the dark abyss in the first place. That's not the way to go, although I totally understand their sense of urgency to get out of where they are. But here's the thing: if you truly want to get better, you don't want to be the same, you want to be better than you were. That means, if you're going to become emotionally more resilient, you must learn what got you here, and which new paths will get you the hell out.

THE TIME TO ACT IS NOW

While periods of depression are the times in which we feel most isolated, sometimes they force us to discover the hidden strengths within ourselves. The personal journeys through which we rise above the paralysis of depression are some of the most courageous endeavors of our lives. They reveal the enormous capacity of the human spirit to embrace the power of transformation in the face of extraordinary odds. Renovating one's soul in this way propels us to heights of emotional and spiritual strength that defy words. But you'll know it when it happens to you.

While it's likely that you can identify some external factors that have contributed to your depression, there is also a high probability that you may be participating at some level, even if you're doing so unconsciously. You see, there's usually some kind of payoff that's reinforcing your depression. I had a friend who loved her sadness and enjoyed sharing how miserable she was with others even more: "My daughter wouldn't bring me a cup of soup when I was so sick; I sacrificed my life for that ungrateful girl; I just give and give and she just takes and takes." What's the payoff? People she'd share these stories with would respond, "Oh, that's just awful. Please, any time you need anything, please call me. You poor, poor dear." This woman's depression made her believe she was only deserving of pity, so she made sure she got it.

We have to separate the emotional factors from who we are and who we want to be. This requires discovering a true image of ourselves. You are truly worthy of great things and of love and re-spect. The self-journeys you must take are the paths to knowing yourself and, more important, knowing what you can do for your-self. You will find that some of the paths are deceptively simple; so much so, in fact, that you might feel silly when you realize how much positive impact you can really have on your mind and body. The best example from my own experience was learning how the simple act of dancing can make one's mind find joy.

The time to act is now. You have the right to be happy and peaceful, but you have to make a move. Success is within your grasp. Say the following out loud right now: *I choose to make a difference in my life, starting right now. I can do this.* Now, say that again. Yes, right now. Excellent. Now, while I rarely insist anyone do anything, I'm going to make an exception: I insist that you make a promise to yourself that you will start today. You are too valuable to waste away in the darkness.

PATHS TOWARD JOY

A diagnosis of depression can indicate many different forms of de-spair and hopelessness, because each person's experience is highly individualized. There are countless volumes written about depres-sion and billions of dollars spent every year in the attempt to break its chains on the human soul. It's not my mission (nor am I equipped) to answer every question about this massive issue, but the depressive brain storm is certainly a part of this complex of terms and dynamics.

Principle I: Neurons that learn together become attached.

Emotions Follow Behavior
Though the brain often directs our behavior, sometimes our actions can direct our brain functions instead. In other words, up until this

point, we've been discussing how our stress storms can create actions that are nonproductive and destructive by the nature of their dysfunction. However, we can also improve the way our brains work by changing our behavior first. What do you think would happen if we began to behave in ways that were inconsistent with what our brain tells us to do? Which would be changed? It might initially be a bit disorienting, but just like a number of other activities discussed (e.g., controlled breathing and dancing), the brain storms and their resulting patterns can be diverted by how we choose to behave.

Consider the action of instigating laughter to facilitate emotional change: a child enters the family room in a mood best described as grumpy, sad, and frankly, unpleasant. Nothing you say appeases her, and she responds only with angry avoidance and harsh words about herself and others. When asked what has occurred that may have triggered her sullen state, she gives you only some vague details about how her friends are treating her poorly, and her desire to jump off the edge of the earth rather than talk to them again. I know this story because it has happened in my household what feels like a thousand times. That said, the following works like a charm . . . well, usually.

What I do is first turn on some music I know my daughter likes. Then I convince her to start jumping and skipping around the room—while she's venting her anger. In no time, her attitude begins to change. Soon I join in and we start tossing pillows or colored tissue paper into the air . . . which makes her smile and laugh. Before she knows it (usually after about fifteen minutes), she's better able to get things into perspective, becoming more capable of realistically dealing with her personal drama. Typically, she resolves incidents with her friends by the end of the next day; and life goes on.

Here are two tips to get younger ones motivated to try this. One, challenge them by saying, "What? Are you afraid it might actually work and make you feel better?" And two, offer to start dancing and skipping around the room first . . . and then do it! Laughter really

can be some of the best medicine when it comes to nipping potentially depressive episodes in the bud. Plus, laughing with your children will do wonders to further the bond you share with them.

On a far more serious note, recent scientific studies investigating
the impact of humor on cancer patients found that its effects include improving the immune system, lowering the levels of stress
hormones in the body, decreasing anxiety and discomfort levels,
relieving physical stress (also measured by hormone activity), promoting a general sense of wellness, and improving patient comfort
levels in ways that help them feel more free to discuss their concerns and fears with others. That's powerful stuff.

In the past, I helped run pain clinics. Patients usually didn't discover us until they'd been dealing with horrible pain for years,
which was such a shame. After they completed their treatment program with us, we'd always do a post-treatment exit interview as
part of our ongoing efforts to provide the best services, results, and
experiences possible. Nearly every patient rated the group support
element and physical exercise programs as top-notch. But the patients who experienced the best success (as defined by them) were
the ones who put five stars next to: "I learned to laugh again."

Exercise

Participating in physical exercise has been shown to be one of the
most powerful (if not THE most powerful) behaviors you can use
to positively impact your mind and body. It works more effectively
than almost anything else we can do for ourselves—especially
when it comes to mood improvement and depression. However,
some people take this to the extreme and exhaust themselves and
their brains, which can do more harm than good; so don't do that.
The secret isn't so much related to the amount of exertion, but
rather, it's the rhythm of the body and breathing that does the
magic. The benefits you will experience by engaging in physical
activity are practically instantaneous. And doing so every day helps
you sustain both your physical and emotional improvements
immeasurably.

Horses have a natural way of coordinating the rhythm of their running because their lungs are like an accordion: as they run, their bodies squeeze and extend their diaphragm equal to their efforts. We aren't built that way, obviously, so we have to train ourselves to get into a rhythm. Some people consciously breathe in certain exercise patterns. If you swim, this occurs naturally because of the breathing patterns associated with the strokes (and not swallowing water). If you walk, you can purposely match your breathing to your stride. I find it easiest to use music and sing along with my exercise; it makes working out a lot more fun, and the music can be inspirational as well.

Exercise is vital to your brain and uplifting for you in many ways: it increases oxygen to the brain, relieves the stress on the brain and body, and strengthens the brain's interactions, helping to facilitate problem solving. Commitment is essential, so if you hate exercising, simply commit to doing some very moderate physical activity (like walking in place and stretching) for just five minutes a day. One of my favorite people on the planet (who detests exercise in all its forms) does something she calls "commercial exercise." While watching television, she only exercises during the commercials. She'll do curls with five-pound weights during the first set of commercials, and switches to lunges for the second set. If she's feeling particularly motivated, she might do abdominal crunches. And when she has no motivation at all, she still does gentle stretches at every commercial. This unique approach has worked wonders for her.

Principle II: Experience and need can change neurological bundles.

Faced with sudden loss of wealth during the Great Depression of the 1930s, some people were known to have said, "I just get busy and work my depression to death." This concept may have some constructive value, in that it offers a way of transforming emotion into a positive force. Certainly the shift in focus brings about a change in the brain. And by changing our focus, we may bring the frontal and temporal lobes into a state of higher functioning.

The primary fear here is being "stuck" in the downward mood

forever. A distraction that shifts the brain into a more active mode will benefit the overall functioning—with the added benefit of improved self-esteem.

Learning a New Skill

Although it can be extraordinarily difficult for someone in the depths of despair to concentrate on learning something new, it can also be a soothing remedy. For example, I bought this wood flute years ago that's musically idiot-proof. Each hole is tuned to play a lovely chord. I enjoy playing this instrument for people because it always sounds good and it never fails to create an air of transcendence. Computerized pianos have the same concept with their chording systems. If you're emotionally stuck in neutral, you may want to try finding your own idiot-proof musical instrument. And if you are musically inclined, 1) start playing every day, and 2) enjoy!

Posture

Mental health professionals know (or should know) that one's posture influences one's emotional state and vice versa (our body posture is an indication of our mental state). For example, if you hold a standing position with your head stooped over, your chest withdrawn, your back bent forward, and your eyes cast downward, your brain will soon follow, and you'll begin to feel down, too. However, if you assume a posture with your head up, your eyes looking straight out onto the world, your chest thrust out with your shoulders back, and your arms spread open like you want to give the world a big hug, it becomes far more difficult to hold on to a negative thought. Of course, you can't maintain that posture indefinitely, but it's a fast and easy tool to get you unstuck.

Medication

Medications for depression would fill a chapter by themselves, since they're among the top-selling drugs in the nation today. I've compiled a list of these medications, which I'm betting you'll find interesting. I'm including it here, as some of them may be of therapeutic value for you and your doctor to consider. Providing you tools, information, and resources to help you get some emotional relief from the high intensity of depressive moods is my number-one priority.

Antidepressive Medications

Tricyclics (TCAs)
TCAs nonselectively block norepinephrine and serotonin uptake into presynaptic neurons.

> ELAVIL (Amitriptyline)
> ASENDIN (Amoxapine)
> NORPRAMIN (Desipramine)
> SINEQUAN (Doxepin)
> TOFRANIL (Imipramine)
> LUDIOMIL (Maprotiline)
> PAMELOR (Nortriptyline)
> VIVACTIL (Protriptyline)
> SURMONTIL (Trimipramine)

Possible Adverse Effects: Blurred vision, dry mouth, constipation, urinary retention, aggravation of glaucoma and epilepsy, cardiac overstimulation, weight gain.

Selective Serotonin Reuptake Inhibitors (SSRIs)
SSRIs are antidepressive drugs that specifically inhibit serotonin reuptake in presynaptic neurons.

> CELEXA (Citalopram)
> LEXAPRO (Escitalopram)
> LUVOX (Fluvoxamine)
> PROZAC (Fluoxetine)
> PAXIL (Paroxetine)
> SARAFEM (Fluoxetine)
> ZOLOFT (Sertaline)

Possible Adverse Effects: Loss of libido, gastrointestinal distress (nausea, diarrhea), insomnia or sedation; may decrease REM sleep; overdose may cause seizures.

Monoamine Oxidase Inhibitors (MAOIs)
MAOIs inhibit any excess neurotransmitter molecules, including serotonin, norepinephrine, and dopamine.

> NARDIL (Phenelzine)
> PARNATE (Tranylcypromine)

Possible Adverse Effects: Severe and often unpredictable side effects; risk of hypertensive crisis; dietary restrictions including foods containing tyramine such as aged cheese, chicken liver, beer; red wines resulting in headache; tachycardia, nausea, hypertension, cardiac arrhythmias, and stroke.

Cognitive Psychotherapy Conceptual Challenges

It would take a whole book, rather than a section, to discuss all the benefits of utilizing the cognitive psychotherapy conceptual challenges for depression. But suffice it to say, these can be very useful for shifting the brain function. Brain maps have shown how the brain's frontal regions can be tuned to problem-solving frequencies that will improve coping skills.

Here are seven of the most common myths associated with being stuck in the stress state:

1. It's a dire necessity that everyone love and respect you, regardless of who they are.
   - Reality Check: It is in fact undesirable for everyone to love and respect you. If they did, you would have no reason to be in the world. You would have nothing to contribute, because you would not want to offend anyone. You would have no identity, and nothing to

say. It would be far better for you to instead focus on extending your love and respect to others who truly matter.

2. There is a right and wrong answer to everything.
    - Reality Check: Every issue can be approached in a variety of ways. Circumstances change, opinions evolve, and the choices one makes should be revised appropriately given new information. A more constructive belief system would be to understand that some answers are better than others.

3. It is horrible if things don't turn out as they were planned.
    - Reality Check: Nothing is horrible or wonderful. We may see things as terrible or good, but this perception is not necessarily shared by the world. Events happen for reasons we sometimes don't have the mental capacity to understand, and accidents do happen.

4. "They" or "it" cause(s) you to feel depressed.
    - Reality Check: Nothing and no one makes us feel one way or another. We control our own reactions. That is our freedom that no one can take from us.

5. You have to be competent and in control of everything you do, or else people won't respect you.
    - Reality Check: People usually respect you because of your courage and efforts, not because of your control.

6. You are the only one following the rules in the game of life.
    - Reality Check: There are no rules to life, only contracts you make with other people about conduct. Unless these contracts are explicit and agreed upon, there are no rules you can apply to anyone but yourself.

7. If you do nothing, happiness will come to you.
    - Reality Check: Happiness is a by-product of how you consciously choose to live your life. This requires action on your part not only to achieve happiness, but

also to do what it takes to maintain it long-term, hopefully throughout your lifetime.

So, challenge your destructive brain patterns. You can absolutely, positively replace them with patterns that work for you, not
against you.

Principle III: Suspension of thoughts or elimination of specific experience can allow neurological changes to happen immediately.

Nutrition and the Depressive Brain Storm

I am a big believer in the motto, "You are what you eat," and I recommend a high mental-energy diet as a front-line offense against
depression. Chances are good that when you're depressed, you
crave comfort foods dating back to childhood, foods that are sorely
lacking in nutritional value. It's not unusual to visit someone at their
home and find fast-food French fries, prepackaged cakes and pies,
pizza, and soda filling their cupboard and refrigerator. To start feeling better, you need to banish the words "super-size me" from your
vocabulary.

It's perfectly natural to want to eat those foods that used to
cheer us up when we were sad and grumpy; if you can do so with
controlled moderation, and only on rare occasions, fine. But consuming high-sugar, high-fat, nutritionally empty foods on a regular
basis will only send you deeper into your depression, and possibly
to overwhelming depths. For the few seconds of mouth pleasure,
junk food truly isn't worth it.

Supplements that are derived from foods have been shown to
be very helpful in facilitating mood changes. But remember, these
supplements are truly powerful and may interact badly with medications you might be taking. Before you introduce any of the following supplements into your diet, you must first talk with your
doctor or pharmacist to ensure that what you are planning on taking is safe for you. Here are seven supplements with positive effects
I've personally witnessed:

1. **Rhodiola** is a new herb that tops my supplements list. It has been shown to have a remarkable capacity to improve moods and energy. Used by Olympic athletes and space walkers to gain strength, this supplement has even been known to ease symptoms of Lyme disease.

2. **Gamma-aminobutyric acid (GABA)** (dosage 200 mg taken four times a day) is an amino acid that appears to prevent the transmission of depressing messages from nerve cell to nerve cell. This is like an anxiety management agent that neutralizes stress and helps you relax without sacrificing alertness. By keeping the system active it prevents you from becoming depressed after the supplement wears off.

3. **Glutamine** (dosage 0.5–5 g daily) is another amino acid that is converted into glutamic acid in your brain. This acid serves as a building block for proteins and nucleotides (RNA and DNA) that stimulate your brain in the mood regions and elevate your GABA levels for stress management. This ingredient is very important for preventing mental fatigue, which appears to be significant in this stress storm.

4. **Phenylalanine** is another building block for brain neurotransmitters that relate directly to depression and sadness. It's helpful in improving memory and alertness, and can also provide a real boost in spirit and libido. Phenylalanine can be found in almonds, avocados, bananas, cheese, cottage cheese, dried milk (nonfat), chocolate, pumpkin seeds, and sesame seeds. It's very important to be cautious about using this substance with other drugs, or while you are experiencing certain physical conditions, such as hypertension, diabetes, and migraine. The recommended dosages are 500–1000 mg daily.

5. **Tyrosine** is synthesized from phenylalanine and is a building block of several neurotransmitters, including dopamine, norepinephrine, and epinephrine. Since depression is associated with low levels of tyrosine, this is an obvious

recommendation. Tyrosine is a natural component in food such as dairy products, meat, fish, wheat, oats, bananas, and seeds. As a supplement, label dosages range from 500 to 2000 mg two to three times daily.

6. **5-hydroxytryptophan (5-HTP)** is a close cousin to tryptophan and a known precursor to serotonin, the neurotransmitter related to high levels of depression, anxiety, and stress. The general recommended dosage is 100 to 300 mg, three times daily. Use caution if you are taking medications such as antidepressnts, or drugs for heart disease or blood pressure.

7. **Ginkgo-biloba** (120–240 mg three times daily) is my favorite supplement. It is believed to enhance the blood flow to the brain, specifically to the temporal lobes. I have seen people make major turnarounds in their lives and say that this supplement was the answer. Don't take this if you're on blood thinners!

Blue Lights and Chewing Gum

As noted earlier, research has shown that brain patterns like the ones that occur for the depressive brain storm can be affected by having a blue light (25-watt bulb) shined on the face to heighten brain energy activities. People of all ages have been shown to be positively influenced and to enjoy better, more optimistic attitudes when exposed to blue light for fifteen minutes or more. It's an excellent tool to embrace in the morning, if you're not a morning person. But it's definitely not good for sleeping.

The act of chewing may also increase your blood flow through the regions of the brain associated with the depressive storm pattern. We recommend chewing sugarless gum frequently to wake up your brain. It also settles your anxiety levels, but I repeat, don't try and go to sleep with the gum. It makes an awful mess in the morning, especially if it gets into your hair.

Principle IV: Times of growth and change are opportunities for learning and relearning.

Psychotherapy and Counseling

Although I emphasize the value of embracing ways of resolving your brain storms on your own, I nevertheless highly recommend psychotherapy and counseling, because this process can be enormously useful in helping you to identify your personal triggers. This is key, because by consciously identifying them, you can dismiss them or develop effective coping mechanisms instead of being plagued by darkness.

Reach Out

This is the right time to reach out to your team of supporters for help and exactly the wrong time to shut yourself in with only perpetual stress as your company. Plan an event with someone else. Go on a trip. Visit somewhere you never thought of going to. A change of scenery can change your vision and perceptions significantly, and the support of friends and those who care for you can make the events more meaningful.

Imagery

One of the greatest gifts you have is your imagination, because it gives you the power to change your body in very specific ways. In order to get "unstuck" from the depressive stress pattern, you have to unload the burdens that keep you on the wrong track. And if you're not sure how to get to the "right" track, you can build a new path in your mind. There are some excellent CDs that lead you through these gateways in a step-by-step manner on the Mind-bodyseries.com website. Here are some suggestions that may stimulate your creative juices:

- Visualize gathering all your problems and regrets in a bag and then emptying it in the ocean and letting them sink to the bottom, leaving you freer and lighter.

- Visualize the problems that keep you from changing. Then write them on a piece of paper and fold it up. In a fire-safe environment (such as a real fireplace), burn the paper and let the problem thoughts disintegrate with the smoke.
- Make a prayer stick. Write down the blessings you want to have on small pieces of paper and tie them on a short stick about a half inch in diameter and approximately sixteen to twenty-four inches long. Wrap the stick with your favorite-colored yarn and decorate it with one or two of your treasured objects. This becomes your prayer stick, which symbolizes the blessings you are looking for.
- Draw pictures of your problem areas, and then either destroy them or paint over them to replace them with your goals and hopes. Be sure to put a lot of detail in them and discuss them with a good friend or therapist.
- Improvise a dance that represents your image of how your brain is working to be free and open. Dance the act of casting off your mental demons and bringing in the blessings you want, and rejoice.

Principle V: New pathways can be changed and improved.

Look for Your Blessings

As I shared with you earlier, I'm sure that there are at least a hundred blessings a day that will happen to you, if you look for them. There are miracles every day that we can see if we focus on them without criticism. There are events of kindness that challenge a pessimistic pattern in the brain. Flowers grow and blossom. Children say the most fascinating things without knowing why, suggesting that angels speak through them. I have the deep-seated idea that some dogs are angels because they have such an open and noncritical assessment of us, and can forgive us graciously. At least my dogs always do.

Create Value from Experience

This is probably the last thing you want to hear, but even the worst thought or circumstance can offer potential for growth. Ask yourself what you learned from going through this experience. Maybe you feel closer to God or your family; or you appreciate each day more because you know how unpredictable life is. Maybe you are able to break out of patterns and limitations that have held you back.

There is value in all experiences; it just may take a closer look or a little extra time to see things for what they really are. Realize that since you don't know when you might lose control of everything, you have to live your life in a way that leaves no unfinished business should it happen. Make the most of the time you have as an active participant in life. Part of getting your mind around the cycle of life (and what you don't control) is making sure that you maximize what you *do* control—and that's the time you have now. Don't waste it focusing on situations you can't change.

OVERALL THOUGHTS

The depressive brain storm exacts a very destructive physical and emotional toll. People can spend precious years feeling enraged, or withdrawing from the world entirely . . . without a clue that escape is possible. You can lose your financial foundation because of its intrusion into your work life, and it can destroy your motivation and concentration. It can disrupt your relationships by causing you to misdirect blame and by rendering you unable to ask for help when you need it. It can also literally kill, as the stress undermines your immune system, hardens your arteries, and diminishes your critical thinking capacities . . . and your capacity to experience love, joy, and happiness.

Stepping out of the trap isn't easy. To escape the swirl of distractions and pessimistic forces, you have to make a concerted, sustained personal effort beyond anything you may ever have done. It's like taking those first steps with an 800-pound gorilla on your back. It's very hard, and I have the greatest respect for those who've made those steps because I know what it takes. If I could, I'd give them all medals for their valor.

Other people have successfully made this journey. While they are all special people, there's nothing about them that is more special than you. You're in charge of turning your own pages . . . and I'd recommend you make that happen.

8

The Chronic Worry Stress Storm:
The Silent Killer

To say that Linda was a perpetual worrier and type A personality would have been an understatement. Dating back to her early teens, Linda believed that she had to be the best at everything she attempted. Being anything less than "the best" caused her great consternation and worry, and motivated her to work even harder. Indeed, at just forty-four years old, she broke the glass ceiling, and became president of one of New York City's top advertising agencies—a position she'd achieved after two decades of working twelve-hour days, including weekends. To be sure, she was financially rewarded for her hard work: she drove a very nice car, owned an apartment in one of Manhattan's choicest neighborhoods, and had a beautiful country home in an exclusive part of Connecticut.

But Linda's worries did not subside with her success. In fact, they only increased. Now a wife and mother of three, she worried that on top of her hectic professional schedule, she had to be the perfect spouse and parent—not to mention the perfect daughter and granddaughter—because achieving this (impossible) standard was strongly "encouraged" by her parents and grandparents. So, she did her best to be the ideal soccer mom, tried to make sure her kids were involved in both intellectually stimulating and creative pursuits, such as music appreciation and dance lessons; and, she tried to be a fastidious housewife and a supportive, loving partner. In fact, to be sure she was up to task in the intimacy department, she even scheduled sex.

Her credo was go-go-go, and the dizzying pace at which she lived kept her in a state of constant stress and worry. She popped Tylenol and Advil on a daily basis to soothe her ever-present tension headaches and backaches. And even though she was fully aware how much exercise had helped release her intense stress in the past, she allowed her exercise regimen (and her gym membership) to fall by the wayside. Instead, she would snack on comfort foods which resulted in her ballooning from a comfortable size 8 (she was very small framed) to a size 14 in just one year.

Afraid to relax and take a break from her self-inflicted nonstop treadmill of tension and anxiety, Linda rarely took vacations, and when she actually did go away, she'd sit poolside furiously typing away on her BlackBerry and fielding calls on her cell phone. Even in the hospital room just hours before delivering her third child, Linda was reviewing advertising copy and having it sent back to her office via the maternity ward's fax machine, worrying that things would crumble if she didn't personally stay on top of every detail, no matter how small. Most people believed her never-ending drive came from her delight in the adrenaline rush; and in part, that was true. But what primarily drove her was her incessant worry about failing.

WAKE-UP CALL

Linda's nonstop world suddenly changed in an instant. She suffered a stroke three weeks before her forty-fifth birthday, causing paralysis on her left side, and slurred speech. This time while in her hospital bed, she was unable to multitask, making her laptop and BlackBerry inconsequential. In that hospital bed, she came to the realization that returning to life as she knew it (the never-ending treadmill of stress and worry) was an option that was now off the table. This was clearly a wake-up call.

Fortunately, she had exceptionally good health insurance, which allowed her the opportunity to receive state-of-the-art care. With the help of ongoing physical therapy, combined with her dedication to getting better, Linda's speech eventually returned; however, some diminished mental capacities remained, leaving her in a hyper-sensitive emotional state.

For the first time in her life, she had to practice patience with herself. Her steel-trap memory (which she had always taken for granted) was gone. Thus, she had to practice using her memory, and had to write things down in order to remember what she had to do each day.

More important, Linda reevaluated what truly mattered. For her, it was the love of her family, the gift of life, her many blessings, and the opportunity to celebrate each of those treasures. Sweating the small stuff was behind her. That being said, experiencing a stark life crisis certainly isn't the ideal path to learning how rigid think-ing and constant worry can hurt you.

Different Kinds of Stress Categories

1. **Aggravating Events**—These are brief, short-term hassles, such as getting pulled over by a police officer for speeding, missing a flight connection, or locking your keys inside your car.

2. **Life-Changing Events**—While people tend not to associate stress with "happy" events, such as getting married or finding out you're preg-nant, these can cause great stress. Of course, sad or upsetting events, such as suffering a death in the family or getting fired, are sources of significant stress.

3. **Chronic Problems**—As the name suggests, these are problems that are ongoing, such as having to deal with a toxic parent, boss, or spouse, or ever-accumulating credit card debt.

THE NONSTOP WORRY STRESS STORM

Of all the stress storms discussed in this book, by far the biggest killer may be the perpetual (chronic, ongoing) worry storm. Most of us know it well, and we might say that chronic worrying is a modern-day plague, with few of us immune to its potential ravages. However, we nonetheless embrace much of our stress on a daily basis. Why?

Stress is defined as a state of hyperarousal. In other words, it's a state in which we get excited—and we do like to get excited about a lot of things. Heck, we even seek it out and pay good money for the experience. We go to carnivals and ride the roller coasters and Ferris wheels to be scared out of our wits—the more frightening the better for some of us. Scary movies hit the top-ten lists as people of all ages enjoy imagining the possibility of evil aliens invading our world, dead people floating through our homes, or ax murderers waiting inside the bedroom closet.

The athlete challenges himself to competition, knowing full well that the risks of experiencing physical harm, failure, or humiliation are high—but choosing to take those risks for the possibility of experiencing the thrill of rivalry and success. Millions of loyal sports fans do far more than just watch their favorite teams compete. These passionate fans identify so profoundly with the action in front of them, they vicariously experience the stress of the battle and can taste the victory (or the defeat) as if it were their own.

Thus, in many ways, stress is what we live for. Indeed, as long as there's some short-term resolution, and we have the opportunity to restore our minds and bodies to some level of harmony and safety, stress can be good. Here's the thing: it is not the event itself that makes stress good or bad. Rather, it is the nature of our *reaction* to the event.

For example, you just finished grocery shopping and you're on your way home when your car breaks down. A gentleman pulls over and offers to drive you home so that you can get your groceries in the freezer, and then offers to drive you back to your car so that you can wait for roadside assistance to arrive. Your stress levels subside and you're grateful for this man's magnanimous offer. Now, let's take the identical scenario, but instead of feeling good about it, you realize that he looks a lot like the guy who has been violently assaulting women at gunpoint using the same *modus operandi* (m.o.). Now your stress reaction would be of the extreme, heart-pounding ilk.

FIGHT OR FLIGHT

The stress response is an evolutionary, highly developed process, one that comes from the brain's instinctive procedures for crisis. A good way to understand what happens when you're stressed is to think about what naturally happens when you sense you're in danger. Most of us are afraid of snakes (except my friend Wendy, who loves them), so let's imagine that you and a friend are hiking deep in the woods when you suddenly hear something . . . something way too close for comfort. Then, you hear it again, except now it's even closer . . . Is it just a rustling of leaves? No. You're pretty darn sure you heard a hiss . . . and a faint rattle. You think to yourself, "Not good." You know that if you don't react quickly, you or your friend may be bitten by some horrid, slithering, venomous rattlesnake!

Within nanoseconds, and without "thinking" about it, there's a dramatic shift in your physiology: like going on autopilot, your nervous system and endocrine system prepare everything within you to deal with this imminent threat. Your heart beats faster, your lung capacity accelerates, your liver releases extra glucose for quick energy, your muscles dilate to receive a flood of oxygenated blood and nutrients, your blood pressure increases, and your body releases a cascade of steroids, neurotransmitters, and stress hormones like adrenaline and cortisol.

But wait! There's more: Your pupils dilate, enhancing your vision, and your brain narrows its focus totally onto the potential foe.

Your sensation of pain becomes muted, and all thoughts that don't concern your immediate safety vanish. Systems and processes such as stomach digestion, reproduction, and your immune response temporarily shut down in order to conserve and divert every ounce of your energy so you can fight the threat or run away. (Or, at least run faster than your friend . . . just kidding!) This reaction to stress is called the "fight or flight" response. Then, once you know the danger has passed, your physiology returns to normal. And chances are, you let out at least one or two big sighs of relief . . . which feels fabulous.

GOOD STRESS

In the above hiking/snake scenario, experiencing stress was clearly a desirable thing, as it helps us to quickly gear up and take appropriate action. Another example of good stress is the surge of powerful focus a parent experiences in acute situations, such as needing to safely transport a child to the E.R. after an accident. And yet another example of "good" stress is how it can help you "get your head in the game" before a challenging competition. Personally, I tend to thrive on good stress and frankly keep my cup running over by design. For example, right now the demands on my time include parenting two young children, writing one book while editing another, supervising a clinic, overseeing a television show, and let's not forget spending time with my wife, who is (thankfully) incredibly supportive and understanding. Failure in any one of these categories in my life would cost me dearly, but for me, the personal rewards of being successful outweigh the efforts and frustrations. Perhaps I feel this way because I consider myself extremely lucky to have such amazing opportunities. But be that as it may, stress is key.

BAD STRESS: WORRY STORMS

The destructive force of stress rears its many ugly heads when your body gets stuck in high-alert mode. Can you imagine all of those "fight or flight" body system reactions *never* returning to normal, including the high blood pressure surge, the muscle tension, the glucose rush, the immune system shutdown, etc.? The results can range from annoying to debilitating to deadly. For example, chronic stress may increase your risk and susceptibility to migraine headaches, depression, back pain, heart attack, diabetes, and stroke. Plus, according to the National Library of Medicine of the National Institutes of Health, severe chronic stress can even lead to cancer.

In the snake story the stress is easy to understand, because we're educated about the danger of poisonous snakes. We can see them for what they are, and we know that we're reacting appropriately. But what about when we don't realize we're in threat mode? Bad worry stress storms can be initiated by stressors that accumulate over time, like having to deal with a horribly unfair boss, ill parents, demanding financial strain, or loss of loved ones. Unlike fleeting stressors—the snake—chronic ones can seriously damage our physical and emotional health.

For example, stress activates the overproduction of a hormone called cortisol. Cortisol increases blood pressure, which can lead to or exacerbate many conditions, including hypertension and stroke. Cortisol causes fat to accumulate around your midsection; and research shows that having excess stomach fat increases your risk for a whole host of illnesses, including type 2 diabetes and heart disease. Cortisol affects bone metabolism, thereby thinning your bones, which increases your risk of osteoporosis; and cortisol negatively impacts your stomach lining, making you more susceptible to ulcers.

Stress also causes you to crave carbohydrate-rich comfort foods—which are usually unhealthy foods, laden with fat and calories. This results in weight gain, which in turn can lead to diabetes, heart problems, etc. Stress also impairs your immune system, making you more susceptible to getting sick and staying sick.

WHEN ENOUGH IS ENOUGH

When the stress reactions linger past their needs and the destructive cascade of physiological events begins to undermine your life, you have to recognize that you're in the chronic worry stress storm. So how do you do that? First, you need to know that experiencing a stress storm isn't a brain dysfunction. Your brain is doing what it's supposed to do; it's just doing it for way too long.

A really good way for you to initially determine whether you're in a chronic worry stress storm is to gauge how well your body is functioning overall. For example, because chronic stress deactivates your immune system, you may find that you get sick more often than you used to. Ask your doctor to run a blood profile for you. You may find that your LDL cholesterol and blood inflammation numbers are running dangerously high, perhaps due to high blood pressure damaging blood-vessel walls and organs. Your muscles might also feel very tense and knotted, perhaps causing headaches, back pain, and even shaking hands.

SELF-AUDIT FOR STRESS

Linda had to have a stroke before she recognized she was living her life in a way that was hurtful to herself and those around her. Here's something I don't often share: I had to have two heart attacks to figure out the difference between good stress and bad stress, before I took the necessary steps to change my life. So I know whereof I speak. And, as is so often the case (as it was for me), many people have told me that they had "no idea" how much stress they were dealing with until the stress was removed (sometimes by their choice . . . but more often by their suffering a life crisis).

The following self-audit was developed for the purpose of helping you determine your personal stress levels. Certainly there are far more sophisticated measures, but this one is reliable enough to give you a reasonable gauge of your perceived stress levels.

INSTRUCTIONS

For each of the following, determine which best describes the extent of your stress experience:

1. I worry excessively and constantly about issues in my past, present, and future.
   (A) Never _____ (B) Occasionally _____ (C) Significantly _____ (D) Severely _____
2. I find it extremely difficult to control my worries and anxieties.
   (A) Never _____ (B) Occasionally _____ (C) Significantly _____ (D) Severely _____
3. When I feel threatened or anxious, I become numb and detached from my emotions and environment.
   (A) Never _____ (B) Occasionally _____ (C) Significantly _____ (D) Severely _____
4. I experience my stress by going into a daze and losing awareness of my surroundings or people I care for.
   (A) Never _____ (B) Occasionally _____ (C) Significantly _____ (D) Severely _____
5. When I have high levels of stress I become irritable, cannot sleep well, and relate poorly to challenges from otherwise normal issues.
   (A) Never _____ (B) Occasionally _____ (C) Significantly _____ (D) Severely _____
6. The stress level impairs my abilities to concentrate and solve problems.
   (A) Never _____ (B) Occasionally _____ (C) Significantly _____ (D) Severely _____
7. I feel constantly vulnerable to any change in my life situation and especially fearful of other people.
   (A) Never _____ (B) Occasionally _____ (C) Significantly _____ (D) Severely _____
8. I become overfatigued easily due to stress.
   (A) Never _____ (B) Occasionally _____ (C) Significantly _____ (D) Severely _____
9. Stress interferes with my ability to perform work.
   (A) Never _____ (B) Occasionally _____ (C) Significantly _____ (D) Severely _____
10. Stress problems have given me high muscle tension and poor eating habits.
    (A) Never _____ (B) Occasionally _____ (C) Significantly _____ (D) Severely _____

Scoring: If you checked (D) five or more times you may be suffering from severe stress and would greatly benefit from professional guidance to help you learn how to manage and reduce the tension in your life. If you checked (C) at least five times or (D) one to four times, you're likely dealing with some moderate but significant levels of stress. You should definitely pay extra attention and strongly consider embracing some self-help techniques for reducing your daily experiences of stress. If you checked (C) one to four times, then you may be dealing with moderate stress that's causing some problems. It would be in your best interest to learn how to better manage these stresses through self-help techniques, which would help you balance your level of peace, control, and effectiveness.

STRESS AND YOUR WORLD

The most common response to "dealing" with the worry stress storm is to engage in unhealthy behaviors such as eating comfort foods, smoking, drinking excess alcohol, and becoming physically inactive. According to national surveys, people experiencing stress are more likely to report hypertension, anxiety or depression, and obesity. Forty-three percent of all adults suffer adverse health effects directly from stress—with women reporting feeling the effects of stress on their physical health more than men. Women also tend to experience stress differently from men. For example, women report that they feel like crying, and often feel a sense of nervousness or exhaustion. Men, on the other hand, are more likely to express their stress in the form of irritability, anger, and intolerance, and report that they have trouble falling asleep or staying asleep.

What's Eating You: Comfort Eating and Poor Diet Choices

According to a survey conducted by the American Psychological Association (APA) in partnership with the National Women's Health Resource Center and iVillage.com, one in four Americans turns to food to help alleviate stress or deal with problems. Comfort eaters report higher levels of stress than average, and exhibit higher levels of all the most common symptoms of stress, including fatigue, lack of energy, nervousness, irritability, and trouble sleeping. Comfort eaters are also more likely than the average American to experience health problems like hypertension and high cholesterol. In addition, 65 percent of comfort eaters characterize themselves as somewhat or extremely overweight and are twice as likely as the average American to be diagnosed with obesity.

- Stress levels are higher for frequent fast-food eaters. While only 13 percent of people who didn't eat at a fast food restaurant in the last week are very concerned about stress, this number rises to 21 percent among those who ate fast food meals in the past week.
- 31 percent of women say they are comfort eaters versus 19 percent of men.
- Men are more likely than women to opt for unhealthy snacks such as potato chips.

WHAT'S STRESSING US OUT

While we have many sources of chronic stress in our lives, it is generally driven by work and money issues, followed by health concerns and children. The most prominent offenders for Americans are listed below. Check and see if yours are among the big seven:

Seven Leading Sources of Stress

- 59 percent say money
- 59 percent say work
- 53 percent say health problems affecting parents or other family members
- 50 percent say health concerns

- 50 percent say nightly news or the state of the world today
- 48 percent say health of immediate family (spouse, partner, or children)
- 41 percent say children

As I suggested earlier in this chapter, it's not the event that causes us stress, it's our lack of flexibility and our rigid reactions. More to the point, it's our *perception* of the event or the *thought* that creates the storm within our brains that eventually erupts into the feeling we call stress.

TRAINING THE BRAIN: STRESS MANAGEMENT

Although we measure the peripheral systems of the body for stress levels (e.g., blood vessel dilation, muscle tension, skin conductance, etc.), the *center* of most stress is in our brains. Stress isn't an abnormal brain function. Rather, it's vital for our very survival. Too much stress is bad, having zero stress is also bad (e.g., you wouldn't know when to run from a dangerous situation); and having chronic stress is definitely bad for your health (e.g., heart disease, stroke, high blood pressure, diabetes, etc.). So while we would never want to totally eliminate the mechanisms of adaptation that create stress, we do want to keep the process in check.

The operative word for reaching restorative patterns is to achieve healthful *cycling*—which refers to a pattern of flexibility, rather than a standard set of healthy responses. In other words, it's not so much the extremes that hurt our health as it is our rigidity. For example, the problem isn't that we may have high blood pressure for some period of the time; that's normal. The problem is when our blood pressure is *constantly* elevated. Thus, it's your ability to respond to crises and challenges with the correct levels of blood flow that protects your health.

Case in point, in several studies for measuring blood pressure, healthy individuals were compared to stressed people by using a mobile self-inflating blood pressure cuff, which automatically took blood pressure measurements at specific times of the day. While, as a group, the healthy individuals demonstrated a great deal of number variability, generally each of them had blood pressure numbers that rose with the sun and dropped in the evening. This was not the case for the stressed individuals. For them, their blood pressure started out high and didn't waver throughout the day—which we know suggests a perpetual state of crisis, no restoration time, and increased risk for organ and blood vessel damage and a host of other conditions.

If you doubt the value restoration time has in your body, then consider how muscle tissue is built. When a person is weight lifting to develop muscle strength, the increase in strength doesn't occur during the lifting process. In fact, the pulling action of the muscles on the bone creates microscopic tears. It's during periods of rest that those tears heal, thus making the muscle tissue stronger.

TRAINING FOR FLEXIBILITY

The roles of stress management and brain plasticity are to train for mental flexibility, thereby creating new neuropathways, instead of rigidity. The more adaptive a system is, the more capable it becomes of responding in appropriate and/or alternative ways. As with strengthening muscle tissue, training for mental flexibility requires a measured application of stress to all systems, so that both elevated levels and restorative levels are achieved. To facilitate a healthy system, you need to learn flexibility and embrace a range of alternative choices in responding to stressors.

Much earlier in my career I had the opportunity to work with a number of high-performing individuals who had high blood pressure, and I was applying biofeedback techniques with them. With the use of very sensitive instruments related to blood pressure, I taught them (as I am teaching you) how to lower it with the use of imagery, hypnotic relaxation, and breathing. The success was quick because they were highly motivated and very smart; however, they refused to allow me to instruct them in maintaining this relaxation all day. They explained that they needed the joy of dealing with stress and performing at top speed. In essence, they were telling me the same story that we all share when we step on the roller coaster or compete. They want the stress.

A similar situation arose when I was training a professional athletic team to deal with stress. Although everyone on the team agreed that they were overstressed, they felt they still needed the adrenaline push to help them perform at the highest levels. They were right. So I taught them both ends of the spectrum: I taught them how to employ and channel their high energy into focused power when they needed it, but I also taught them how to restore themselves through relaxation. In other words, I taught them to have balance in their lives, and the approaches worked well.

The largest portion of what we term stress is worrying too much. Everyone worries to some extent, and clearly worry can serve as a constructive bridge to preparation for future problems. But too many of us worry out of balance with reality. We worry about too many things, and even become apprehensive when we think we're not worrying enough about something. As one of my patients bravely admitted, "If I don't worry about something happening, then it will happen." This type of magical thinking is not productive. We need to conquer our fears in more constructive ways.

HEALING PRACTICES OF STRESS

There have been hundreds of stress management programs that purport to relieve stress. I've explored everything from crystals to acupuncture, and everything works to some extent . . . if you believe it will work. However, there are some paths that actually can harm you. For example, if your idea of stress relief is coming home, popping open a few cans of beer while you watch wrestling matches until you fall asleep, you are playing with fire. That is avoidance, which is bad, and candidly, emotionally lazy.

Stress management approaches have verbs in them for a reason: you have to *do* something to make change happen. For some of my patients, the biggest challenge I ever gave them was asking them to commit to setting aside forty minutes a day (divided into two twenty-minute sessions) when they were not talking on the phone or doing something else. That was an incredibly tough step for some of them to take, but it was also a necessary one. If you're not willing to commit part of your day to restoration, you're setting yourself up for failure.

Regardless of what you've learned thus far in this book, the question comes down to whether or not you want true balance in your life. This takes a willingness to change. You have to want to improve your mental health, your physical health, your emotional life, your happiness, and your prosperity. This is not a passive process. You must act deliberately. You have to participate.

In facing chronic stress storms, you must act to increase the *flexibility* of brain plasticity and to facilitate your ability to let go of stress ties. The broader the range in your responses, the more adaptable and free you can be to deal with upcoming stresses and move on. Based on the principles of brain plasticity, I will give you some ideas on exercises you can do to strengthen these skills.

Principle I: Neurons that learn together become attached.

This principle can be applied as an ongoing practice, using the neurons in the motor strip of the brain as leaders in creating direction for other cell bundles in the frontal and temporal cortex.

Alternating Exercise
When heart-rate variability became the hot topic in stress research, a set of exercises soon swept the country, which aimed to cycle back and forth between high performance and relaxation. The regimen went as follows:

1. Start exercising (jogging, swimming, walking fast, treadmill, etc.) until you reach your target heart rate.

*Note: As a general rule of thumb, your maximum tar-
get heart rate is 220 minus your age.*

2. Upon reaching this high level of exertion, immediately lower it to below normal (according to your normal rate). Take as much time as needed. *Note: Average
beats per minute (bpm) for adults range from 70 bpm
to 75 bpm, for men and women, respectively.*

3. As you reach the lower level, rest for a few minutes
and repeat as above.

The objective is the training of your body and brain to find the
methods that you could employ in periods of highest stress to create a natural cycle of restoration. Remember, flexibility is key,
whether it be physical or psychological.

Biofeedback

A similar program can be developed with self-monitoring devices.
As mentioned earlier, biofeedback is a self-training method that
uses sophisticated computer technology to monitor stress-related
levels in your body, such as blood vessel dilation, muscle tension,
breathing cycles, heart rhythms, and even brain waves.

My favorite is peripheral temperature, which is an indication of
vessel dilation and restriction. Basically, the idea is that the more
relaxed you are, the more relaxed your blood vessels are, and thus
the warmer your hands and fingers will be. As you get stressed,
your blood vessels constrict, limiting blood flow and lowering finger temperature. The average temperature for a relaxed state in the
fingers is about 90° F. The advantage of using a biofeedback instrument is immediate sensitivity to change and measurement in
the hundredths of degrees. However, you can also use a hand-
held thermometer. My high chronic stress patients nearly always
share that they find it extremely useful to observe the temperature
change measurements and to see that they really can affect those
measurements.

Music

Music and dancing are probably the oldest forms of stress management. Even in biblical times, David was known as a musician with the primary job of creating relaxing music to help Solomon go to sleep. You've certainly noticed how music sets the emotional tone when you're watching a movie. For example, sometimes the music alerts us to impending doom, and other times to jocularity. That said, music affects different people differently. For example, I can enjoy just about every type of music, but country music doesn't "calm" me . . . even though I like it. For me, listening to classical and flute music has a particularly amazing impact on reducing my stress levels.

Principle II: Experience and need can change neurological bundles.

During the time in my life in which I was very involved with counseling terminally ill cancer patients, one of the characteristics of these patients was their honest way of interacting. As one of my peers remarked, "A sure cure for neurosis is having cancer. You don't have time for anything but truest integrity." I found that when death is at your doorstep, a lot of things we stress out about become distant second concerns.

Most of our stresses are issues of little major importance when the most important parts of our lives are being threatened. This insight is perhaps the product of experience and life's solutions. But the "need" for brain change is the rethinking process of what you are going to devote your mental and emotional energies to. I have seen too many people stress themselves needlessly, develop very destructive results, and inject new stress into the scores of Little League baseball games, who gets the promotion, who is right, what is the sin, etc.

This is the time to grow out of the stage where your values are confused with what the trillion-dollar media industry tells you. Truly investigate what you need and appreciate. You don't *need* a new car when you are sixteen. You don't *need* a new computer or the latest fad clothes. Make a deal with yourself to decide what you need and want, what you should pay attention to, and where your values lie. Then stop worrying about the rest.

Principle III: Suspension of thoughts or elimination of specific experience can allow neurological changes to happen immediately.

The basic concept of this principle is to be able to suspend worry and stress. A couple of approaches are very helpful in this regard.

Time-out

Even my most stressed patients realize that they worry too much, and very likely are in my office because they want to stop. However, eliminating stress altogether isn't a good idea—you don't want to be a zombie—so we can have time-outs for stress instead. I realize that this may seem counterintuitive, but having the ability to worry in proper measure is essential, as stressors will always exist.

Pick out the best times of the day for worry and keep it within the limit of thirty minutes. For example, depending on your scheduling issues, the best times for you might be 10:00–10:15 a.m., 2:00–2:15 p.m., or 4:00–4:15 p.m. These are your times to worry and fret over things you don't have supreme control over. It could be rising gas prices, your best friend's concern with infertility issues, who gets elected president, or whatever you have on your list. Allow yourself to feel as stressed as you want during these times you set aside.

Distraction

I know that I will never play professional golf, and my bowling leaves a lot to be desired for consistency, but these two activities have probably kept me from staying stressed over my limit. It started in college when my friends would encourage me to play golf to relax a little. I spent most of my time looking for the ball in trees and sand traps. But what it offered me was a distraction from my worrisome obsession about school. Bowling was also a great distraction from my stress while I fought the battles of dealing with a failing business situation. Sailing is my current favorite distraction because it takes me out in the middle of a lake where cell phones have a way of drowning, and it takes forever to return to land.

I think nearly everyone would greatly benefit from having a sport or hobby to distract from life's stresses. Although it would drive me bonkers, needlepoint is the savior for my brilliant friend Dr. Larry Dossey; and Rosey Grier, former all-pro football star, is a major needlepoint fan, too.

Vacations

Although vacations are not the answer to dealing with stresses back home, they can suspend life between worries and provide you some joy and peace for a while. Take advantage of the rest and be sure to schedule some restoring time for yourself. You might even think of educating yourself on more productive methods of dealing with stress, as the new surroundings may help with your objectivity. I've enjoyed spending my vacation time at exercise spas. Instead of vegetating on the beach somewhere (which for me is anything but relaxing), I exercise to build up my endurance. Hopefully I shed a few pounds and lighten my load along the way, too.

Good Sleep Restoration

Sleep is probably the chief method for our bodies and minds to find flexibility in our lives and to balance our incessant worrying. Without question, reintegrating our experiences while we're sleeping is an extraordinarily important brain function. If that process becomes stymied, worrying really can mean the death of you.

Most sleep problems emerge from circadian rhythm disruption. That means that your brain is not sleeping in the natural patterns it was designed to do. You should be getting at least eight, and ideally nine hours of sleep (during the time the sun is not exposing you to light), especially if you're undergoing stress of any kind. This comes down to a scheduling and prioritizing issue. You're going to have to turn off the television and computer earlier than you're used to, if you're to optimize your brain health.

Arguably, the hardest habit to break is turning off the worry factor. Many people with insomnia have "performance anxiety" in which they worry about not getting enough sleep . . . which can be maddening. CDs designed for relaxation have helped many of my patients. That said, the most frequent barrier to getting a good night's sleep is worrying about the next day (not ruminating about what happened today or yesterday). When you plan for the next day, your brain goes into a complex processing wake-up mode. No wonder you can't sleep: you're calling your brain to action when it needs to be at rest.

Principle IV: Times of growth and change are opportunities for learning and relearning.

Breathing Techniques

While I feel that I've discussed the power of breathing more than enough as an effective method for reducing stress levels throughout one's body, its application is unique in stress management. To get your body and mind into the highest and most powerful state, breathing in cycles of highest oxygen absorption levels is the way to go. This means that you should cycle to the counts of 5–3–4, what is known as the *Pythagorean pattern* (like the triangle formula). The concept is to inhale to the count of 5, hold it for a count of 3, and exhale to the count of 4. (These are counts, not seconds. I don't want people hyperventilating in this exercise.)

Some studies show that his breathing exercise can improve memory, focus, muscular strength, and eyesight. However, continuous breathing in this pattern can also exhaust your system. So proceed with caution.

Another take on the Pythagorean restorative breathing pattern is to do it in reverse, with a cycling of 4–3–5: inhale first to the count of 4, hold it for 3, and make the longest part the exhalation. You magnify the relaxation effect by humming a long vowel sound, such as "O-o-o-o-a-a-a-a," as you exhale. The vibrations of your voice may help you to focus on the process and could relax your muscles more quickly. The vibrations of saying the vowel also stimulate the nasal passages and help produce better metabolism and clearer thinking.

Cognitive Psychotherapeutic Approaches

Psychotherapy can be enormously helpful for learning why we're stressed, and for identifying the destructive baggage we're carrying around. For example, if you feel you were mistreated as a child by your parents, and you're allowing those past experiences to deleteriously affect your adult life, your stress levels (and the accompanying ill health effects) aren't going to diminish. You can't change the past, you can only change your reaction to the past.

You can't predict the future either. It may be true that future behavior is best predicted by past behavior, but that doesn't mean that everyone is going to abandon you, nor are you destined to be the failure you thought you were when you were seven. It's entirely your choice as to how you frame events in your mind. And if you're choosing to blame the past for your current "reality" as an adult, then you need to figure out what the payoff is for you. In other words, why are you trapping yourself? How is that choice benefiting you? Are you using it as an excuse for not attempting new challenges? Are you afraid to fail? Do you like the attention you get for being fearful of something? Maybe you're simply stuck in an unwanted neural pattern, and the payoff is a nonissue. Whatever the reason(s), you can change how your brain stores, processes, and experiences your world and, more important, you can change yourself.

Otherwise, if you continue to do what you've always done, you'll always get what you've always got. Yes, there are stresses you don't have the power to change, such as the financial markets, but how you choose to deal with those types of stresses is entirely within your power. If you "get" that critical distinction, then you're on your way to better mental health.

Bibliotherapy and Media Attention

This is one of my favorites. I like to refer people to go to the movies or read books for help with chronic stress. Many morally inspirational movies and television shows are basic stories that feature transcendence, which is a basic tenet of stress reduction. *Enchanted, Bee Movie, Star Wars,* and a whole host of inspiring stories are great choices. Also, these types of movies tend to be family-friendly. Of course, profound life truths usually are.

Principle V: New pathways can be changed and improved.

Celebrate the Good Things

Stress may be always in your life, and some of it is actually good for you. Take time to rejoice in the good times, especially when you've learned something valuable. Congratulate your friends for overcoming their struggles too, because what you give you also receive.

Take Care of You

Find ways of keeping yourself healthy by eating the right foods and exercising. The healthier you are physically, the healthier you will be mentally. Make a plan to give yourself the present of healthy thinking and doing.

Walk the Talk

Too many people can give you good advice, but too few actually walk their talk. The brain knows this and stress can come from discrepancies in our actions and words. Be clear about what you want to be and what you need, and guide your actions toward those goals. Be proud of who you are.

REMAINING THOUGHTS

Chronic stress exists in every corner of the world. But it's not the demons outside of us, or the weaknesses within us, that defeat our health. It's our lack of understanding and our inability to employ efficacious coping skills. There are also environmental factors involved. Exposure to heavy metals, pesticides, and other pollutants increases our physical and mental vulnerabilities. And restorative resources, such as extended family support and close, caring communities, have become more the exception than the rule, leaving us feeling more isolated than ever before in history.

Most of our chronic stresses are learned behaviors—which become habits. We learn to worry, we learn to create obstacles when there are none, and we get in our own way. But you must understand that you have what it takes to turn all that around. Your brain is designed to do that! Our bodies and minds are armored with all the necessary tools and weapons. Our brains are specifically prepared by their own plasticity to adapt to our challenges, if we allow them to resolve these issues.

I believe in the human spirit and our special heritage of going to higher levels of enlightenment. I've witnessed this countless times. Allow me to be your friend who walks this path with you and supports your journey. You can achieve a joyous life.

9

Training Two Brains:
Interpersonal Stress Storms

The weather metaphors I've been using throughout this book are particularly well suited for looking at temperament currents and stress storm patterns. It's a basic fact that the winds usually have a set pattern to them, often crossing the country from west to east. Sailors have been counting on wind patterns to speed them along since the inception of seafaring commerce, and a clever navigator can do the same using water currents, too.

Not all currents run to our liking, however, and some are not predictable; even so we try in earnest to bend them to our will, often with little result. Seafaring explorers have regaled eager listeners for centuries with stories that warn us about the importance of respecting the power of the sea—and learning to navigate it successfully requires that one be willing to interact *with* the sea, instead of trying to work against it.

Just as the winds and seas have particular currents that have impenetrable patterns, so do humans. Whether we're born that way, or whether they come from some unknowable source, each of us has a built-in tendency toward a certain temperament. What's fascinating is that temperaments are extremely difficult to predict or understand from pure biological logic.

NO CARBON COPIES

On the surface, it seems puzzling to many of us that children from the same gene pool (parents) aren't born with similar personalities. But fortunately, there is a special pattern within each of us that is entirely unique—even in identical twins. Besides, one can only imagine how dreadfully dull our lives would be if the world were filled with carbon copies. Yet despite our individuality, those who don't "blend in" are all too often branded as deviants, and are given labels such as hyperactive, lazy, antisocial, eccentric, resistant, loose cannon, or just plain odd. It is this friction between who we are and who the world expects us to be that often creates stress. Tony was one such individual.

Tony's Story

From the time he began school, teachers thought of Tony as an odd boy who didn't fit in. He preferred to read his own books (hidden behind his schoolbooks), and loved to imagine himself on wonderful adventures, rather than listen to his teachers. And although Tony scored very high on all of the intelligence tests, his school grades were relatively poor. His teachers found this discrepancy tremendously frustrating, which bothered Tony. In fact, whenever he sensed their disapproval of him, he would consciously try to further hide his intelligence. This passive-aggressive behavior was his way of coping. He thought of himself as being like Superboy, hiding his true talents to protect himself from evildoers. How did his parents feel about all this? His father was a mean drunk who couldn't have cared less, and his mother was ineffectual.

Tony was saddled with several diagnostic labels, ranging from ADD to retarded with special talents (savant), Asperger's, communication disorder, and conduct disorder. He also had a mild stutter triggered by anxiousness; his cruel classmates smelled blood and would go on the attack. But that didn't go on for long. Far from being a weakling, Tony was very strong and fast, and his refusal to submit to his bullying peers soon earned him the reputation of being a good fighter.

Tony really never enjoyed life much as a child, largely because he had no true safe place in the world. He moved out of his family home at age fifteen, or rather, his family left him without a home because they moved to another state, supposedly for his father's work. Tony found a garage apartment that he could afford on his newspaper route wages, and from the tips he'd get for his excellent service. Rather than bemoan the bad hand he was dealt, Tony not only embraced his self-defined life, he thrived on it, gaining more and more self-confidence every step of his way.

Tony the Tiger

Tony's naturally strong temperament of adaptability, intensity, and persistence helped him to flourish and grow into a very powerful young man. When it came time for college, he was able to complete a four-year program in just two and a half years—which he did *after* developing and then selling a lucrative Internet-based consulting company. In his early thirties, Tony found a wonderful woman to complement his powerful abilities. She knew just how to be supportive of his strengths and understanding of his weaknesses. They married, had a couple of kids, and are still very much in love.

Too many of us are not that lucky. The one-size-fits-all system eventually breaks a lot of us down, compelling us to repress who we really are, so that we'll fit in. Don't allow your authentic self to disintegrate. No matter how far down you've fallen, you can turn things around.

TEMPERAMENTS AND STRESS CURRENTS

In psychology, temperament begins with the innate aspect of an individual's personality, and is often defined as that part of the self-structure that is brain based. Along with character, and those aspects acquired by learning and reshaping our brain function through socialization, it is said to constitute our personality. Researchers have shown that temperaments can be recognized in infants as young as three days old!

Since a person's general temperament, character, and personality are something he or she is born with, it can be celebrated as unique, but it can also be a source of tremendous stress—particularly if the person is your child, and his or her innate style is not to your liking. And clearly, loving, but not "liking," one's own child is something a parent has to come to terms with . . . and get over. Otherwise, the stress that's soon to follow will surely cause great pain and emotional suffering for everyone involved. But know this: this is not an issue of fault. No one is at fault. You simply need to understand that different types of people will rub you the wrong way. And when those people are family, or even just someone you must deal with or work with on a regular basis, you need to find a way to accept it and deal with it wisely.

Nine Temperament Characteristics

Rejecting the commonly held belief that parents were the sole cause of a child's problems, a team of five brilliant researchers sought to discover a way to explain why one sibling, for example, would develop undesirable characteristics, while the rest of the siblings would not. Their research culminated in the identification of nine temperament characteristics in infants that can serve as indicators as to how well a child might navigate his or her life. Here are the nine characteristics, along with brief descriptions, which will serve as our basics:

- **Activity Level**—Where a person falls (on a spectrum of high to low) with regard to his physical and/or mental activity levels. For example, does this person tend to sit quietly and read, or does he need to be constantly moving? Is he curious about the world around him or not?

- **Regularity/Rhythmicity**—Describes the extent to which a person's biological functions are predictable, such as when someone awakens in the morning or becomes hungry. For example, a predictable child may always want breakfast the moment he wakes up, while an unpredictable child doesn't have set times for meals.

- **Initial Reaction**—Also called "approach" or "withdrawal," it describes how a person first reacts to being placed in unfamiliar situations. For example, at a large conference, does she walk right up and introduce herself to the first person she sees, or does she stay back to evaluate the situation before proceeding?

- **Adaptability**—The adjustment period that someone requires to feel comfortable in a new situation after their initial reaction. For example, when new standard operating procedures are required in an office setting, how resistant or compliant is that person to dealing with the changes?

- **Intensity**—The energy level a person exhibits with regard to positive and negative situations. For example, upon learning that he is getting a long-overdue promotion, does he jump up and down with glee, or does he merely smile to show his pleasure?

- **Mood**—This describes a person's general outlook on life. For example, does she tend to be a happy or unhappy person, i.e., is her glass half full or half empty?

- **Distractibility**—This is the ease with which a person is sidetracked from what he is doing. For example, does his mind easily wander, as he notices every little thing around him, or can he stay focused on the task at hand, regardless of outside distractions?

- **Persistence and Attention Span**—This is a person's ability not only to stick with something that takes a long time, but also to do so despite its difficulty level. For example, is this person able to finish putting together a complicated toy, or does he stop soon after feeling frustrated?

- **Sensitivity**—Also called "sensory threshold" or "threshold of responsiveness," this is a person's ability not to get bothered by distractions that are occurring around him. For example, is the person able to easily return to what she is working on after being momentarily disturbed by the phone ringing?

Influences of Temperament Currents on Family, School, and Work

While genetics and biology are believed (and in my opinion, rightly so) to have a substantive impact on a person's temperament, that is not to say that other influences, such as environmental factors, don't also play a role in how a child's personality develops or is expressed. Bearing that in mind, a person's temperament profoundly affects his or her family, school, and work life. For example, some children are "easy." Meaning, they easily swing with changes in their normal routine, such as going on a family vacation and eating different foods at different times, sleeping in a different bed, etc. Conversely, other children may suffer a major meltdown, and may have a horrible time trying to adjust to the changes. This is where storms start to brew.

Sometimes a child's particular temperament doesn't emerge as an issue until after he or she starts school. For example, a child who displays the combination of distractibility and high activity temperaments is bound to be diagnosed as ADHD sooner or later. Diagnostically speaking, these behaviors aren't necessarily interchangeable, but to too many general practitioners, medication is the one-size-fits-all answer.

Of course, none of the nine temperaments is inherently good or bad. In fact, knowing one's own tendencies can be particularly instructive when it comes to choosing a vocation. For example, people with high activity and highly responsive temperaments are often outstanding salespeople.

Familial Mismatch

An additional nuance that's important for you to understand is called "goodness of fit." This refers to how someone's temperament may affect his relationship with others: people can be matched or mismatched. For example, a classic parent-child mismatch would be that of a parent whose temperament is generally one of low activity and is rhythmically predictable, with a child who has a highly active and easily distractible temperament. One can imagine how overwhelmed or irritated a parent (or perhaps a teacher) could feel dealing with this mismatch day after day.

The key here is for a parent to figure out the general temperaments of all family members (including one's spouse). This knowledge can be extremely helpful in being able to differentiate between behavioral problems and temperamental differences. Moreover, understanding and taking into account anyone's temperamental tendencies is profoundly helpful for resolving conflict in nearly any life situation.

Using the Universal Five Types

Nine temperaments may be a bit complex and awkward to handle for a lot of us, so I've combined them into five types of individuals with common clusters of behaviors and attitudes that are considered hardwired in our brains. I've come up with general categories in which most people will belong; however, you may see yourself as belonging to more than one—and possibly even to all of them to some degree.

The five basic groupings are:

- **The Teacher** bases his primary values on respect for tradition and its messages for the present. He loves detail and enjoys structure, inasmuch as he enjoys realistic goals that are based on his values.
- **The Pathfinder** focuses on the future and values completion of tasks by whatever means are

necessary to do so. She is often seen as emotionless because of this powerful focus, but is also usually considered a great leader.

- **The Empathizer** focuses more on personal power and is motivated by inspiration. The means by which this is accomplished is most important to him, and he invests huge amounts of energy in unifying feelings and emotions. He is known to embrace lofty, romantic ideas.
- **The Magician** enjoys chaos and relishes crises as opportunities. She loves drama and will instigate chaos when things become too calm and routine for her liking. She is a risk taker and enjoys living on the edge.
- **The Warrior** is the one who maintains his personal integrity above all other influences. He is the one who knows that, regardless of the outcome, victory or defeat ultimately rests on his shoulders. He is seen as an authoritarian.

Do you see yourself in one or more of these descriptions? Can you pick out the types for someone else that you interact with on a daily basis? If so, how well do the two of you get along? I will help you find the category that fits you best in the following audit of types.

AUDIT OF BASIC TEMPERAMENT TYPES

In the statements below, indicate the course of action you might take in each scenario. For those situations in which you find it hard to imagine yourself, make your best guess as to what your natural reaction would be. Be as honest as possible. You can also use this conduct audit on someone else and match your observations to the results.

1. When describing your major personality qualities to another person, what words would best reflect what you would say? (A) Kind, truthful, peace-loving person who cares most about relationships. (B) Trustworthy, obedient, respectful, and a thinker. (C) Curious, logical, clever, visionary. (D) Energetic, playful, fun, free. (E) Independent, self-sufficient, obedient only to your own values.

2. What are some of the behaviors you enjoy the most? (A) Doing good things for others, helping others, and making peace. (B) Showing that you are responsible and productive. (C) Thinking about possibilities and creating innovative approaches to life. (D) Seeking action and adventure, experiencing what life has to offer. (E) Serving your mission alone and without interruption from others.

3. How do you like to interact with other people? (A) By listening so you can better understand other people and show them you understand. (B) By focusing on the current communication style so you can be heard correctly. (C) By expressing your thoughts openly and clearly, while being impartial and nonjudgmental about others' views. (D) By being witty and enjoying the give-and-take of banter. (E) By respecting other people's right to be themselves, but not allowing them to dilute your purpose in life.

4. What kinds of descriptions would you use for yourself as a leader? (A) You're more of a democratic leader who serves the people. (B) You set the rules first so everyone knows and abides by them. (C) You weigh your actions against future benefits and choose talented people to assist you. (D) Planning is not your forte but you go full steam and try everything. (E) You are neither leader nor follower; you are your own person, which is enough.

5. What are your favorite recreational activities? (A) It is not the activity but the friends and family whom you're with. (B) You like well-structured activities, especially family favorites. (C) You like activities where there are definite goals with competition. (D) You like to create your own fun, and partying is your favorite sport. (E) Hiking alone, praying and meditation, self-exploration.

6. How would you describe your childhood? (A) You spent a lot of time in dreamland and fantasy. (B) You were the favorite child because you were very obedient and respectful. (C) You were always making and inventing things. (D) You were usually in trouble because you were so mischievous. (E) You spent a lot of time alone and created your own entertainment.

7. How were your teenage years? (A) You had lots and lots of friends. (B) You were always busy doing things for some organized activity. (C) You were usually the leader of a team trying to change things for a better future. (D) You were a risk taker,

always driving wildly and being the clown. (E) You enjoyed activities, although you were alone much of the time.

8. What were your favorite subjects? (A) Drama, literature, and the arts. (B) History, government, social studies. (C) Science, engineering, mathematics. (D) Athletics, music, extracurriculars. (E) Reading, doing individual research, writing.

9. How do you handle relationships with the opposite sex? (A) You are romantic and like to be more than a "boyfriend" or "girlfriend." (B) You like the traditional relationship where the rules have been set and respected. (C) Your relationships have to fit with your plans and goals. (D) You want someone you can laugh with and have fun. (E) You have had only one friend and girlfriend or boyfriend.

10. What kinds of friends do you have? (A) You have loyal friends whom you care for and nurture. (B) You have friends who fit a role in your life, such as church, work, and family friends. (C) You have few friends except those who work with you on specific projects. (D) You have lots of friends from all kinds of backgrounds. (E) Friendships are how you are supported and support others in their private missions.

11. As a parent you behave: (A) As a nurturer, being responsive to the child's needs. (B) As a teacher, being sure the child understands the rules and boundaries of life. (C) As a leader, with specific goals set for both of you to achieve together. (D) As an example of having fun for life as a rule. (E) You support your child in his or her personal and unique way of life.

12. What kind of work do you think you would enjoy? (A) Working with living things, like people and animals. (B) A steady job that has security and acknowledges your efforts. (C) A creative outlet where you can see your future. (D) Not tied down to a desk or set times, but able to express your needs through your job. (E) Forestry, consultation, writing.

Scoring: Count up the number of times you chose an A, B, C, D, or E and sum the five categories into ranges from 0 to 12, writing them down below:

12	____	____	____	____	____
11	____	____	____	____	____
10	____	____	____	____	____
9	____	____	____	____	____
8	____	____	____	____	____
7	____	____	____	____	____

	A's Empathizer	B's Teacher	C's Pathfinder	D's Magician	E's Warrior
6	—	—	—	—	—
5	—	—	—	—	—
4	—	—	—	—	—
3	—	—	—	—	—
2	—	—	—	—	—
1	—	—	—	—	—
0	—	—	—	—	—

Your profile may be flat or hilly, based on your defining yourself within these five groups. For example, mine looks something like this:

	A's Empathizer	B's Teacher	C's Pathfinder	D's Magician	E's Warrior
12	—	—	—	—	—
11	—	—	—	—	—
10	—	—	—	—	—
9	—	—	—	—	—
8	—	—	—	—	—
7	—	—	—	—	—
6	X	—	—	—	—
5	—	—	—	—	—
4	—	—	—	—	—
3	—	—	X	—	—
2	—	—	—	—	X
1	—	X	—	—	—
0	—	—	—	X	—

This pattern would be primarily that of an empathizer, but I also have pathfinder, warrior, and teacher tendencies as well, which means that people are my first concern. I also like to be alone at times, however, and as a teenager I was pretty conservative.

You may find you have traits of more than one temperament,

too. But becoming more aware of the different aspects of your personality is important, because that self-awareness can help you better understand the stressors in your life.

MAKING SENSE OF THE TYPES FOR LESS STRESS

Each type of basic temperament can produce varying levels of stress depending on the culture you're raised in. I'll summarize some of the probable positive environments where you'd likely be very well received (meaning, less stressed). I'll also highlight environments that are likely to be more stress filled. I'll then suggest how you can create a game plan to achieve a better balance between your authentic self and your world.

Empathizer

If you found yourself in this category you are likely the type of person who invests your time and energy in people. You can be inspired by honorable goals that you work tirelessly and devote your entire self to accomplishing. These goals usually have to do with human improvement or helping charitable causes. As a true empathizer, you tend to be unselfish in your needs and have very high, perhaps too high, levels of trust, so you can sometimes be vulnerable to people who might want to take advantage of you. Perhaps you see the good in everyone and don't always recognize their undesirable character traits.

People with whom you will likely have relationships with minimal stress:

- You would likely find that the teacher type would applaud your sensitivity to everyone's individual needs, although there might be issues over setting comfortable boundaries.

- You would probably find some common ground with the warrior because of his desire for personal support, but it could be a one-way relationship.

- More than likely you would enjoy a relationship with another empathizer because of your mutual interests, especially if you're both inspired by the same goals.

People with whom you may have problems:

- The magician will likely drive you to highest stress levels because of your respect for others' feelings and his lack of inspirational and honorable goals.

- The pathfinder may find you difficult to work with because of the conflict over the relative importance of external, objective goals and the internal personal goals of the people involved.

Pathfinder

This cluster of temperaments demonstrates what would be considered the most productive leadership style in many industries. You are a good idea person who can muster a game plan easily and realistically. You will extend everyone's talents to the maximum, and share the results as a whole. You are very calm on the exterior, but intense on the inside. You appear to have great patience, but it would be more accurate to say that you have a calculated time plan inside your head. You can see all sides to an argument or problem area, which makes you a good problem solver.

People with whom you will have the least stress in relationships:

- The warrior will likely be helpful to you as long as you recognize his independence and need for his personal fulfillment. In fact, the warrior may be a very good ally if he buys into your plan and it supports his strengths.

- The teacher might serve you well in your goals, as long as you can recognize her need for respect—not only for herself, but also for the traditions or structure of the project.

- Other pathfinders may resent your leadership, so you will need to create special projects for them to handle. They can be very helpful because you use the same playbook; but don't cross them or they may turn on you and become your greatest enemy.

People whom you will likely find stressful:

- The magician will be difficult because there are few values you share and the last thing she would want to do is focus on a small objective that isn't fun. That is the key to decreasing potential stress storms: making a project fun and reminding the magician of that fact as often as possible.

- The empathizer is going to buck you if you mistreat or slight someone for the sake of progress toward the goal. However, a good pathfinder knows that group success is based on the success of each individual involved. You will have to focus attention on the subtle ways you motivate the people on the team in order to keep the empathizer off your back.

Magician

If you fit primarily into the magician category, you are likely to be a person who lives in the present, rather than dealing with past issues or future promises. You dislike being bored so much that you get stressed just thinking about sitting in a class or working all day without some relief. Consequently, you create your own style of life as a clown or instigator of mischief. You probably find gossip to have some entertainment value, and you thrive on crisis because it adds spice to your life. These factors do not have negative value. They equip you to be a great negotiator because you can deal with ambiguity and confusion very well. The basic spontaneity and creativity of your approaches increases others' attraction to you.

People you likely have good, low-stress relationships with:

- You will likely find the warrior to be a very positive personality type to work with, largely because you can bring the fun out in him and give him balance. This type is typically very closed off, and he may be more balanced by your interactions.

- The empathizer could be very positive in a relationship because of his sensitivity to your nature and support for your own good. The empathizer also is present minded, so you would have some overlap in focus in terms of goals for individuals.

- You would embrace other magicians as brothers and sisters because you would have similar games you've played and enjoyed in the past and recognize the rules immediately. If three of you got together, it would probably shift the dynamic into a partylike atmosphere.

The people you may have issues with:

- The pathfinder would have considerable concerns about your ability to be serious about focusing on future goals. Your stress would rise to the top and become even more acute as you attempted to undermine authority. It would be more productive if you could offer your creativity as a major contribution toward achieving the goal, which would give more value to the relationship as well as minimize the stress.

- The teacher would likely have complaints about your style, because of your lack of respect for the rules and tradition. (You may have had this experience already with actual teachers in the past.) You will also likely be criticized for these factors, so to minimize stress in this relationship, it would be prudent to reorganize the situation to create a friendly competition. In this way you can be seen as supporting respect for the individual while using your wits.

Teacher

The teacher cluster of temperaments has a number of very strong traits and exists in every culture I've studied. This figure stands for the history and basic values for any community and family. You serve a vital function for everyone as a historian and stabilizer, so you are to be honored and respected. But there will always be a force for change, and you may be standing in the way at times. This possibility requires strength as well as tolerance.

You possess a deep sense of loyalty and enjoy the feeling of being responsible. You probably also understand the need for rules and policies. Perhaps you've seen the chaos and anarchy without the standards of civilized behavior, and may even fear some loss of control.

People with whom you will likely have less stress in relationships:

- You would likely find common ground with the empathizer because of your similar respect for the individual, although there may be some conflict when it comes to making exceptions to rules to allow for individual needs.

- You will also probably enjoy relationships with the pathfinder because both of you seek to join forces to achieve an external goal; however, if you focus too much on the rules and insist on deferring to past processes without reference to the immediate goal, you may find yourself in direct opposition to the pathfinder.

- You will probably find other teacher types as allies because of your common belief in rules and procedures. You would probably gain a lot of support by finding kindred spirits.

People with whom you will have problems and stress:

- The magician will probably be your worst nightmare because he or she will counter every value of respect and obedience you stand for. Your goals will be at almost opposite ends of the continuum for external versus internal goal satisfaction.

- The warrior might also give you some stress, because the goals for him tend to be very inward, as opposed to yours, which are externally focused. There will also likely be major communication and semantic issues.

Warrior

You will likely come from a background in which you grew up in a very independent way. You have found ways for self-gratification through personal achievements, and you still hold to those behaviors and consider them more important than others' opinions. For example, you may have become a fast runner or a good speller, and you feel that these accomplishments were attributable to your own efforts rather than your coaches.

People with whom you will have less stress in relationships:

- You might find the pathfinder as a suitable working relationship because you probably have some talents and abilities he can see as part of accomplishing a goal. The more similar you are in having the same goals and needs, the less stressful the relationship will be, especially if you learn to trust each other's motivations to that end. The age-old example is two people who marry with goals of high intensive emotional commitment and being a "team" at beating the business world. But with children and other home demands, their common goals diminish and high stress invariably emerges.

- The empathizer will likely be a good supporter if you can open up to him or her for your needs, especially if you need help with something. He will probably feel privileged to be part of your confidence, and you could enjoy his company a great deal.

- Depending on your balance, the magician may become your best friend, not because he knows and accepts you so well, but because he gives you a sense of joy and having fun. Not being experienced so much in relationships, he accepts you when he feels you have a fun side and will delve into you to find it and bring it out in you.

People you may have greatest stress with:

- It's likely that you might find interacting with other warriors stressful, because all of you are so self-contained. You don't communicate very well outside yourselves, so there's often a void in your interactions.

- The teacher will likely doubt your motivations because you don't express them, and any negative or positive projections will be the reaction of the teacher. If it's a positive or negative projection, such as "You are the exact image of John Wayne—I am going to treat you as him," this could be trouble, because you may not like being John Wayne and the path of stress will be riddled with expectations not your own.

BRAIN TEMPERAMENTS AND INTERPERSONAL STRESS

All of the above begs the question: how can we learn to get along to make this world a better, more enjoyable place . . . when we're all so different? The answer is, we do that by learning how to interconnect directly through brain channels. These communication/interaction pathways in our brain are flexible. Thus, we can reroute and develop them to better work with the innate tendencies and orientation of the people with whom we interact.

Learning to Connect at the Brain Rhythms Level

There is much to learn from other cultures about changing brain patterns for the sake of communication with minimum stress. Many of the American Indian tribes would wait for three days before convening their powwow conferences. The preceding period was used to listen to the drums and smoke peace pipe tobacco, while contemplating the Great Spirit and creating the right atmosphere.

Contrary to popular belief, the most profound communication can occur without the use of verbal language. Several years ago Elmer and Alyce Green conducted some research they later reported in their book, *Beyond Biofeedback,* which offered exciting prospects for people to learn to communicate and empathize at higher levels.

They set up two people with EEGs who could see both their own EEG monitor as well as the other person's. They were instructed jointly to make their EEG frequencies as similar as they could, which they did after spending some time in learning how to control their own frequency. What was so amazing was that when the matching occurred, each of them felt that they could "hear" the other's thoughts. Indeed, a good deal of evidence suggests that there is a scientific basis for creating common brain patterns through sonic stimulation.

For individuals seeking higher communication and empathy with each other I would recommend selecting a rhythmic beat or using something like the BAUD device, or just beating a drum, so as to find a similar brain frequency pattern as a regular practice. Dancing and moving to sonic patterns together would also be a natural way of relating. Given time, a connectiveness emerges that guides people into the bond.

Learning Basic Communication Cultural Rituals

A few years ago, I had the pleasure of working with a group in Wisconsin on an imagery workshop. In so doing, I realized that I was in a culture far removed from my Texas roots. Here's what happened: we needed open space for the workshop, and we found a house that was almost perfect, if we just removed one of the walls. This, of course, required our using a professional carpenter. The property owner highly recommended a local carpenter named Bill, whom we found sitting in the town hardware store in front of a wood-burning stove.

Right off the bat, Bill started to size me up. He commented on the weather, then asked about my Texas roots, whether I was married or not, how many kids I had, whether we might know some people in common, what my vocation was, my political tendencies . . . until finally, something clicked with him, and he shifted gears and got down to discussing the particulars about the house alterations I needed. He then said, "I'll consider doing the job, but I'll have to think about it. Come back in an hour or so." I returned an hour later, as he requested. He looked at me for a long time and then agreed to do the work. Incidentally, he did a fine job.

Every culture has its own communication rules, which sets the tone and receptivity for interaction. But there are underlying themes. The general format usually goes something like this:

Phase I: Exploratory phase—initial questions such as:

1. What kind of language (technical) are you going to use?
2. What kind of relationship do you want with me?
3. How demanding are you going to be in working toward some goal?
4. How amenable are you going to be concerning my input?
5. Are you going to understand me?
6. Am I going to understand you?
7. How trustworthy are you?

Phase II: Coming to terms

1. What currency are we going to use (praise, money, respect, etc.)?

2. Am I going to get what I want?
3. What kinds of behavior am I going to want to see, and what do you want to see?

These subtle—albeit incredibly important—kinds of rituals set the brain on a course to satisfy the need to relieve tension in communications between personality types. This is exactly the kind of process I was taught by my parents in dealing with problematic teachers. If you know what the teachers want, in terms of behavior and words, you can determine what their needs are, and you can adjust your brain agenda accordingly.

Any interaction with another human being is an educational process. Both of you are attempting to decode messages from each other, and your brains are working hard to educate yourselves for survival's sake as well as to find success in your interaction.

Learning to Listen to Brain Messages

Better communication and empathy skills on the cognitive level would also help immensely in regulating your brain as you deal with each other. Just the behavior of active listening gives you a tremendous advantage, as it increases your ability to identify potential stress, so that you can nip it in the bud. Your brain uses both content (words) and feeling (emotions) components to size up a situation, so you have to listen for both.

The most severe mistake you can make is to assume you know what the other person means based upon their word choices alone. This whole chapter is intended to impress upon you that brains are different and words do not mean exactly the same thing to different people. You also need to bear in mind that sometimes the other person doesn't actually know what he wants—and he may or may not realize that fact himself.

The art of communication requires modifying your brain to receive communication from another—assuming you care to make the effort. This is called empathy training, which is the ability to show understanding of the feelings and intentions of others. Without this foreknowledge, proceeding is often ill advised.

The process requires sensitivity to another person's feelings, which is hard for some individuals, especially individuals who've been trained to avoid such things. The idea is to use feedback to increase awareness while making sure the two of you are on the same frequency, language-wise. The format for practicing empathy interchange is as follows:

1. Person A makes a statement.
2. Person B reflects on what he understood in terms of content and emotion and requests accuracy.
3. Person A confirms or restates statement for clarity.
4. Person B reflects what he heard again for accuracy. Upon acknowledgment that his understanding was correct, Person B then responds to Person A with his own ideas. Person A in turn begins the process of reflecting his perceptions for accuracy.

This process gets easier and smoother with practice. For example, the following is an interchange between two beginners learning the skills of empathy:

Dialogue I:

PERSON A: You know that I wanted to go shopping tomorrow afternoon?

PERSON B: Are you asking me if I know your plans or are you telling me you want to go shopping?

PERSON A: Actually I was wondering if you knew I wanted to go.

PERSON B: It sounds like it's really important for you to go, and you would be pretty disappointed if you didn't.

PERSON A: Yeah, I guess I would. I've got so many things I want to do.

PERSON B: Yeah, I can tell it's important to you. Can you

tell me what you'll be doing and how long you will be out?

PERSON A: Yeah, I can. Probably from three o'clock to six-thirty. What are your feelings about my plans?

PERSON B: I'm OK with them, just wanted to know.

PERSON A: You sound sad or even a bit angry. Are you upset?

PERSON B: Yes, I guess I was looking forward to some time with you watching the game. But let's make a plan to do that the next day, OK?

Now, compare that dialogue to this.
Dialogue II:

PERSON A: You know that I wanted to go shopping tomorrow afternoon?

PERSON B: What for? (Didn't answer the question.)

PERSON A: I wanted to go get some things.

PERSON B: What things? (Still evading the question.)

PERSON A: Oh, some shoes and some groceries. (Feeling defensive.)

PERSON B: OK. (Still no communication.)

The second communication left both of them hanging (and annoyed). Nothing was really learned about what each was thinking or feeling. In order to connect effectively, you have to listen and question your own perceptions as well as the real messages behind what is spoken.

CONCLUDING THOUGHTS

A major challenge in life, as stated earlier, is to maintain the "you" in contrast to the world's reductionist expectations. Stress results from our efforts to reconcile these conflicting demands, while still maintaining authenticity. This process dates back to the time in which survival was based upon building community power to thwart threatening forces. It's still the first task of life to learn a common language, cultural customs of eating and eliminating our food, and developing roles in our families and communities.

This process of integrating our authentic selves within a whole that contains many different personalities can cause us doubt and frustration. However, there are steps we can take to make it less frustrating at the most basic level, regardless of which temperament we were born with.

If you are part of the human race, escaping from stress entirely is not an option. Besides, stressors themselves are not the enemy. It's how you react to them that makes all the difference. And knowing a person's temperament gives you a serious leg up.

10

Gender Stress Storms: Special Edition

The interpersonal dynamic between men and women has been fraught with stress and confusion since the beginning of recorded history (and undoubtedly before). Accordingly, few of us are surprised to learn that the male brain isn't wired in exactly the same way as the female brain. However, this is not to say that our respective brains aren't well matched. On the contrary, it appears they are designed to work in a complementary fashion, so as to optimize each other's strengths and provide backup for each other's shortcomings.

Sean and Judy would be described as fairly ordinary people. Both had parents who married more than once, and both had a few childhood problems adjusting to their blended families; but that's perfectly normal. They were also both generally happy people, and when they met, the sparks flew. Eventually they fell in love and were married in a traditional ceremony, including all the customary rites and celebrations befitting two terrific young individuals embracing the next level of maturity and obligation to the community. In fact, all their friends and family considered them the "perfect" couple.

Fast-forward five years and they're meeting in divorce court for "irreconcilable differences." What happened to this couple? Did their love simply vanish? Were they ill suited to each other? Were they immature?

These questions surround nearly every marriage, even ones that don't end in divorce. Of the 50 percent of marriages that don't legally end, far too many would nonetheless be described as so empty and void of meaning that divorce would be a blessing; but often neither partner has the emotional courage (or perhaps the financial resources) to pursue it. These are lonely, devastated people who dread every day of life with another person, and find themselves stuck in psychotherapists' offices, or wishing for a magic wand to wave away their troubles and deposit them in the land of happily-ever-after. But the reality is, a good marriage takes ongoing effort and commitment. Even the best of marriage partners go through rocky, stressful times. What makes the difference is whether or not you have the skills to address and resolve those conflicts in ways that are kind, respectful, and loving.

We all experience stress in varying degrees, some of us starting at a very young age. Children may be raised by parents who are addicts, or full of rage, or mentally ill, or even just intensely self-absorbed. But as stressful and tragic as these childhood experiences can be, they have relatively little to do with one's future quality of marital satisfaction. In fact, sometimes having survived a dreadful circumstance fosters our having a deeper, more profound understanding of what truly matters in life, thereby helping us to develop and nurture our relationships, rather than sabotage them.

Shacking Up—A Statistical Fact

Whether you lived together prior to getting married for a few months or for years, your chance of having a successful marriage isn't any better than if you'd only met each other on your wedding day.

MARRIAGE AND HEALTH

A twelve-year study of 9,011 British civil servants (both male and female) found that those with the worst close relationships (which could be with a spouse, close friend, or relative) were 34 percent more likely to suffer a heart attack or have other heart troubles than those with good relationships.

This study, published in 2007 in the *Archives of Internal Medicine,* supports previous research that has linked health problems to being single and having few close relationships. Another recent study found that there was no association between marital woes in general and increased risk of heart disease or early death. However, what it did find during the study's ten-year follow-up was that wives who kept silent during marital arguments had an increased risk of prematurely dying, as compared with wives who expressed their feelings while the fights were in progress. For men what appeared to matter most was simply being married, i.e., married men were less likely to die during the ten-year follow-up than single men.

Thus, the science strongly suggests that men and women are different in more than just physical ways. This chapter is designed to help equip you with the tools and understanding necessary to facilitate your embracing these differences, instead of struggling against them.

PROBLEMS IN HAVING DIFFERENT BRAIN NETWORKS

Few would argue that marriage doesn't introduce a whole new set of stress storms, regardless of how good one's coping skills are. But in my view, too many psychotherapists continue to be blind to the possibility of creating positive synergy to address our inherent differences.

When brain imaging became available to psychologists and neuroscientists, it provided us our first clues as to how the male and female brains worked in synchronicity. The science suggests that we're actually designed to work as an *integrated* whole. Perhaps this intertwining of abilities felt more "natural" back in the days when our ancestors had to combine strengths to survive: in order to achieve a secure and predictable lifestyle, each partner required the highest levels of coordinated strengths, such as hunting, gathering, constructing, farming, child care, etc. However, in today's world (where, for the most part, our physical survival doesn't actually require we work together), these very powerful forces instead are often a source of confusion, which we know leads to stress storms.

MALE AND FEMALE THINKING PATTERNS

Note: When I'm discussing either the male or the female brain, I'm talking in generalities. There are of course individualistic differences, and all brains are plastic, especially in the formative years. Plus, most people are somewhere in between the extremes of what would be classified as a male versus a female brain.

Ask any man if he thinks he understands women 100 percent of the time, and he'll surely say no . . . unless he's fooling himself. In fact, many of us find humor in that statement; and the long-running Broadway show *Defending the Caveman* attests to that fact. That said, sometimes these differences are anything but a laughing matter. For example, as recently as the twentieth century, academic professors have stated that a female's thinking patterns are too petty, irrational, and emotional for a career in science! That just makes me mad. So here are some myths (about the male and female brains) that I'd like to bust for your edification:

- **Myth:** Men only use half their brains at times.
  Busted: This myth comes from the naïve concept about the narrow use of the male focus abilities. Both men and women use all their brains, but they do so in different ways.

- **Myth:** Women possess better verbal skills.
  Busted: There has never been any valid research to support this myth, but it is true that female and male brains are different, and females may have a broader range of emotional integration in their expressions. They also learn writing skills earlier than boys do. However, if one thinks about some of the world's greatest authors, there's little basis for this generalization.

- **Myth:** The female brain has a better capacity for memory.
  Busted: It's not that the female brain has better memory capabilities; it's that it remembers different types of information as compared to the male brain.

- **Myth:** The male brain is better suited for leadership.
  Busted: While it is true that historically, there have been more male leaders, that doesn't necessarily mean that they're good at it. The attributes that make up a leader can vary considerably, and the situation oftentimes defines the leadership.

- **Myth**: Women have better coordination.
  Busted: This myth has been argued from both sides. Men can do some things better than women, women can do some things better than men, and some skills are evenly matched (thank you, Billie Jean King).

MALE AND FEMALE BRAIN STRUCTURE, DEMYSTIFIED

An adult male brain tends to weigh from 11 to 12 percent more than a woman's brain; and men's heads are usually about 2 percent bigger than women's, too. Of course, absolute brain size is not a good measure of human intelligence. Conversely, there are recent studies that suggest that the corpus callosum (the big bundle of axons that connects the left and right hemispheres of the brain) in women is bigger and more developed than a man's—suggesting that women have a greater capacity for superior intellectual activity. This supposition is based on the belief that having a bigger corpus callosum allows women to make and process more interconnections between their emotional side (the right hemisphere) and their rational side (the left hemisphere). However, there are also recent studies that disprove that contention, such as a 2003 study that concluded that men's corpora callosa are bigger; and researchers of this study also cautioned readers *against* concluding that bigger means better.

There are additional significant differences, in terms of size and shape, that are less well known. For example, it's well documented that the preoptic area of the hypothalamus (which has to do with mating behaviors) is clearly different between women and men; the men's is more than twice as large, and has roughly double the amount of cells. And of course, women and men don't share all of the same hormones; and these chemical messengers impact a huge variety of functions, including (but certainly not limited to) metabolism, mood, mating, growth, the "fight or flight" response, the immune response, and caring for one's offspring.

Hormones and Women

Women have three particular hormones that regularly catalyze a wave of changing brain connections. These hormones are estrogen, progesterone, and oxytocin. Estrogen is the accelerator of brain functions, and progesterone is the brake and inhibitor, making the relationship of these two hormones a sophisticated checks-and-balances arrangement. Oxytocin is best known for being the hormone that stimulates contractions to help the birthing process, prompts the breasts to secrete milk, and triggers the feeling of deep caring and protection of one's newborn. It's less widely known that oxytocin is also released into the bloodstream when you fall in love, and that it serves as a memory stimulant to help you remember the people you fall in love with. Recent studies suggest that oxytocin is associated with healthier social relationships. All of this suggests this is one powerful, extraordinarily vital hormone.

I'm going to focus on two aspects of a woman's brain: 1) balance and 2) multiple capacities. The female brain is built on a balance of attention. A woman has to contend with balance all of her adult life: balance between her goals and her mate's goals, between her job and family, between a child in pain and attending to her other children, and between her dreams and her responsibilities, to name just a few.

I have observed female leaders expertly balancing the need of a group to move forward with an ambitious goal, while simultaneously nurturing one of the group members who is suffering through some personal challenge. But add too many important issues that require her focused attention, and that sometimes tips the balance. Perhaps that's why so many women who strive so hard to "have it all" are sometimes so frustrated: when is enough, enough?

Of note, a careerbuilders.com online survey of six hundred full-time working moms with children under the age of eighteen found that one in four responded that they were dissatisfied with the balance between their work and their home life, and were actively taking steps to find jobs that would allow them more freedom. An AOL online survey asked women who worked outside the home what caused them the most stress: their jobs, their children, or both. Nearly half responded "both." That said, a scientific study published in the *Journal of Women's Health* found that, regardless of how stressful either of their roles are (worker and mom), employed moms enjoy a mental health advantage; and this was the case regardless of whether these women were married or not. Incidentally, the scientific community refers to this work-related mitigation of stress as *positive spillover.*

Mood Management and Brain Function

Mood can be a tremendous asset, triggering inspiration and creative thinking, and it can be deleterious, triggering depression and anxiety. Because of women's hormonal makeup, their brains are inextricably intertwined with mood. For example, many women experience mood changes preceding their menstrual cycle. This shift in mood can range from mild to intrusive to overwhelming.

It's also been reported that women have more insightful and creative dreams during menstruation. In fact, it was common practice among some Native American tribes (and other cultures in South America and northern Europe) to isolate women during their period for fear of their tremendous magical powers.

If we look for a theoretical reason for having this cycling mental ability, we can surmise that its survival basis might be the need for emerging skills at specific times, to allow women to balance their obligations. For example, women can bring a broader perspective to tasks, such as more creativity and rationality. It is this "flow" into one state and another that defines the process of passion and mystery.

Spatial Orientation

In a multitude of capacities, women often serve as mentors and teachers to others, and these tasks call for orientation to different points of view in order to be able to put feelings, thoughts, and even spatial constructs into practice and application. For example, it's difficult to create a plan to build a house without some concept of direction; it's hard to direct a person on a journey if there are no guideposts; and it's hard to see an object from other perspectives than what you see directly, without a sense of orientation. Indeed, creativity requires one be able to imagine that which is not readily apparent or already there.

The brain's right hemisphere is dominant for general orientation to visual/spatial imagery, including noting the angles, distance, and widths of objects. However, the details of these images are often in the left brain. In real life, this usually means that the male brain will orient itself according to general characteristics, such as "go north for three miles, then turn west for four miles, etc."—whereas the female brain would be more likely to provide more specifics and confirm details with accuracy. For example, a woman might offer directions this way: "Go up this road for about five minutes, until you see a blue house with lots of gingerbread details along the roofline. You'll know that's the one I'm talking about because it has an incredible garden with four magnolia trees framing the entrance-way, and tons of rosebushes surrounding the house—and all of the other houses have no landscaping at all. Right after this house, you'll see a rusted old wheelbarrow sitting in a huge ditch on your left; at the very next intersection (which has a stop sign), turn right. If you went too far, you'll see a graveyard on your left. But that's no big deal, just make U-turn . . ."

There are advantages to both approaches. Which type of directions you prefer is a matter of your brain processing style. But here's the thing: when you're *giving* directions to someone, it behooves you to ask how the *other person prefers* to have driving directions given to him or her. Why? While it's often true that the above male/female distinction of spatial orientation applies, it's certainly not necessarily always the case. One very good female friend of mine (who is particularly directionally challenged) prefers both the "male" and the "female" version be provided to her, so that she can not only use her dashboard odometer, but also keep track of confirming visual details.

Memory and Gender

When it comes to what and how people remember events, there are differences in the male and female brain. They're related to the kind of details one remembers. In fact, there's a psychological concept (which applies to both men and women) that can provide some immediate insight as to why a person behaves in a certain way, and what motivated that behavior in the present.

The technique comes from the famous psychologist Alfred Adler (the person who coined the term *inferiority complex*). Adler introduced the principle that we all learn from the past but we behave for future events. Put simply, we have over 210,240,000 seconds of waking experience over any ten-year period (60 seconds × 60 minutes × 16 hours awake each day × 365 days a year × 10 years of life); and if some event happened every ten seconds, we'd have over twenty-one million events we could remember by the age of ten. By that early age, or even sooner, we might be using this vast collection of memories to form lasting norms of behavior and expectations of success and failure. For example, if your memories prior to age six all told you that your very existence in the world was totally insignificant, it's likely that in your present life you would still be behaving in ways that react to that memory. Whether your behavior was confirming that prediction or rebelling against it, you would still be reacting to those childhood memories.

Betty's Story

For a real-life example, let's take Betty. A nurse by profession, Betty was twenty-five years old and very unhappy with her life. She came to the clinic because she thought she had ADHD, a conclusion she based upon her inability to concentrate at her job, which had led to her being repeatedly passed over for promotions. When asked what she thought were the five defining moments in her life, she shared the following:

1. People bragged about her brother . . . for something she had done.
2. She won a medal for a music competition, but she never got to tell her family because a crisis happened that day . . . and nobody ever asked.
3. One day a wasp stung her, and everyone paid a lot of attention to her while she cried . . . so she intentionally cried more than was justified by the pain she actually felt.
4. She made money in high school by ghostwriting papers for the other students. She liked that because she made good grades for them, made friends with popular kids, and didn't have to defend the papers to a teacher.
5. She was at a concert with her family and was in total rapture at the artist singing.

It quickly became clear that Betty was probably seeing life as a stage—one where other people got the credit for her success; and that she was actually more comfortable with being in the background. She liked being in the audience for a hero, rather than being the hero herself. In fact, I eventually discovered that it was self-sabotage that thwarted her promotions.

The point about memory is that instead of remembering every event in one's life (which is impossible), we choose the events that define our perspective on life. We all do this, consciously or not, and we continue to look for events that validate our life summaries. If Betty doesn't change her thinking, she will continue to look for events that she perceives as substantiating her role as the invisible martyr. When she experiences new events that don't support the sad, limiting stories she tells herself, she'll dismiss those events as not valid, or she may not recognize (and certainly won't commit to memory) that non-sequitur event at all.

Details, Details . . .

When you ask a man about what he remembers, he's likely to share memories about events that relate to his achieving or not achieving a goal. Women's brains are much more detail focused, rather than outcome focused. As an example, let's suppose a man and a woman were witnesses to a bank robbery and each was asked to give a description of the robber. The man would likely give a description of how tall the robber was and how much he probably weighed, maybe what kind of gun he used. The woman would likely report what color and style the robber's clothes were, the way he walked, the port wine birthmark on his face, and his voice quality.

Testosterone levels influence attention and concentration, making men more impulsive in their emotional reactions and behavior. In other words, men's brains are more reactive—which can be either a good thing or a bad thing. Men want to fix things quickly, not talk about them. This makes them very frustrating to deal with, for those who prefer to carefully plan things out and weigh the options. Yes, it's true; men's memories tend to be more receptive to facts and figures, like baseball statistics and football standings. Of course, men are also very visual, but that's another book, entirely.

A woman's brain is less testosterone driven because she produces far less of that hormone, which often means she's less inclined to make a quick fix, and is more inclined to first investigate multiple solutions. A woman's brain also records much more emotional content. Now, if the emotional content is stressful, cortisol (discussed in chapter eight) will be activated. Cortisol actually increases our ability to remember things and adds to the clarity of our memories.

Sometimes, when the brain is severely stressed, memories are planted in the depths of the unconscious. On a physiological level, the hippocampus (which is involved with verbal memory) becomes overwhelmed, and the pain of remembering the event shrinks memory capacity. This is a protective shield, but when you have to perform, it can be a huge problem. That's the reason hypnosis often works. You get in a relaxed state so you can revive those brain functions by relieving them of the emotional baggage.

Pain Sensitivity and Mental Functions

A woman's brain reacts differently to both physical and psychological pain than a man's brain. Men's brains are geared toward goals and ignoring pain—possibly because pain is perceived in the male brain as an obstacle to achieving end results. Throughout history, great conquerors have sacrificed hundreds or thousands of lives to obtain their goals. Whether or not you would make a similar decision, it's undeniable that their progress would have been greatly compromised if the welfare of these individuals had been as important to them as their goals. Perhaps it takes such a brain mechanism to help a society as a whole to overcome major challenges to progress; or perhaps this mechanism operates only to the detriment of society, depending upon your perspective.

A woman's brain has more cellular receivers to detect pain than a man's, thereby increasing her sensitivity responses, especially in the joints and lower digestive tract. Women are also generally more sensitive to touch and color.

It's unclear whether or not having an increased sensitivity to pain is the reason why women are more likely to seek medical and psychotherapeutic care than men. The difference may be a function of societal norms, i.e., men are more often taught to "suck it up." Of note, a woman's more acute awareness of discomfort and imbalance may be one of the many reasons why women are more likely to function as caretakers in so many cultures; and historically, women were often healers and expert providers of medicinal herbs and other natural approaches.

Further, a woman's brain is particularly well suited to sensing the imbalances within her body and correlating them to possible cause-and-effect events. Now, if you've ever thought or said things like, "I feel it in my heart, "I know in my gut," or "I know something is wrong because my nerves are so agitated," those are messages your brain is providing you. In fact the brain serves a lot like a biofeedback machine. This intuitive skill that so many women have (and to a lesser extent, men) may also be why—at least in my personal experience—it is almost impossible to lie to your mother without her sensing your deception.

Maximizing the Combined Gifts

The best answer to the challenges that give rise to gender stress is that we have to return to our basic brain dispositions. To the best of my knowledge, we're the only animals on earth that haven't worked this out yet. Other species have no problems integrating their respective abilities and talents for the best resolution for all parties concerned. Not to be overly simplistic, but the fact that human beings ostensibly have more complex social interactions is not the problem. The problem is our failure to understand and work with our respective natures—which is key.

The primary triggers associated with stress between couples are most often the ego, miscommunication, and misunderstanding of each other's respective experiences and expectations. Cultures differ, time demands are ever-increasing, and people change. But resetting long-held concepts and beliefs (even when everyone involved is on board) is still a difficult adjustment. We need to train our brains to make these changes—and to make them stick. Otherwise, our brains will revert to older patterns as the default position. But you can change those patterns.

To be clear, understanding this evolutionary process that has led men's and women's brains to develop the way they have is in no way a reason to want to return to those caveman days. Indeed, that is a very, very bad idea! What I am suggesting is that we have the capacity to learn and even reprogram how we interact with each other and with ourselves.

Principle I: Neurons that learn together become attached.

The approach of correlating brain frequencies discussed in chapter nine has special relevance to gender communication and the lowering of stress. The same problem-solving tools for communication are useful for people who have a mixture of other kinds of relationship dynamics. Couples can use the problem-solving mode of interaction necessary for successful working relationships, but there are also independent dynamics of sexuality, affection, authority, friendship, and team participation that must be addressed. If one person is in one frame of reference, and the other person has another agenda, any progress toward either concentration will end in frustration and stress.

Review the approaches in the last chapter and make clear preparations for significant relationship communications. Play music, listen to drums, meditate, dance, whatever you think might help the other person relax or become inspired for what comes next. Too often individuals dive into a serious discussion without any preparation, catching the other off guard, and both respond emotionally as if they were being trapped or sabotaged.

In one family I consulted with, being served a nice turkey dinner was the clue that an important discussion was about to take place. Two brothers I worked with used cigars: if one offered the other a cigar, that was the clue that one of them needed to talk. Each of these techniques for clueing the other in not only sets the stage for emotional preparedness, it also makes the initial phase a pleasant one. And we listen, process, and think better when we're not stressed.

Principle II: Experience and need can change neurological bundles.

The operative words here are experience and need. This principle sets the needs of the individuals involved, which will always be in a state of change. This is the reason for continuing to make time for interactions. You have to be aware of what needs aren't being met for the other person you value as well as for yourself. The general step-by-step process goes as follows:

- Survival
- Belonging and being protected
- Stability and security
- Love and affection
- Self-esteem and identity
- Expression of the authenticity of the self—standing for values
- Spiritual connection—the meaning of life

If one member of the couple is still searching for survival and the other is searching for love, and they form a relationship on that basis, then as long as they stay in that mutual need mode, their stress will be kept relatively in check. But if one or both people progress to the next step (which is perfectly natural), that's where the conflicts begin. For example, let's say one person's need for survival is satisfied by the other partner's generous financial savings, and the need for love is satisfied by the other partner's nurturance. They have made a contract, knowingly or unknowingly. But then, once the survival needs are met, there are needs for belonging and security, so this person may require additional support systems, perhaps involving other people in addition to his or her partner. The other partner may see this new need as a shift suggesting that each other's needs are not being met, which can cause stress. As the growth process progresses, each individual will be presented with new challenges, and for most people, that too spells stress.

There are other stress factors that are more easily recognized, such as external issues of family, business, children, etc. These are common factors that shift a low-stress relationship into a more stressful one. However (and borrowing from the serenity prayer), taking the steps necessary to change the things you can, accepting the things you can't, and having the wisdom to differentiate the two, is the key.

Principle III: Suspension of thoughts or elimination of specific experience can allow neurological changes to happen immediately.

This principle is very difficult for individuals involved in conflict-laden relationships to implement, but it can be done. The objective is to find a way to avoid dead-end discussions. Perhaps someone you both trust to be fair, or a therapist, could assist in this effort.

When you observe the exchanges of people suffering from gender stress, you will see the same interchanges occur again and again. All too often, someone dredges up something completely off topic, which invariably (and needlessly) exacerbates the situation. Other times, someone brings up an incident that went very badly and throws it in the other's face—even when that issue had been previously "resolved." These behaviors serve no one well.

Why? When the same issues are brought up over and over again, the brain begins to stop processing that information, because it already "knows" it. Then, over time, as these "heard that already" topics continue, the brain does make some new connections: it starts associating that worn-out topic with increasingly negative feelings. In order for the brain to shift out of this trap, these topics have to be put away. Otherwise, the stress becomes dominant and overtakes the feelings of happiness and pleasure with the other person, which may lead to the termination of the relationship.

Principle IV: Times of growth and change are opportunities for learning and relearning.

This principle is crucial in the effort to manage feminine and masculine factors, since if we can learn to highlight the strengths of the other and the self, the couple may become more powerful than the self alone. These are the steps in the natural process of reduction of gender stress storms.

1. ***Learning to listen:***

    As I have tried to convey, women probably listen to more of the metacommunication in conversations, while men tend to listen for the most linear content. This means that women want more information to make the concepts clearer, while men want to "fix things" with the information they have. Men probably have more pressure on them to be absolutely clear and consistent with all the information they offer, including voice, tone, breathing pace, information content, and body posture. If they're missing any of these elements, this triggers a woman's brain to want the situation/problem/solution to be far better clarified.

    There is also the reality of women's intuition. No, I can't prove it exists . . . but it does. Some women I know will stop at practically nothing to glean more information if their intuition is in conflict with what their other senses are telling them. I've observed this phenomenon in clinical practice more times than I care to say. And just for the record—and I know it's cliché, but—if you sense your spouse is having an affair (and if you're generally a secure, happy person), then there might be some truth to it. Of course, that "truth" may simply be that your spouse is feeling particularly vulnerable and/or is in need of some extra attention, so don't jump to conclusions. For both men and women, the key is to speak your mind frankly and kindly and ask questions to clarify meaning. Truth plays a huge part in the connection between two people, especially in gender relationships. You just have to honor how the brain works and to respect the integrity of it.

2. *Learning to integrate each other's needs:*
Problem solving and conflict resolution are seen largely as a psychological strategy, but the process is deeper than mere steps along a continuum. There are five phases that have to be dealt with in an honest and forthright manner; otherwise, the process only builds stress. They are summarized as follows:

• One person goes first, here we'll say the male. He explains his needs in as complete detail as possible. His partner will attempt to clarify them with empathic listening skills so at the end of this phase, both of them understand his physical and emotional needs. For example, if he says, "I want to play golf on the weekends," she may convert this to an emotional need, "I need time alone" or "I need some control of my life during this time."

• The other person goes second, with the same agenda: to explain what she needs, with her partner clarifying emotionally what she is asking. For example, she may be asking for him to spend more time with her, and his clarifications might evolve to: "I want more attention" or "I want to be heard more."

• Third phase goes back to him. He is to think of as many ways as possible that he can realistically give her what she wants. For example, he might offer dedicating a special time for them to talk, going on dates, talking on the phone during the day, or traveling once a month together. This is not the time to negotiate, and this is not a list of all the things to be offered, just some ideas.

- Fourth phase is her turn to offer ideas on how she might support his needs. For example, she might suggest that he take three hours each weekend to do whatever he wanted; that he consider making a plan at the beginning of each week to see how he could arrange for the best time; or, for both of them to have a scheduling session once a week (say Sundays) to plan for the next week.

- The fifth phase is the opportunity for each person to find at least one way that they could support each other's needs. After all, one of the most important aspects of any relationships is providing and receiving support for each other's day-to-day responsibilities, as well as for each other's dreams. Take a specified amount of time to discuss how things are going; and, be willing to discuss new possibilities. Lastly, take to heart the profound importance of nurturing and respecting each other, so that you honor the relationship as precious, special, and valuable.

Principle V: New pathways can be changed and improved.

Inasmuch as the principles are new challenges for any individual or couple in the developmental process, the last principle is usually the easiest to embrace. In fact, I suspect that the pleasure principle is the reason for most people to want to have a relationship in the first place. The goal here is simply to renew this powerful incentive to maintain a healthy, integrated relationship. I never cease to be amazed how loving relationships can be rekindled when the stress is minimized.

For loving relationships between men and women to endure and mature into the integrated model presented, the definitive word must always be *support*. If you want this relationship to make you a better and more effective person, you have to bear in mind that both of you must actively participate. There is an explicit assumption that you intend to support your partner in his or her needs. This is not a conditional deal where you say, *"If and when you demonstrate that you're going to support me, then I'll take the risk to support you."* No, this contract has to be mutual to work. You may also be surprised when you feel (probably for the first time in a long time) how supporting the other person will help you better meet your own needs. If both of you can commit to this strategy, then you're truly on your way to enjoying a better, more fulfilling relationship. The point is to embrace each new chapter of your lives in an integrated way.

Rejoice in Your Relationship

There's nothing so deadly as taking each other for granted. If you once felt how enormously lucky you were to have found someone with whom you could have a meaningful relationship, then chances are, you can get there again . . . if both of you want that. If you can problem-solve at any level, and utilize the full potential of your combined brainpower, you'll achieve great strides. Celebrate every single successful step you make in the right direction—no matter how small. A supportive, loving handwritten note slipped in a brief-case or taped to the coffeemaker is one idea—whatever it takes for each of you to make the other feel how truly and deeply your partner matters to you.

OVERALL THOUGHTS

The power struggle between men and women is real. Perhaps one of the reasons it exists is because men are fearful that if women take power, then men will be left feeling that they aren't necessary. However, in a relationship, as in a community, we're losing huge human capital by ignoring the value of integrating the best parts of the female and male brains. Why are we depriving ourselves of this joy? Maybe too many of us lacked good role models. It's not that we don't have the capacity to change. We just need to know how to do it.

You have the power to make these changes happen together with your mate. Together, you can create the reality you both want. Two brains really are better than one.

11

Recognizing Triggers and Resolving Stress Storms

Understanding how stress storms get started in the first place is essential. You need that information if you're going to be able to effectively manage, and in some cases prevent, those storms—which is where neuroplasticity comes in.

If you've been reading this book in sequence, you certainly know by now that stress storms aren't always the result of stressors or events outside of your control. They are the results of triggers that manufacture the storms within our minds. To deal with the storms, our brain tries to cope by developing a response. Sometimes our brain gets "stuck" in that response, even when new information is presented that's counter to what we thought was true. We "learn" to become hurt, angered, or frightened by words, thoughts, or situations that actually remind us of past situations. But with the right tools, you can create new neuropathways to replace the ones that are serving you poorly.

Changing trigger responses is similar to changing other habits in terms of creating new neuron connections. Whenever you stop an unwanted habitual behavior, the neurons that have attached themselves to that old pattern will begin to detach and start looking for another group to join. As you practice and repeat your new desired response, those neurons will begin to cluster around this new pathway and, with repeated practice, will grow deeper and deeper roots. The trick is knowing how to stop the knee-jerk response you don't want and replace it with clear thinking, so that you can make new and better choices based upon what's true, instead of basing your response upon what's no longer true.

DELORES'S STORY

Delores was probably one of the smartest people I've ever worked with in a therapeutic capacity. She resolved her stress storms very quickly by embracing one of my favorite combinations: cognitive therapy, a breathing technique, and physical exercise. Here's her backstory: Delores came to us for one basic problem—marital unhappiness. She had been previously diagnosed as having a personality disorder, ostensibly due to her inability to carry on stable intimate relationships. She complained that she couldn't communicate with her husband because he was constantly putting her down, although she couldn't think of any specific examples during our initial consultation. She was always on edge around him, and she never trusted him with other women.

Delores was a very attractive forty-year-old mother of two children. She was a teacher who liked her work very much: she frequently talked about her students, and she'd never missed a day of work. She didn't report any specific traumatic events in her past, or anything else that she thought of as out of the ordinary.

When discussing the problems she was having with Marcus, her husband, she exhibited a great deal of stress about what he *might* do to disrupt their relationship, not what he had done in the past. More curiously, she even described him as a "great husband" who did all the things she expected of him. I asked her how they met. She said their courtship lasted a year, and that he had swept her off her feet. She was a junior in college when she first met him. He was a teaching assistant in one of her classes, and they were inseparable from their very first date (which they had on the last day of the class). She went on to say that he was handsome, smart, generous, and kind; she considered him a great father. Now, if you're wondering what the problem was, so was I.

The Problem

The problem started when Delores was a child in a family that wasn't so wonderful. Called a "family legacy" in professional jargon, this occurs when, as an adult, you superimpose onto others (usually unconsciously) expectations, behaviors, and motivations that you experienced or witnessed as a child growing up. In Delores's case, she viewed her father as the worst of devils. When Delores was only three, her mother had divorced her father. Delores grew up listening to horrible tales of his adultery and laziness, and witnessed some of his very "bad moods," which became the only thoughts and images to stick in her brain about her dad.

Over time, these thoughts colored how she felt about all men. And of course, repeatedly hearing her mother say things like "Men are bastards—they only think of themselves" went a long way toward deepening neuropathways that damaged Delores's spirit. That's the thing about unwanted neuropathways: even when you rationally know something isn't true, it still "feels" true. For Delores, even though she admitted that her view of her husband was totally distorted and based on irrational thinking patterns, she couldn't shake it.

Not unexpectedly, as her story continued to unfold, it became more and more apparent that her ambivalence toward her husband wasn't actually about her husband at all, it was about her perceptions of her dad. And unfortunately, the kinder, the more thoughtful, and the more supportive her husband tried to be, the more untrusting and suspicious she became. Why? Because he wasn't acting in accordance with the belief in her head that all men are evil. So, without consciously realizing it, she would try to provoke him to make him fit the mold in her head. The irony is that if he'd treated her badly most of the time, it might have actually reduced her stress. Of course, she'd have lived a horrible life, but it would have been the life she expected. This is one of the many reasons why some people stay in genuinely abusive relationships. It fits their expectation, which is very sad.

It only took two sessions for Delores to see how her thinking patterns from the past were damaging her current life. But that insight, while helpful, didn't provide her any real relief. Her brain was in a stress storm that she didn't know how to reason through. She'd become a victim of her habitual emotional reactivity, which left her feeling unable to find alternative, constructive pathways.

A Path to Happiness

Cognitive therapy is especially helpful for those individuals who have irrational thinking patterns, as Delores did. In this type of therapy, the assumption is that the problem may arise from faulty social learning, or from a lack of experiences that would encourage the development of coping skills, or even from dysfunctional family experiences.

Delores delighted in her ability to "rethink" things, literally. And as she began to leave behind the destructive, faulty assumptions she'd made about men, she began to appreciate and enjoy her relationship for the first time in a long time. She realized that she always had choices; and now she not only knew how to cope with her anxieties, she understood where they came from.

At our last follow-up visit, Delores was positively glowing, and smiling from ear to ear. When I asked her what was the source of her wonderful smile, she shared that things with Marcus were going splendidly, and that she was excited about her life. Oh yes, and that they were expecting their third child. I just love happy endings, don't you?

TRIGGER RECOGNITION

Stress storm triggers are learned from a wide range of situations, and the first step is to be aware of what they are. It might be very useful to take the following questionnaire to see what triggers you may have.

Please read carefully the following items and determine what your most likely emotional response would be for each. Here's a guide to the choices: (N) no emotional response expected, (M) moderate and controllable emotional responses, such as becoming agitated but not openly confrontational or retreating, or (H) highly charged responses. Indicate how often in the last year the following fears and rages have triggered stress storms in your life, and mark their intensity in the appropriate column.

Fears and Rages	(N) Never	(M) Moderate	(H) High
Fear of embarrassment	___	___	___
Fear of failure	___	___	___
Fear of success	___	___	___
Fear of insects	___	___	___
Fear of criticism	___	___	___
Fear of intimacy	___	___	___
Fear of rejection	___	___	___
Fear of death	___	___	___
Fear of pain	___	___	___
Fear of humiliation	___	___	___
Fear of poverty	___	___	___
Fear of germs	___	___	___
Rage from embarrassment	___	___	___
Rage from failure	___	___	___
Rage from criticism	___	___	___
Rage from intimacy	___	___	___
Rage from rejection	___	___	___
Rage from pain	___	___	___
Rage from humiliation	___	___	___

For the following, indicate the situations in which you still assign blame and withhold forgiveness. These may be relevant to severe or minor issues, but they still bind you to stress storm cycles.

Unforgiveness	(N) Never	(M) Moderate	(H) High
Childhood abuse	_____	_____	_____
Childhood neglect	_____	_____	_____
Spouse abuse	_____	_____	_____
Spouse neglect	_____	_____	_____
Work molestation	_____	_____	_____
Work discrimination	_____	_____	_____
Work unfairness	_____	_____	_____
Unfairness unspecified	_____	_____	_____
Lack of perfect body	_____	_____	_____
Lack of opportunity	_____	_____	_____
Other:	_____	_____	_____

Your particular triggers may not be listed above. So please, take the time, think about your past, and try to remember what has triggered some of your past stress storms—particularly those that made you feel as though you'd lost control. Look at the situations for which you marked "High" responses and consider these your top triggers.

Top Triggers: _____
                       _____
                       _____
                       _____
                       _____

HOW TO PREVENT STRESS STORMS AND BUILD HEALING RESPONSES: RECONSIDERING YOUR PERCEPTION OF THE EVENT

Now that you've gone through the above section, consider how these triggers have placed you in stress storms and led to your missing opportunities for joy and resolution. It's time to stop the destructiveness of your stress storms by dealing with the triggers. Putting this as kindly and as plainly as I can, the reality is: all events are only perceptions of the real truth. What we actually see or hear are only messages from the sensory nerves in our bodies and brains that interpret the world for us. For example, we don't actually see a bird fly directly. What we sense are the light rays being bounced off a birdlike object, which are then focused by the lens of our eyes, as tiny vision cells in the back of the eyeballs are stimulated. We call on our memories of similar patterns to identify that object as a bird.

Reality is different for everyone, and social perception is the most complex of all. The question we all have to ask about everything we think we see or hear is, *Is it true?* Is it true that this person just insulted me? Is it true that I am being treated unfairly? Is it true that I am weak and stupid? Is it true that I am being victimized?

Most important, you need to realize that no matter what anyone (and I do mean anyone) has ever told you, you aren't stupid, weak, unimportant, a waste of space, insufficient, or any other demeaning label that someone else gave you and that you may now believe to be true. It's not true. These misconceptions stem from the distortions that you have embraced. This is not a problem with the world; it is a problem in how you see yourself in relationship to your world. What you need to do is change your own self-talk, meaning, the negative things and beliefs you say about yourself in your head. These are only distortions of the truth.

Take my advice: STOP THE CASCADE OF SELF-DEFEATING EMOTIONAL RESPONSES, RIGHT NOW. Go no further in your self-limiting internal dialogue. This is not the time to argue with yourself (or anyone else) as to your limits. If you have to put a rubber band on your wrist and snap it hard to get yourself to stop thinking bad thoughts about yourself, then do that. You can try splashing water on your face, or counting to ten or one hundred. Stop beating yourself up. Grin and ground yourself. Challenge your perception of reality. Put an end to your self-doubt.

Assessing the Agenda from the Other Side

People trip your triggers either unintentionally or intentionally. In other words, there are those who make you vulnerable to distractions

without meaning to, and then there are those who purposely distract you as a manipulative technique. There are many incidents in
which someone can innocently arouse your emotions, the kind of
thing little kids do when they don't have sensitive social skills, like
when they say "You sure are fat, aren't you?" or "I think that woman
is prettier than you." In this case, you can chalk such comments up
to ignorance or lack of consideration; or, you may even choose to
feel sorry for their lack of understanding. The goal I want you to
embrace is this: release their ill-considered comments to the wind.
They have no power over you.

If you are the intended victim of a trigger-pusher, such as an ex-
wife who intends to hurt your feelings with indirect insults, you
have to dig a bit deeper for alternative thoughts, instead of choosing battle. Mothers-in-law can really have an impact on you, especially when you can't escape, such as during a car ride. Avoid these
circumstances at all costs if you anticipate trouble. If staying out of
their way is not possible, try the following: switch topics and create
alternative arguments (one of my personal favorite diversionary
tactics) by bringing up issues like war, politics, near-death experiences, religion, and euthanasia. Or just tune out and go to your
own happy place.

If that doesn't work for you, make a Plan B—well ahead of time—
to escape this emotional bully. I'd also recommend making a Plan C
and D. You might consider talking with a trusted friend or therapist
to help you come up with plans that would work best for you.

Assess Your Destructive Response Set to Stress Storms

- The ravages of fear
- The traps of anger
- The emptiness of unforgiving
- Ambivalence about choice
- Expectancy incongruency

Fear has to be the most basic of all triggers of stress storms. Most of the individuals I've helped have enormous capacities, but they're wrapped up in the pain of fear. The fear of death is instinctual from the first months of life and embedded in our unconscious survival behavior; however, fear of rejection is probably the most powerful conscious trigger. Whenever we're threatened by isolation, our brains go into a major meltdown and can become locked up in a never-ending hurricane.

Anxiety is an extension of the dynamics of fear. It's the feeling of fear without an awareness of the object of your fear. All you know is that you're fearful, but you can't specify exactly what you are afraid of. You just worry about everything. It's worth noting that phobias and obsessive-compulsive behaviors are only a fraction of the issues that come under this general heading.

As there are several kinds of fear triggers, there are several kinds of stress storms. But the common denominator among all of them is a high frequency in the beta range, in which the "noise" of the fear shuts off the mind's ability to create solutions.

Fear and anxiety usually impact the brain by increasing activities in the nerve cells and producing high-intensity brain waves. This may serve as a survival function, since rapid thinking and problem-solving abilities may be needed to quickly face or flee danger. However, when the activity *overwhelms* the rational processing, and the cycles of high intensity appear to build on each other, all you have is unbridled panic. It's like having a frightened horse that's out of control—it will run in any direction, even straight into a fire.

Anger and resentment are the triggers of rage, driving us into and the trap of self-defeat. Anger can serve a useful purpose if it is justified and directed appropriately. But when it's only a substitute for self-loathing and a justification for cruelty to others, the trigger in your brain can become horribly destructive and addicted to that emotion. It's like a tornado that blows away all of your pleasure and replaces it with emotional poison. Like fear, the brain reacts to anger with high intensity, probably as a way to focus. But without resolution, the brain can go into rage without reason. And rage is a sure road to defeat because there's no precision of action and no resolution.

The emptiness of unforgiving is a spiral into the void. Too many people are still wrestling with their past, especially those who were offended or assaulted in ways that diminished their dignity or self-respect. Some people have great difficulty letting go of these injustices and remain stuck in the anger and suffering. This trigger deadens your brain and makes it numb to your passions. By identifying with your pain, you force your brain to either distort or deny your real feelings.

Ambivalence about choice is a trigger that sets one part of the brain against another. It divides the self and creates chaos. When choices are presented, you have to speak up for what you value and meet the consequences. It can be a no-win decision in which neither choice has a good outcome, but you have to choose the least harmful option. For example, you may have to choose between working on Saturday or forfeiting your vacation. There are also more positive situations in which both options have good outcomes, like having to choose between two good jobs.

The trigger that really sets the storms in motion is the one psychologists call the *approach-avoidance conflict.* You know you have to confess your misdeeds in order to reestablish your ties to someone you love, but you also know it will have painful consequences. Or there are the *avoidance-avoidance conflicts* where you have to decide which option would be the least painful, knowing that neither is to your liking.

The most powerful trigger of a stress storm is to avoid making choices altogether. Often people who have spent their childhood at the mercy of a troubled parent who applied discipline harshly and unpredictably wind up in a state of *learned helplessness,* similar to lab rats that have received random electrical shocks. When the rats discover that no behavior they can muster alters the pain, they become paralyzed and will not move. In the same way, when a person is emotionally paralyzed, the brain loses functional capacity quickly, because interaction with the world is so painful. This is even more true as one gets older.

Expectancy incongruency is perhaps the most acknowledged of the triggers. This occurs when you are surprised by the outcome of your behavior. We develop certain predictions as we grow up that we begin to count on. We expect people to be nice to us when we show courtesy and respect. We predict that when we work hard we will be rewarded. Our brains develop circuits that define a predictable world, and our sense of stability is based on those learned expectations.

Then one day you act in a predictable way, such as being nice to your spouse, and the response is totally different. He or she acts hostile and angry and you can't understand what you did to provoke such a response. Your brain goes reeling into chaos because your set expectancies have been destroyed. Another example is suddenly getting fired from your job, even though you've worked your heart out and made personal sacrifices for the company. It feels as though they've cut off your legs. Your sense of support and stability vanishes. You can't find a rational answer or explanation, and your stress storms erupt.

ACTIVATING YOUR ADAPTIVE RESPONSE CHOICES

Using cognitive approaches to deal with triggers and emotional cascades has significant advantages for your overall health. Creating a reservoir of helpful responses, in lieu of falling into the trap of stress storms, can open up your life, allowing you to take advantage of important opportunities.

One of the most fascinating research findings I've come across was a comparison of the impact of the cognitive approach with the effects of medication. The findings suggested that antidepressants dampened activity in the limbic system, which is the emotional center of the brain. Conversely, the cognitive approaches calmed activity in the cortex, the part of the brain that controls reasoning and processing. The implications of these findings are profound. Medications reduce emotions and numb your pain, whereas cognitive changes can help process emotions in healthier ways. This finding may explain why there is a greater likelihood of relapse into destructive stress storms with medications alone than with cognitive restructuring. Medications, of course, are an excellent tool, but in my view, without understanding the cause and making the appropriate emotional shifts, the storms are only being temporarily quelled; and you deserve better than that.

The Basics

There are basic methods that are simple yet effective in preventing triggers from cascading into stress traps.

Face Your Feelings and Emotions

Feelings and emotions are normal, and it's not necessary (or even wise) to try to block them in order to prevent a serious stress storm. The better you can recognize what you are dealing with, the better you can make good choices about how to prevent your feelings from taking over your life.

For example, it would be completely natural for you to feel hurt by someone who uses your feelings against you. But here's the key: face your emotions in a constructive way. Instead of escalating your reaction to the point where these thoughts become your master, find ways of resolving the deepest underlying feelings, such as insecurity or your need for everyone to like you. Recognize that competing with another person or beating yourself up by focusing on these issues will only magnify them; be honest and open about the situation. If you're afraid of looking stupid or anxious, announce your anxieties or fears and ask for help in understanding them. Yes, put them right out there. You'll be amazed how people respond to candor. Don't hide your emotions, or else they'll fuel the furnace of negativity inside you.

Use Time: "And This Too Will Pass"

The wonderful thing about time is that regardless of what you do, time passes. Our memories are relatively short, and we remember very few events in our lives unless they are associated with something. The key is not to stamp an event with a negative emotion, but to allow the emotion to dissipate. If you attach a powerful emotion to an event, time cannot erase it. The idea is to learn from your mistakes, but then let them go and concentrate on the next moment. For example, if you are embarrassed and angry because your pants split at the seams, creating problems with a person you were trying to impress, do not try to hold on to that memory and invest it with great power. Let it go as an event that happened but that had no real significance. Find a moment of strength, make a joke, and move on.

When we connect events with great emotions, these become triggers for future similar incidents. Using the example above, if we attach a great deal of shame to that memory, we will start to fear similar reactions when we are trying to impress someone else. The fear becomes greater and our triggers become more sensitive until we are on the verge of a stress storm days and weeks before it happens. Allow time to separate you from the event. Other people will also forget quickly unless you give them a negative emotion to attach to you.

Forgive Yourself

Everyone makes mistakes. This is one of those life truths that unites all of us, regardless of culture or generation. But this truth rarely makes us feel better about the mistakes we've made. After all, history can't be changed. But there is something you can do, and that's learn to forgive.

One of the factors that distinguishes a superstar athlete from an average one is the capacity to forgive himself or herself. For example, whether the wide receiver misses a pass that sails through his arms, or the soccer player completely misses the ball and allows the opposing team to score, the great stars don't deny the event. Instead, they learn from their mistakes and get better. They make their mistakes productive. So can you.

What's Your Best Advice?

It always seems easier to look objectively at someone else's behavior and circumstances and figure out how to help, as opposed to doing that for ourselves. So try this: think of yourself as your own client and give yourself advice. After all, who is a better expert on who you are than you? Ask your therapist self what would be the best manner in which to respond to a situation to avoid a stress storm. Listen to what you have to say, because given enough time to really listen, the brain will usually create the best solution on its own. Trust your intuition and your wits. With enough space to process the challenge of reducing stress to acceptable levels, your brain will rise to the task.

I've always found it useful to take some time and write down my best responses to stressful circumstances before they happen. When you write them down, you remember them more easily and can readily access them when needed.

Become Your Own Hero

More times than not, you already know what situations are likely to cause you stress, because you've dealt with them before. For example, if you go into stress storms whenever you have misunderstandings with your spouse or significant other, it's likely to happen again. If you get agitated whenever your teenager wants to drive the family car to a party, it's highly probable another similar situation will emerge. You need to make a plan.

One of the best plans that will work with your brain plasticity (instead of against it) is for you to make up a story involving exactly what each of your expected challenges will be. Creating the setup will surely be easy—as you've been there and done that. But what I want you to do is change the outcome! In fact, I want you to come up with different scenarios in which you are the hero who resolves the situation. If you want to enlist suggestions from your friends, a trusted family member, or a therapist, that's a really good idea, too. However you get there, this is a positive, proactive method of managing your triggers.

Many examples come to mind that might help you with your triggers, but my favorite is one I call "Jim's Folly." His recurring trigger was his children's fighting and his lack of control in responding to it. All three were under the age of ten, and they'd always choose the worst times to act out. Their behavior would set off Jim's stress storm and he'd be stuck in it for days.

We got Jim together with as many family members and friends as possible, ten of us in all. We made suggestions about his hero stories and had a good time. One of the stories went as follows:

Jim was driving along a covered bridge en route to a vacation spot, when his children in the backseat started fighting over a box of cereal they'd been munching on. He took a deep, cleansing breath and then silently said a magical word inside his head. Then, poof! Jim was instantly was transformed into Clever Dad, CD for short. Without saying a word (and with much wisdom), he pulled over to the side of the road and stopped the car. It was a hot day, but he kept the windows rolled up, so the temperature inside the car began to soar. Puzzled and distracted, the children asked what he was doing. He explained in barely audible tones (so they'd have to make a concerted effort to hear him) that he wouldn't continue driving with such a ruckus occurring, so he was stopping until they cleared the issue up.

The children immediately started to point fingers at each other, in the hopes that Jim (aka CD) would assign blame and punish the wrongdoer (as he had done before). But this time Jim refused, explaining that this was their business and it was up to them to resolve the issue; the ability to make the vacation trip resume was entirely up to them. The children's first impulse for conflict resolution was to continue fighting it out and get one another to either admit blame or apologize; which of course only led to more fighting. Without an umpire (their dad's attention), the conflict lasted about forty-five seconds and another ten degrees of heat and body odor level. Then silence. The oldest one, unprompted, said, "Um, Dad, we're ready to go now." Without explanation or singling out the initial problem, Jim started the car and drove on.

Throughout the next family vacation, the exact same backseat fighting situation occurred four times, and each of these times Jim went into hero script mode. And instead of having a long drawn-out conflict, the boys acquiesced more and more quickly. Since that trip, the boys no longer fight excessively in the backseat. They learned that there were consequences for their actions, and they learned what they needed to do to avoid an unwanted result.

If you have the opportunity and are so inclined, and if someone you care about has a quick stress trigger, you might want to share with that person the value of writing his own hero script. You could even help him do that. As I noted in chapter three, it's also one of the most productive processes I've found for people who are addicted to alcohol and need a plan to refrain from their stress storm.

Celebrate Your Good Choices

In concert with what we know about brain plasticity and habit-forming mechanisms, it's important to celebrate each positive, constructive behavior and success in managing your triggers. Celebrations like this can be private or public. It can be an announcement to your loved ones or friends that you conquered a trigger response, and that applause would be greatly appreciated. It can be a cake or special meal to support a new positive way of managing stress. It can be a personal gift to yourself, such as giving yourself the luxury of reading a book, getting a manicure and pedicure, taking a bubble bath, or going to a movie you've been wanting to see. If nothing else, at least give yourself a well-deserved pat on the back.

Enjoy any success you feel, every time it happens. Please don't fall into the trap of thinking that you have to establish a track record of success before you celebrate positive movement in the right direction. It's the positive reinforcement that solidifies the behavior; and getting into the practice of enjoying your successes as they happen is essential for building new, desirable neuropathways.

CONCLUDING THOUGHTS

Triggers are like doors to disaster, but they can only be opened by you. This is a major principle that is always true, regardless of what happens externally.

Remember our motto from chapter four, and emblazon it deep within you: YAHOO, or "You Always Have Other Options." You *always* have control over what you tell yourself about what you perceive and how you want to react. This is the freedom of being human.

12

Training Your Brain Past Aging Stress

There are many stress storms yet to be defined, and as technology advances, we will surely learn more about the brain. Doing so will enable us to explore new protocols to mend the brain and take constructive (and possibly even preemptive) steps to bring about optimal, lasting change. As I shared with you at the beginning of this book, brain scans give us a glimpse into the problem dynamics. However, considerable work needs to be done for us to better understand what brain scans show us about stress and the human mind.

AGING AND STRESS

In my work on the sources of stress, one of the most important things for me to master (particularly at my stage of life) is the process of aging. Statistically in the United States, if you've made it to age sixty-five, the expectation is that you'll reach the age of eighty-five. However, living longer and living well are two different things. For example, in the United States, the Hispanic population lives longer than both Caucasians and African-Americans, but the quality of their life, in terms of health, is far worse. Additionally, the expected time to live in poor health for men is 8.7 years. Women, who generally live longer than men, live in poor health for 11.6 years, on average.

I know I don't want to live a dismal, passionless life in ill health for the last 30 percent of my life. But the good news is, we have more control than ever before over how we lead our lives. Indeed, contrary to popular belief, we don't have a finite number of brain cells, and we do continue to learn and build new neuropathways throughout our entire life. Our brains absolutely have the ability and do continue to change according to our experience until the day we die. So, if you know the secrets of nurturing your spirit and your mind, your fate is primarily in your hands, genes be damned. Seriously, your genes are responsible for about 10 percent of what happens to you. The rest is a combination of your environment and the choices you make.

A WORD ABOUT MEMORY LOSS

We hear a lot about the terrible illness called Alzheimer's disease, but that term is often used incorrectly to describe simple forgetfulness in the elderly. Alzheimer's disease is a specific type of progressive neurodegenerative disease. There are other medical terms like age-associated memory impairment or mild cognitive impairment that describe less severe memory loss in the elderly, although in some cases, these can be a warning sign that the individual is at a higher risk of developing Alzheimer's disease. Dementia is the more general term for a serious decline in mental faculties, particularly memory. And senile dementia describes a loss of cognitive functions that is generally attributed to aging.

That being said, with age also comes a special type of wisdom. The things we've learned and the experiences we've had can certainly be sources of insight and much-needed clarity for the younger generation. The point is that the extent to which you enjoy and celebrate your life is within your power. But you need to commit to nurturing your brain.

You can overcome nearly any challenge if you use your natural capacity for brain plasticity. Throughout this book, I've laid out a number of ways to do this, but there are many more. So, let's review (and possibly project) some of the ways in which you might embark on this new challenge. Perhaps you will see a specific plan for modifying your own neurological network and conquering your problems.

THE LAST FRONTIER: AGING STRESS

Charlie was one of my best buddies in college and we never lost contact through the years, regardless of marriages, job changes, geographic relocation, or children. Every time we met it was like we'd only been apart for a few days. There was always that friendly smile and hearty handshake. Friendship and loyalty are of paramount importance to me, so having Charlie as part of my life forever was unquestionable. But five years ago, his smile was only half a smile and his handshake was weak. I was terribly worried about him, and feared he might have cancer.

I was relieved to learn Charlie didn't have cancer, or any other medical problems, although there was definitely still something wrong with him. I worried that even if he wasn't already sick, he might be more vulnerable to becoming sick.

As I've known Charlie for years, to me it was obvious that he was depressed, although he denied it. During the five years since I had seen him, many significant life-altering changes had occurred for him. His wife had died after battling a disease for a very long time. They'd lived way out in the country, so he'd been her sole caregiver for much of her illness, and we talked about the strange mixture of relief and sadness he felt. He also had retired during this time from a very intensive administrative post (in order to take care of her), and he talked about the isolation he felt, and how he had underestimated how helpful the distractions of work had been for him, for giving his emotions downtime.

Being the inexhaustible change agent that I am, I convinced him to come to my clinic for some brain scans. I wanted to help him, and I was pretty sure I knew what I would find: Charlie's brain scan was rather normal in its balance, but instead of the high frequencies associated with an active brain, there were none above the slow alpha levels. This meant that, as I suspected, Charlie was coasting. This was the way he was acting. He wasn't processing new information from inside or outside himself.

Charlie's well-being became my primary focus. I got him to promise to exercise on most days, and made sure we had many stimulating discussions about anything from current events to trying to identify what secret spice a local diner used to make their grilled fish taste so good. I researched and sent him loads of information about cool and interesting opportunities for education and even dancing lessons.

After a couple of months, I reassessed his brain scan and found even lower frequencies bouncing around the theta range. In the crudest of terms, it was as if his brain wasn't present most of the time. An MRI showed that his brain was shrinking, and there were signs that were suggestive of pre-Alzheimer's. If he continued to deteriorate, he was destined to end up in the delta state, which means that he would be in a sleep zone and unable to communicate in any meaningful way. I was terribly upset for him and for myself; I was losing a very dear friend, of which I have too few. Like a hungry dog with a bone, I grabbed on to the principles of brain plasticity, and had no intention of letting go.

Phase one of my plan was to get his brain stimulated. Whatever it took, I was going to help him fire up his brain and get his neurons dancing around that fire. I tried three campaigns. First I used the BAUD with an EEG monitor attached to Charlie's skull to measure how his brain frequencies were affected by the sonic frequencies. It took about five minutes to see positive results; I required him to listen to these settings for at least one hour (total) a day. To be certain he wouldn't forget, I made sure someone else helped him stay on schedule.

I also asked him to participate in twenty sessions of hyperbaric chamber time, during which you sit in the chamber, the way sea divers do, and experience increased air pressure. Why did I have him do this? There's good research to suggest that stroke victims who are placed in a hyperbaric oxygen chamber within the first few hours of having a stroke may greatly benefit by the infusion of oxygen into their tissues. Furthermore, while the scientific jury is still out, using hyperbaric oxygen chambers is also currently being researched as a potential treatment for patients with other types of severe brain injury.

Thus for Charlie, it was hoped that the combination of the sonic stimulation and the chamber sessions might facilitate coherence among the nerve centers of the brain and increase his frequency levels. Fortunately, Charlie responded very quickly to this powerful combination. He began to talk more passionately and began to process new information far better.

But there was more to be done. Now, since I knew he used to be quite the dancer years back, I introduced him to my form of dancing exercise. I sent him home with an armload of my drumming CDs and went over to his house every day to dance with him. I invited mutual friends to have "exercise parties" with him and hired a dance instructor to continue with some special dances, making them social interactions. Charlie loved this attention—especially from the ladies.

Of course, the sadness of his past would always remain a part of him. But it didn't have to control him. I embraced fun and joy with a vengeance, because I knew that his brain learning centers would open up only if he could break the depression mode to allow joy back into his life again. I knew he liked funny movies, so I rented or bought Dean Martin and Jerry Lewis movies and watched one with him every night. I can't even describe the sheer bliss I felt when I heard Charlie laugh! In time, the twinkle in his eyes returned.

Granted, this transformation took an enormous commitment of time, effort, and know-how. And perhaps this level of drive on behalf of others is rare. But for me, Charlie was more than worth it—and it proves that change on this level is possible.

Charlie was tested again for cognitive capacity and was found to be in the above-average range for his age group; and he was visibly happier. How's Charlie doing these days? Well, he's ninety years old now, and while he's no spring chicken, his dignity is intact, and he swears he gets up and dances whenever the notion strikes him.

A PROTOCOL FOR OLD AGE

Should you ever have an accident or trauma that restricts your capacity to the point that your brain begins to shut down, you should be clear about how you want to be treated and what you want done so you can have a chance to experience the smell of roses, the tenderness of a kiss, and the passion of one more idea before you leave this world. You do not want pity or sympathy. You want dignity and hope that you can think for yourself and enjoy relationships as a living soul, not as a passive recipient.

Here are some minimum requirements for any caregiver who takes on the challenge of your rehabilitation needs. The first prerequisite would be that this person be a believer in brain plasticity. This person must not form their expectations of you and what progress you're able to achieve based on statistics. He or she needs to understand that the brain isn't dead until you are dead. Until then, an older person's brain cells are capable of growing and developing just as a child's are, although not as quickly or robustly.

Your caregiver must have extraordinary patience and be supportive of your interests, however eccentric or ambitious they may look. You don't want to hear or overhear anyone talk about how grim your chances are for success. I remember running on the treadmill while being tested for my heart condition when I overheard one of the doctors say "That is bad" as she pointed to the computer monitor measuring my heart rhythms. I was working very hard at that time, so I didn't feel like confronting my own sense of defeat or her insensitivity, but at a later discussion with my cardiologist, I knew the tests were disappointing. The next assessment I had, I made it clear to the technicians and doctors that if they had nothing nice to say during my assessment, then I preferred they say nothing at all. No one needs a toxic critic.

Principle I: Neurons that learn together
become attached.

Ask your caregivers to administer the BAUD stimulation to your brain in such a way that you can see your brain leap to the higher frequencies of low beta, especially in your frontal lobe. Calibrate it so you can turn it every two or three hours to ramp up your brain energies, but please don't sit in front of the television set (except for watching *Dr. Phil,* of course). I believe that watching television generally slows down our brain frequencies and numbs us to our passions. It has been shown clearly that any time beyond one hour a day can create terrible walls to learning in our children, and you will not need any more walls to break through.

You will need brain fuel in the form of food and supplements. Protein, like that found in fish and eggs, will be part of your daily diet. Complex carbohydrates should be integrated for energy reserves, and fiber will be crucial. Fiber is required to reduce toxicity as much as possible and keep your brain from being poisoned by your own inflammation process. You must avoid constipation at all costs. Constipation can cause toxicity and brain cross-circuits.

Challenge yourself with intellectual games so your capacities can be directed toward recreating nerve patterns around coordination of memory and organizational skills. Have people talk to you about meaningful things, like politics or religion, even if they have to go slow at first while your brain catches up. The best way for the brain to cluster brain cells and grasp concepts is through stories. Stories have a natural way of uniting different concepts and splicing cell networks together. This is also a powerful way of connecting up some memory cells along the way. But be patient and go slowly, because frustration in comprehending can defeat you quickly with negative experiences. Once those patterns get enough brain players working together, you'll catch up quickly.

Exercise your limbs with a rhythmic beat so you can remember or relearn how to coordinate your muscles. Swimming and moving through the resistance of water would be a great way to help your brain learn coordination again, and this strengthening would be consistent with the earliest forms of developing motor skills. This will take time, much longer than in the beginning, so try to always have people encourage you to make the effort. Your tolerance may be short, but you should be trying as hard as you can.

Another way the brain can bring together networks is to sing songs. Musical melodies provide some of the most powerful ways of combining many sensory inputs and collecting those matrices of nerve connections. The A-B-C song would be good for the beginning, but use whatever types of songs are embedded in your brain and might be easiest to access. Be sure to emphasize the breathing component.

Principle II: Experience and need can change neurological bundles.

Practice is critical, so be consistent with your training. Remember that your brain may be upgrading another part because the original networks may have been destroyed. This is like scientists' hooking up the visual nerve to the auditory regions of the brain of ferrets and discovering that the animals could eventually learn to "see" through their "ears" or auditory regions, although not with as much definition as originally.

One of the brain plasticity pioneers, Dr. Paul Bach-y-Rita, invented a device to help people (sometimes called wobblers) whose sense of balance has been disrupted. His ingenious invention was first used to treat a woman whose vestibular system had been wiped out by disease. Doctors believed she would never walk again without falling. The device looked like a hat, and it had stabilization measurement sensors that connect to a strip the wearer placed on her tongue. As the various sensors detected imbalance, the strip's 144 electrodes were immediately initiated. The subject reported sensations like bubbles on the tongue, which were usable brain messages! After the first session, the woman could walk without falling for twenty minutes, and eventually could dance and walk normally. She has regained full function and no longer needs the device.

Another story I love is the one Dr. Bach-y-Rita told about his father, Pedro Bach-y-Rita, a poet and scholar. After suffering a stroke at the age of sixty-five that paralyzed half of his body and left him unable to speak, he was pronounced incurable and was deemed unfit for any of the rehabilitation centers in New York. Dr. George Bach-y-Rita, Mark's brother, decided to work with their father on his own. He began with having him crawl like a baby. After a few months, his father began to crawl partially upright along the wall, using his hands and knees for support of his left side. Months of intensive practice led to walking. His speech started to return, and coordination of his arms was improved with exercises such as teaching himself how to type again. After a year, he returned to teaching full-time at City College at the age of sixty-eight. His physical condition improved to the point that he was able to climb mountains as high as nine thousand feet with his friends.

This story is extraordinary because when Pedro died of a heart attack at the age of seventy-two, the autopsy revealed that his brain was severely compromised, and over 97 percent of the nerves running from the cerebral cortex to the spine had been completely destroyed. This meant that his brain had almost entirely reorganized itself in twelve months to return to what would be higher-than-average performance. This is the amazing process I think everyone is capable of, including you.

You will need to persistently practice to reorder your brain and relearn your abilities. Start with simple exercises such as playing with marbles and picking up objects from the floor. I use the term *playing* because this process should be fun and exploratory. You need to crawl as best you can before advancing to higher functions. If need be, one of your arms might be tied in order for the other one to be used more intensively. That's fine.

Principle III: Suspension of thoughts or elimination of specific experience can allow neurological changes to happen immediately.

The brain works best by suspending existing habits of thought. This is how we power creativity itself. Inventions come about from thinking "outside the box." We usually discover our potential through trial and error.

I'm reminded of Bob Beamon, who broke the world's long jump record by two feet. He did it by entering a state of mind in which he felt no limits to himself. The great football player Jim Brown often talked about the imagery he would visualize as he ran through tackles, and many premier athletes discuss how, when they're in the process of completing some extraordinary play, they experience it in slow motion, actually seeing themselves doing it. How cool is that?

In order to create a new order of performance, you have to learn to suspend your old beliefs. I use an example known by millions, and though it lacks scientific validity, here it goes: according to Matthew 14:26, there was a time when the disciples of Jesus were gathered on a boat in a storm and were afraid for their lives. Then they saw their leader walking across the waves and were called to join him. I take some privilege in paraphrasing the words, but the message was to have faith in their own abilities. Peter ventured out and got partway walking and trusting totally in this ability. But he turned back to his friends, looked at the waves, and grew afraid and immediately he began to sink. The operative term is *turned back* to his old way of thinking.

You will need to suspend old habits of thought, and there are ways to accomplish this process. Using imagery is excellent for achieving this. In my own research I've seen many people use visualization to enhance their immune systems enough to destroy tumors; I've witnessed other people learn to extinguish their pain symptoms and walk without discomfort by using imagery.

A fascinating aspect of imagery is that the body and brain don't seem to see differences between objective reality and your personal reality. Therefore, the brain will develop the pathways *you experience*. For example, if you believe that I placed a red-hot poker in your hand, when instead I just handed you a cool metal bar, your brain would serve your perception first, and if the belief was great enough, a blister could even form. I've seen the eye color of a person change from blue to hazel when imagery was used. This is a very exciting process that you can practice with the help of the right person.

Principle IV: Times of growth and change are opportunities for learning and relearning.

The primary growth factors are basic neurotransmitters and hormones that are related to emotional contexts. For example, there are definitely links between our immune systems and our emotions. Our organs, such as our heart, have a very intense connection to our emotions in terms of their coordination and pace as well.

Speaking concretely (not figuratively), what you want are parties, and I have clear justification for this phrase. You want celebrations of what you achieve and what you are. In my case, I also have a large appetite for competition. I love to engage in sports like football, tennis, badminton, and sailing. It's not the winning or losing I crave, but the effort of achieving my best and beyond.

So what I would want is a friendly, competitive game of some sort, to raise the standard for effort and celebration. You might want something similar that suits your interests. Need more convincing? Okay, in order to open your brain to new vistas, the last thing you need is healing done for you by others. Request an opportunity to earn your healing. Set goals for yourself, and reward your efforts and achievements with something you consider worth struggling for—a trip to Hawaii, a series of CDs, or a gift for someone else, like a computer for a poor child. You may be your harshest taskmaster, but you'll feel stronger if you earn your steps into whatever chapter lies beyond this day.

Principle V: New pathways can be changed and improved.

Once you have mastered a skill, changed a habit of thinking or a cognitive ability, you want the brain to retain and maintain that template. This is the time for reflection. This is when you need to be alone and allow your brain to organize itself around your new learning. This can be accomplished through your dreams as well as when you are meditating. This is your time to relive the image of what you've accomplished and relish the feeling of celebration within.

SUMMARIZING THOUGHTS

You should expect your quality of life to be the highest you can make it. Though I'm sure few would argue against that outcome for themselves, the difference is that you now know some basic principles (that I've shared with you throughout this book) that will help you reach toward that end.

I'm not afraid of death, largely because I was once declared dead when I had my heart attack. I remember the process quite vividly as being welcomed to a "sweet" place where all I felt was love. In fact, I wasn't eager to return to this reality, but I did with the conscious decision to do all I could to contribute to the overall quality of life for others and for myself. That said, I'm not afraid to return, because I know of the blessings on the other side. When it is my time, I will rejoice in that return.

Personally, I doubt it would even be a good thing to have immortal life, because it is death that defines life for us. Quality of life and how I can continue to do what I was supposed to do are uppermost in my mind. I am equally sure that my brain, indeed my entire body, was designed with that purpose, as was yours.

It's also my belief that part of my mission in this life is to live the most honorable life I can, with the awesome responsibility of being a model or mentor for someone else. If I can walk my talk in the integrity of my values, then perhaps someone else can find the purpose to do the same. I have to maximize my strengths to benefit the world, my family, and my loved ones by both word and deed. I would ask my future caretaker to please bear that in mind, as it is my desire and intention to continue striving until the final moments when I take my last breaths.

In closing, it is with great humility that I hope this book has brought you even a modicum of understanding, so that you can start your journey down the path of living your best life.

Kind wishes,
Dr. Frank

Exercises

Although the exercises are broken down to about two per day, this is a self-paced and -directed process based on greatest areas of need, so feel free to see them as more of a guide than a rigid schedule.

Day One: On the first training day of the 45-day stress program, your first exercise is to begin to recognize the various levels of activity your brain goes through during a typical day. Normally you will reach an apex in which you have highest thinking and concentration capacities during certain periods of the day. You will also experience low energy points. Focus on a three-day period and make a diary to record your observations.

Mark the time periods in which you felt you had the best concentration and problem-solving abilities (high beta frequencies).

Mark the period of time you felt the most relaxed (high alpha frequencies).

Mark the times you felt the laziest and lowest energy (delta and theta frequencies).

6:00 A.M. _____		6:00 P.M. _____	
7:00 A.M. _____		7:00 P.M. _____	
8:00 A.M. _____		8:00 P.M. _____	
9:00 A.M. _____		9:00 P.M. _____	
10:00 A.M. _____		10:00 P.M. _____	
11:00 A.M. _____		11:00 P.M. _____	

12 NOON _____	12 MIDNIGHT _____
1:00 P.M. _____	1:00 A.M. _____
2:00 P.M. _____	2:00 A.M. _____
3:00 P.M. _____	3:00 A.M. _____
4:00 P.M. _____	4:00 A.M. _____
5:00 P.M. _____	5:00 A.M. _____

From these observations, see if there are consistencies across days and note the times your brain was most active. From now on, to the best of your ability, try to address challenges and deal with problem-solving issues during those times when your brain is known to be functioning at its highest capacity. The slower frequencies may be your best times for relaxation and restoration.

Day Two: In comparison to the noted times for best situations based on your normal brain activities, please note for the next couple of days (or more) the times in which you have the most stress (scored on a 1–10 scale, with no stress as 1 and high stress as 10).

6:00 A.M. _____ *Stress* = _____	6:00 P.M. _____ *Stress* = _____
7:00 A.M. _____ *Stress* = _____	7:00 P.M. _____ *Stress* = _____
8:00 A.M. _____ *Stress* = _____	8:00 P.M. _____ *Stress* = _____
9:00 A.M. _____ *Stress* =_____	9:00 P.M. _____ *Stress* = _____
10:00 A.M. _____ *Stress* = _____	10:00 P.M. _____ *Stress* = _____
11:00 A.M. _____ *Stress* = _____	11:00 P.M. _____ *Stress* = _____
12 NOON _____ *Stress* = _____	12 MIDNIGHT _____ *Stress* = _____
1:00 P.M. _____ *Stress* = _____	1:00 A.M. _____ *Stress* =_____
2:00 P.M. _____ *Stress* = _____	2:00 A.M. _____ *Stress* = _____
3:00 PM. _____ *Stress* = _____	3:00 A.M. _____ *Stress* = _____
4:00 P.M. _____ *Stress* = _____	4:00 A.M. _____ *Stress* = _____
5:00 P.M. _____ *Stress* = _____	5:00 A.M. _____ *Stress* = _____

Compare these findings to the times of your brain activity levels. Is there a pattern to how your brain is performing and the intensity of your stress? Is there a specific time you feel the most stress? Are there consistent times you are relaxed and have little stress? Note connections between your perceptions of your brain activity and stress.

The purpose of these exercises is to prepare you to become sensitized to the different levels of brain activity you can detect. The levels are all normal because the brain adjusts as different demands are placed on it. The brain's strength is its flexibility. We feel out of control when it is stuck in the wrong gear or pattern.

Day Three: This exercise will be focused on Principle I of brain plasticity: forming new neurological bundles. Decide to change a habit, and for this exercise the task is to start a new brain bundle that will result in automatic behavior (new habit). You can use this for your children or spouse if you want to.

Step one: Form an image of your new behavior. Let's assume that you want to begin a new behavioral habit of being happy most of the time, regardless of what else is going on in your life. The first step is to call up an image of how that would be in your usual life. How would you look? How would you show your pleasant disposition with your body, such as smiling and attending to others instead of yourself? As you increase your imagery, consider how you would greet others and address problems, or how you would handle fear and stressful situations from a happy perspective, such as being optimistic and focusing on new possibilities. How would you handle an aggressive person? Try focusing on areas where you have fears or confidence issues holding you back, like public speaking or confronting others. Imagine yourself smiling while confidently navigating each situation. You might want to discuss this with your friends to work out what the behavior would look like and how you would feel inside. Write down some expectations from your experience with the imagery.

_____

_____

_____

Step two: With the imagery notes as your guide, engage in the world all day as a "happy" person. This does not mean you are superficial or not involved, but being a happy person you will look on the more optimistic side. Practice this attitude and associated behavior. Intentionally deal with stressful situations and maintain your happy disposition, because few problems are life-threatening and you always have options and choices. Get feedback on how much friends and coworkers may be noticing more smiles and laughter, and pay attention to how others are responding to you; see if strangers relate to you differently.

At the end of a time period in this exercise, record how you feel and what successes you may have made as a "happy" person. Write down the differences you saw as people dealt with you. In some cases, people may have tried to drag you down to their levels of depression. In other cases, others might have been encouraged by your optimistic view.

Step three: Reinforce the new habit of neural networking. For each time you were successful being a happy person, give yourself a gift. When I was playing football for the University of North Texas, many of the players would hand out candies called Kits to the teammates who performed the best during practices and games. Kits were squares of taffy you could buy in a package of four for a penny. These little rewards were magic because they represented support from our teammates and also tasted good after a hard practice. I often wondered if this trick was significant in our performances as we won the league championship and played in the Sun Bowl.

If you have changed a neural network by using the plan in the exercise, you have made a huge step in creating better ones. You can learn to play sports at a higher level and reach far advanced training in whatever career you want.

Day Four: This exercise will be focused on Principle III, disrupting neurological programming and behaviors. In order to deal with stress successfully you will need to learn ways of stopping the destructive stress storms in the brain.

Find an external source that your brain will listen to. This is a task in which you will need to identify at least one resource that will alter your brain activity, especially if it seems to be churning out of control. This may arise when you get angry or hurt and want revenge or relief from some injustice. Events that threaten you or your safety can also cause you to obsess over the situation.

Evaluate these positive resources to determine if they can alter your consciousness to break the stress cycles, and report on each. You can add other resources as well.

Music (be specific): _____

Exercise _____

Walking in another environment _____

Talking _____

Singing _____

Reading _____

Meditation _____

Offering help to others _____

Day Five: There are many ways of getting your neurons firing in a positive direction. My favorite exercise is breathing. Practice the breathing and relaxation script on pages 60–61. Determine its impact on how you feel emotionally and physically before and afterward. For example, before practicing the breathing exercise, rate yourself on the following dimensions:

How tense do I feel?

Extremely tense _____ Very tense_____Moderately tense_____

How effectively do I problem-solve?

Unable to think clearly _____ Poor planning _____ OK processing_____

How would I rate my sense of self-esteem?

    Very low _____ Fairly low _____ About average _____ Above average_____

How physically strong do I feel?

    Very weak _____ Weak _____ About average _____ Above average_____

Now, begin the breathing and relaxation technique in the script. You can read it or record it and listen. Also, you can have a friend read it aloud for you.

Now reassess using the same rating scale provided above.

Practice the breathing techniques often and do this as a regular part of your day. Be sure to write down your impressions, so that you can follow your progress.

_____

_____

_____

Day Six: Explore ways to apply Principle II to disrupt the anxiety cycles by participating in the following:

Listening to music: _____

Exercising to the beat while listening to rhythms: _____

Meditating (perhaps while listening to music): _____

Talking to someone helpful: _____

Walking or driving in a new environment: _____

Reading: _____

Watching an inspirational movie: _____

Hearing a powerful story: _____

Others: _____

Be sure to keep track of which of these methods best helps to distract you from the spiral of your stress storms. That way, you know what to do as soon as they begin. Replace destructive feelings with good ones.

Day Seven: This exercise will help you to establish new brain modeling, taking advantage of the disruption of the anxiety cycles and implanting new constructive habits of thought. I would recommend the imagery exercise below as you strive to implement Principle III.

Imagine yourself as the most powerful, wisest person in the world. You are your own hero. You may even choose a new name for your hero-self. See yourself as having many ways to deal with the world's stresses, such as breathing and seeing yourself growing stronger. See yourself as having wonderful ways of using your mind to devise problem-solving processes and give good advice to others.

Now make up a short story in your mind in which you, as your hero, deal with a problem you know a lot about, because it may be one of yours. Be engaged in the problem not as the victim, but as an observer and hero. As the process goes on, give the characters good advice about possible positive outcomes. It might be good to tell the story to someone else.

What were the results? How do you feel about being a major hero? Did you feel stronger when you found new information available to you through your hero? Write about your experience and repeat as often as needed.

Extra Smart

You know those times when you're giving advice and what comes out of your mouth is . . . really, really wise? And you think to yourself, "Where did that come from? That's smarter than I am!" Well, that's your true self making him- or herself heard!

Day Eight: This exercise will help you to apply Principle IV and eliminate stress triggers form your life. Whenever an anxiety stress storm occurs there are usually triggers involved, like an insult from someone or a fear-based response. What are your anxiety storm triggers?

Name at least one trigger per category and note why you believe they're present. Then eliminate them by confronting them and changing your brain reactions to ones of relaxation and confidence.

Becoming a victim (such as giving up control and surrendering to the fear) _____

_____

Aggressive reactions (such as rages and fighting) _____

_____

Avoidance of fear (such as running away or using substances to numb your emotions) _____

_____

Day Nine: Apply Principle V by celebrating your positive changes in brain response. Being a big fan of celebrations, I would make a big deal out of each successful way you re-model your brain to deal with the anxiety stress patterns. For each success, give yourself a prize—whatever jazzes you, e.g., going out for an ice cream cone, going to the movies, giving yourself permission to eat a wonderful dessert. Even a manicure and pedicure can work wonders (or so says one of my good female friends!).

How Do You Plan to Celebrate the Next Time . . .
You successfully deal with an anxiety stress situation by engaging in healthy behavior such as breathing slowly and deeply or using another stress-reduction technique.

_____

You successfully calm an anxiety stress storm by using distractions or other forms of mental modification to free you from stress.

_____

You successfully use mental imagery to keep you from engaging in anxiety stress.

_____

You successfully eliminate a trigger or change your behavior to a more positive way of dealing with your anxiety the way you want.

_____

You successfully celebrate yourself and your positive reactions to stress.

_____

For your last exercise, write down how you feel about your newfound abilities to modify your brain in the face of anxiety and other fear-related situations.

_____

Day Ten: Application of Principle I—Probably the most powerful way of getting your brain neurons to begin working together is to start moving your muscles in a unified manner. For you to achieve the best possible benefits, please do the following exercise for thirty minutes every day. If that means you must wake up thirty minutes earlier, then do that. Choose the kind of music or drum rhythms that are upbeat and put you in the happy place. Turn it up loud enough so you can feel the vibrations and start moving to the beat. I don't care how you move, just move. I often have people just shift their weight from one foot to the next to the beat and move the rest of their bodies in some motion to add to their movement. For example, I have them focus on the knees, hips, back, shoulders, and head progressively in order to get the whole body moving in a unified process.

After each movement session, answer the following questions to acknowledge your efforts:

1. Do I feel more alert than before the exercise? _____
2. Do I feel happier or less depressed? _____
3. Do I feel more flexible and balanced? _____
4. Do I feel lighter? _____
5. Do I feel that I can concentrate better? _____

If your answers are not a resounding yes, choose different music.

Day Eleven: Application of Principle II—To best shift your brain from the attention deficit stress storm, breathing is the most immediate method that you can do anytime and anywhere, even in a

classroom. The breathing pattern you need to use is the one described on pages 85–86 in which you start timing your breathing
pattern to about ten to twelve respirations per minute. That aver-
ages out to be about one respiration for every five seconds.

The secret of really making this work best is to remember to
breathe in through your nose (and out through your mouth). This
method excites your brain and signals lots of your neurotransmitters to go into action, essentially instantly making you smarter, because your connections improve and your stress levels drop.

Practice this method for ten minutes for maximum fog lifting.
You should remind yourself of this approach every time you are
faced with a challenge. Jot down how you felt before and after
going through this breathing pattern:

_____

_____

_____

Day Twelve: Application of Principle III—For optimal neural network connectivity, eating nutritiously is essential. Using the information on page 89, develop a menu for breakfast and stop eating
and drinking foods that literally work against you, such as highly
processed, saturated-fat, and salty or sugar-packed foods. That includes most fast foods, too. I would certainly make eggs part of
your first meal of the day and definitely include a complex carbo-
hydrate, such as whole grain toast. Describe your menus for the full
day below:

Breakfast _____

Lunch _____

Dinner _____

Snacks? _____

Foods to avoid: _____

With your plan in your pocket, observe your energy flow during
the day. Do you have the same energy drops you had before? Can

you focus better? Are you as hungry on this plan? How do you feel at the end of the day?

It may be important to use more than one day to get your body into the routine of a better nutritional plan, but you should be able to see some difference right away.

Notes: _____

_____

Day Thirteen: Application of Principle IV—This approach is for brain stimulation, to get your nerve cells perking up on a more consistent basis, and I think the most fun way is through games with others. Select a game such as checkers, chess, card games, or any game of your choice. Invite friends over to play (make it a routine, regular gathering) and engage in the games, regardless of how well you do. Teach yourself to be more skillful, and by all means have fun. This is often challenging to those individuals who fear losing and begin to act out in amusing ways to compensate. It's perfectly fine to be relaxed and have fun, but hey, if you win, that's awesome.

Notes: _____

_____

Day Fourteen: Application of Principle V—Increasing concentration requires effort and may take some time. I'd suggest some exercise to reinforce the efforts, especially with children. Choose an activity that requires concentration, such as reading a book or solving mathematical problems. Using a ten-minute guide as a start, commit to a period of time in which you will give 100 percent effort, not stopping for any rest. However, at the end of the ten-minute limit, stop your activity and review your performance. If you completed this period without fogging over, give yourself a reward (brief), such as a three-minute rest, and stretch your muscles.

Continue for another ten-minute trial with the same conditions. Continue this process for an hour, or at least five trials. This process is training your brain to concentrate; however, you may have limits. Thirty minutes would be tops for most people, so your trials may increase your concentration for any period of time, but know that it's normal to need to break your concentration every once in a while. Practice—practice—practice.

Day Fifteen: Application of Principle II—One way to avoid the cyclical downward spirals of the obsessive pattern is distraction, and physical distraction works best with many people. Of course, shifting your focus when you're already in an agitated state can be particularly difficult. So, know that it's hard, that it's the nature of the beast, and that it's best to get ahead of the storm, whenever possible.

This exercise works to dispel the neural storm by way of required attention. I would suggest trying a sport that you might not be great at, but one in which you can easily participate. Bowling, golf, hiking, shooting, and fishing have been very good distractions for me and many of my patients. All of these activities do require our total focus and involve a change in environment.

Choose an activity, such as one of these sports, and engage in it with the intention of fully participating. Even if you're frustrated with your performance, the outcome will be positive because that level of investment will shift your attention and brain pattern. After your participation, write a note about your emotions and possibly the shift from your ruminations or worries.

_____

_____

_____

Day Sixteen: Application of Principle III—A technique that has been of enormous benefit to individuals suffering from the obsessive stress storm has been to visualize their brain functioning more calmly while breathing very slowly. Remember that the brain is being destabilized by the lack of connections among its various parts, so it will help to focus on images that suggest a unity of mind and breath.

For this particular process it may be very useful to listen to one of the professionally developed CDs for relaxation and de-stressing because they can give you step-by-step processes. If you go to MindBodySeries.com/DrFrankLawlis on the Internet and enter the number DFL3528, you can download a free relaxation CD for your computer or iPod. Use it repeatedly over a hundred times and your brain will eventually learn unconsciously through brain plasticity by association. It is especially useful to teach your brain effective quality sleep habits. But many people prefer to set their own pace with their breathing. Both are fine choices. The imagery you focus on could also include a musical arrangement, and the visualization would be one of conducting the various instruments to play together in harmony, much like what you want the brain to be doing. You can also draw or paint your image, using the circle for integration as you breathe and relax. Start with a circle and practice drawing various symptoms on it—just free-associate. Some examples are below:

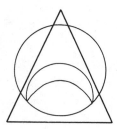

FIGURE EX.1

Use the visualizations and breathing to calm your brain. You might also use some nutritional aids to help you, such as chamomile tea or almonds.

Day Seventeen: Application of Principle IV—Halting the rampage of the obsessive storm can also be achieved by visualizing time and using your imagination to slow it down. You might practice with your watch, focusing on the second hand as it swoops around the dial. Concentrate on the hand as it moves and imagine you are slowing it down. Try to see every aspect of its movement, its color, and every other tiny detail of the watch itself. Breathe slowly and give this exercise your full attention. Then, observe other parts of your environment, such as a person shopping or a dog walking nearby. Play around with setting everything in slow motion. You might even imagine voices in slow motion, slurred and drawn out. I have a patient who does this whenever her "drama-queen daughter" or "goth son" go into their occasional tirades about how the world's not fair if they can't have this or buy that.

Practice this process many times until you can master the feeling of slowing down, which will be vital to managing the anxiety component of the obsessive pattern. This practice could also give you relief from time urgency and a sense of crisis.

Notes: _____

_____

_____

Day Eighteen: Application of Principle V—Avoiding rumination may take a lot of effort, especially if your brain appears to slip quickly into an obsessive pattern that creates anxiety. Small steps should be recognized and celebrated. Get your friends to help you recognize any positive improvements in your behaviors. Try having some meetings with a group of people to help you make the changes in your stress storms on a regular basis. During these meetings I would discuss the following topics:

- What techniques you've learned to change your responses to anxiety situations and obsessive thoughts.
- What recommendations would help you develop new approaches. Keep in mind the brain plasticity principles.

- Ask for feedback concerning how you felt you handled specific situations, such as controlling your emotional ruminations.
- Close each meeting by thanking your friends for their continued support in helping you work on and discover the joyful, loving, and lovable person you truly know you are inside.

Day Nineteen: Application of Principle I—Probably one of the most difficult things to do when you are in a depressive stress storm is to move physically, since you are "stuck" mentally. But it is very clear that physical exercise is the best thing you can do to stop your brain from swirling into an emotional vortex. For an exercise plan you should choose activities that do not require exertion beyond your endurance and that have some rhythmic quality. If you go to MindBodySeries.com/DrFrankLawlis on the Internet and enter the number DFL3526, you can download a free rhythmic drumming CD for your computer or iPod. Expose yourself to its sounds for at least twenty minutes twice a day, preferably while moving your body, for maximum benefit. You can even use it in the car, provided you stay alert to drive safely. Here are some recommendations:

- Walking to a rhythm (even on a treadmill)
- Swimming or hydro-movement
- Yoga exercise
- Dancing or movement therapy (tai chi)
- Bicycling
- Drumming (conga)

You would need to be consistent in your participation for at least twenty-five minutes daily. More strenuous exercise is fine; however, it is important to maintain this activity and not to approach it as a competition. In order to maximize its benefit you should recognize the differences in your emotions after completion and celebrate your spirit.

Application of Principle II—This exercise may sound extraordinary, but I think it will demonstrate how your brain can be influenced by your body. If you have a depressed brain you will likely have depressed body posture. You know what I mean. If you see someone with stooped shoulders, downcast head with eyes to the ground, bent back like the world is weighing them down, and sunken chest, you will likely predict correctly that the person is depressed. The curious factor is that if you assume this position long enough, your brain will actually initiate a depression state as a result.

But if you can make yourself depressed by assuming poor posture, then conversely, you can also shift yourself out of a depressed mental state by improving your posture. This exercise is to help you realize that connection.

Assuming that you are in the "blues" mental state, move your body into the "eagle" posture, which is described by the following behaviors:

- Extend your chest outward and thrust your arms back.
- Raise your arms into the victory or "V" position, using your arms as if spreading wings.
- Tuck your chin so it is resting even with your shoulders.
- Raise your eyes skyward and let out an expression of celebration.

Hold this position for a minute or two. If your arms get tired you can drop them, but rest your hands behind your back so you can maintain the forward thrust of your chest. Breathe deeply and fully.

If you are depressed, this posture may be difficult to get into and maintain because your muscles are so tight and bound to the depressed state. You may find it difficult to breathe for the same reason. But hold this posture and you will find it almost impossible to be depressed. You don't have to maintain it for the rest of your life, but it is an easy technique you can use to shift your mental state.

Day Twenty: Application of Principle III—Turn back to pages 136–38 and consider the myths that make you unhappy or depressed. Read carefully the seven myths and determine if they are part of your belief system:

Myth one: Necessity for love–? _____

_____

Myth two: Right/wrong answers–? _____

_____

Myth three: Horrible outcomes–? _____

_____

Myth four: "It" causes–? _____

_____

Myth five: Competent–? _____

_____

Myth six: Only one–? _____

_____

Myth seven: Doing nothing–? _____

_____

Other myths: _____

Consider the myths that you find to be depressing to your spirit and determine if they are true or false. Dispose of those that either are not true or do not serve your best interests.

Day Twenty-one: Application of Principle IV—This exercise is related to the one above. Assess all the beliefs you have about yourself and your life that are creating stress. These beliefs may involve guilt trips you have placed on yourself or ones that others have placed on you. They may also be rooted in old grudges that you have held against people who have hurt you. These are attachments that keep you stuck in the past, so make a list of all the beliefs and thoughts you hold that are related to negative emotions.

_____   _____

_____   _____

_____   _____

_____   _____

_____   _____

When this list is as complete as possible, you need to find a way to burn it safely. This can be in a fireplace, a campsite-type fire, or even in a bowl. Enact a ritual in which you say aloud, "I am burning these thoughts away. I will have memories and may remember some of the events associated with these beliefs, but I am freeing myself of their bondage and their drain on my joy and happiness." Create whatever ritual is most meaningful for you. I usually recommend that you make a big noise to shake your brain up a bit, such as beating a drum or breaking a plate.

Day Twenty-two: Application of Principle V—To properly seal a change in your brain pattern it's important to make your experience meaningful and to take some joy in your ability to make this shift. For example, if you have been depressed for some reason, perhaps grieving a lost person or mission in life, see your meaning in light of the process that you passed through. If your stress storm is related to being out of control, become aware of the control you needed to make the change. See your meaning as a valuable lesson in life. You might ask your friends to discuss some of these considerations in order to gain a deeper and richer appreciation of your process.

Above all, celebrate your victory over the "stuckness" of life. Sing and give praises to those who have helped you, including those who offered spiritual help. Tell people how important they have been to you and make time to enjoy what treasures you have in life.

Day Twenty-three: One of the most ancient ways of shifting brain patterns is chanting or repeating words or phrases. In order for the brain to start creating new networks, consistent actions must take place. A repetitive action done in a calm setting is a process your brain will easily take to.

Select a phrase or set of words that has meaning to you. I emphasize the vowels as easiest to bring a sense of relaxation. Some recommended phrases are:

I am enough	I can do it	I am
I am all	God is all	Love and peace
All is good	You and I are one	Brothers and sisters

Begin to repeat the phrase and continue for a certain length of time instead of trying to count them. Soon you will discover that there's a rhythm to the phrase, which actually has the most powerful impact on your brain. Practice this for twenty minutes, then assess your emotional state.

Day Twenty-four: Mental rehearsal is the process by which you imagine the meeting of a stress trigger and teach yourself to go through a ritualized behavioral activity every time you meet the situation. The idea is twofold: one, to learn a process through calm brain activity, so the trigger is associated with relaxation instead of stress, and two, to learn the process so well you don't even have to think of your reactions. You just "automatically" respond according to your rehearsal.

For example: choose one of your dreaded situations as the rehearsal focus. Imagine being confronted with your triggers or threat; however, envision the entire process in which you meet this problem with complete confidence and relaxation. Go through the imagined experience with perceived expertise. If you have some anxiety, do some relaxing breathing and talk yourself through it as slowly as you can, focusing on each second of your success. Repeat the process faster as you gain confidence in completing the total action plan without undue anxiety. Assess your emotional state. And practice, practice, practice.

Here's a tip: You might want to try chewing gum while you rehearse your action plan, as doing so has been shown to be helpful with stress reduction. People experience pleasure from the fresh taste, which is another positive reinforcement.

Day Twenty-five: The alternate nostril breathing exercise would be great in order for you just to become aware of the potentially excellent effect of brain shift it offers. As described on page 111, practice the breathing exercise, and experience the shift of the brain pattern after ten minutes.

Day Twenty-six: Develop a team to work with. Meet at least once or twice a week in order to create a deep sense of group support for yourself. This can be a social activity, or something to work out solutions toward upcoming activities. You might find it very helpful to develop new activities, such as learning to fish or cook.

Day Twenty-seven: Restoration is a way of rebuilding your energy to cope with stress. Give yourself plenty of time to relax (minimally eight, ideally nine hours of sleep). Use music, massage, listening to sleep or relaxation CDs, meditation, or any approaches that you experience as soothing. You may not experience success overnight, but stick with this. I'll say it again: you can do this.

Day Twenty-eight: Practice raising and lowering your activity and stress levels as described on pages 159–60. The act of increasing and decreasing intensity will create more flexibility in your ability to deal with the perpetual stress pattern because it varies the stressors instead of holding one level all the time. Several activities can be performed, such as walking fast and slow, jogging with a rest period, lifting weights with periods of rest, or creating activities of your choice. The basic principle is to develop a balance between high and low activity levels. These practices should be done every day for a minimum of twenty-five minutes.

Day Twenty-nine: Since Principle II of brain plasticity suggests that we need to vary levels of activity to interrupt the perpetual worry brain pattern, the exercise recommended would be a kind of biofeedback using temperature. All you will need is a thermometer or some way of measuring skin temperature, such as a mood-type color patch. For example, some stress cards have color-coded patches; you place your finger on the patch, which then turns different colors depending on your temperature. For instance, black might mean lower than 80°F, blue 80–85°F, and green warmer than 85°F.

The goal of the feedback is to learn to raise and lower the temperature measured on the finger. The warmer the temperature, the more relaxed you are, the cooler the temperature, the more stressed you are. The goal is being able to reach each point of the color/temperature spectrum at will.

Day Thirty: Time-out is probably one of the most difficult exercises when you are facing a perpetual worry storm because of the long-term intensity of stress at the highest level. Practicing taking time-outs will break the pattern. The important thing is to predetermine periods of rest and restoration when approaching a task. Purposely take time-outs for relaxation and to distract yourself from stress. (This is sometimes referred to as "learning to delegate" and can be very helpful for long-term health.) This approach is critical to applying the shifts in the perpetual worry profile. Evaluate your level of effort and performances.

Day Thirty-one: The breathing pattern of 4-3-5 described on pages 164–65 would be an excellent method for demonstrating to yourself how breathing patterns can influence levels of brain stress. Practice the pattern of inhalation and exhalation for ten minutes and assess how you feel. Attempt this approach several times during various activities of the day to demonstrate how flexibility in brain activity can be expanded.

Day Thirty-two: Develop a plan to balance your daily activities based on anticipated intensity of demands. For example, if you expect a heavy level of stress during the day, plan for an equal or balanced level of relaxation. In the case of worrying, if you have frequent worry periods, plan on a specific time for these activities with a balanced time for non-worry. You might even plan to have a friend do the worrying for you while you take a short vacation from that stressful time (no kidding). This exercise requires conscious planning and awareness of your stressful times, not to delete them, but to balance them.

Day Thirty-three: Listening to common rhythms can modify the brain patterns of groups of individuals. The same holds true for creating rhythms. The exercise calls for you and one or more other people either to select a music piece (or drum sounds) to listen to or to make the rhythmic music yourselves. If you play musical instruments, this would be the preferred method; however, if you don't, I would suggest getting some drums and beating out similar rhythms.

This exercise is especially good if you're all experiencing different moods or have different issues on your minds. Listen or create your rhythmic experience for at least fifteen minutes and assess how you're feeling and what issues are at hand. Note if your communication is better or if your tension has lessened. Note any additional positive reactions from the experience.

Day Thirty-four: This exercise may take some extra practice, as it requires some fine-tuned, active listening skills. To begin, allow someone else to choose a discussion topic. Your job is to show how attentive you can be to the feelings of the other person. Be sure to look into the person's eyes and concentrate 100 percent on the emotions expressed either verbally or in body cues. Attend to the content of the conversation as well, sharing your thoughts and observations, but be sure to follow the concepts on pages 187–88. Clarify how you perceive the other person's feelings in the context of what's being discussed. Be clear on what you're hearing by giving feedback, not advice.

Assess how the other person felt during the discussion and if your relationship skills were helpful. Show support, regardless of the conclusions. Of note, you needn't only do this as an exercise. In fact, it is optimal that you practice this type of listening during most any discussion.

Day Thirty-five: These exercises are focused on cross-gender relationships, so if you aren't concerned with these stress provocations you can feel free to skip forward. However, I would bet that most of the readers have some curiosity and are willing to invest some time in learning how to better relate with the other half of the human population.

This exercise is based on the descriptions of the principles on pages 208–10 that pertain to getting both brains in sequence. Take this opportunity to create a ritual in which both people find ways of working together with their talents. Start with the selection of music, and turn it on for the duration of the activity. I would suggest music without lyrics and with a strong bass beat, because this level of intense rhythmic quality is required for the brains to start harmonizing.

The next event will focus on preparing foods together. Each individual contributes, but shows respect for the other's ideas. This is both an effort to share new ideas and a chance to discover common feelings about what foods best fit the desired mood.

The third segment of this exercise is to create a written story in which both parties participate. One person starts with the beginning, but stops at a set time or number of words, requiring the other to add the next part. Each can give support, but this interaction should continue for about forty-five minutes. After that time, the couple can discuss the story and their respective contributions.

The fourth and last part of the exercise is feedback. At this point, each person should take turns giving feedback to the other on any aspect of the exercise, whether it's about the music reaction, the food preparation experience, the story, or just behavior in general. This part of the exercise should last about thirty minutes, but it can go longer if you both agree.

You can build your own exercises with these same four dimensions:

- Preparation
- Food or nutrition
- Project
- Feedback

Day Thirty-six: The exercise requires you and your partner to engage in a productive dialogue. It is based on two steps: 1) a statement of values and 2) prioritizing your needs in interactions.

Step one: Each of you writes down and describes the values you feel are essential for positive interactions with others. The list on page 206 may be helpful to get you started. List at least seven values and describe how they were recognized before and why you see them as important.

Step two: Each of you takes a turn in prioritizing and applying the values on the list to specific relationship situations. These may or may not pertain to your relationship, but might be discussed in a context you find interesting. The specific areas of relationships are:

- Problem-solving in finding solutions to common problems
- When one person is in a subordinate role and following directions of another (such as worker)
- When one person is in a superior position and is required to be responsible as leader (such as boss)
- In sexual relationships
- In relationships showing affection
- In relationships showing support (friends)

Assess what you may have learned from the other values and in what context they'd be best addressed. Discuss the differences and similarities.

Day Thirty-seven: This exercise addresses the transformative aspects of gender relationships. Assuming that the relationship has some history and certain roles and expectations have been set, the first step is for each person to describe, in written form, how the other person is seen and perceived to act and react to situations. Using everything from body signs to specific words, be as clear as possible as to the nature of the perceived behaviors of the other person. Be sure you write this exercise in a nonaccusing/nonattacking style. This stage can be funny or serious, but be sure to articulate each element of the behavior and not the conflicts that arise.

With these descriptions in hand, the individuals exchange roles, taking over the other's behavioral manifestations. If one person appears not to invest in the other's problems as a typical behavior, the other person assumes the same behavior. This exercise can last from one hour to a week.

Assess how accurate you felt the perceived behaviors were and what changes in attitude came out of the exchange. For example, sharing the idea of accepting more responsibility for the outcome of interactions might help create new relationship dimensions.

Day Thirty-eight: Utilizing the list on page 217, indicate the intensities of fears and rages you may have that trigger your stress storms. Be careful to consider those that keep you in a state that you think you can't escape.

_____   _____
_____   _____
_____   _____

Day Thirty-nine: Identify your most frequent responses that fail to satisfy your emotional needs and intensify your stress storms. Be sure and describe the situations in which these responses occur.

_____   _____
_____   _____
_____   _____

Day Forty: For each of the unhealthy or destructive responses to your triggers, describe a more constructive approach that might bring about a more satisfying result.

_____   _____
_____   _____
_____   _____

Day Forty-one: Give a description of some activities you would like to try to encourage your brain to learn new skills by creating high cohesion in nerve sets (Principle I). Note: Feel free to use some of my ideas discussed in chapter twelve if you like.

_____   _____
_____   _____
_____   _____

Day Forty-two: Give a description of some activities you would like to use during the aging process to retrain your brain by substituting a new behavior, such as using the other arm if your dominant one was to become less functional. In other words, what demands would you want created for you to relearn habits and strengths?

_____   _____
_____   _____
_____   _____

Day Forty-three: Describe some possible beneficial ways that someone might be able to get you to suspend your current conclusions and open your mind to new ideas and concepts (Principle III). I have offered some of my personal experiences on pages 239–240.

_____   _____
_____   _____
_____   _____

Day Forty-four: Name some activities that would be new opportunities to learn something. Think about what might get you enthusiastic about learning in new areas and discovering new concepts. What conditions turn your brain on?

_____   _____
_____   _____
_____   _____

Day Forty-five: What kinds of celebrations would or do you enjoy most? Name the situations in which you would feel most joy and appreciation, especially as a result of something you have accomplished.

_____   _____
_____   _____
_____   _____

References

ADAA. (2007). 2007 Stress & Anxiety Disorders Study. *Anxiety Disorders of America.*

Aftanas, L., & Golosheykin, S. (2005). Impact of regular meditation practice on EEG activity at rest and during evoked negative emotions. *Int J Neurosci, 115*(6), 893–909.

Allman, J. M., Hakeem, A., Erwin, J. M., Nimchinsky, E., & Hof, P. (2001). The anterior cingulate cortex. The evolution of an interface between emotion and cognition. *Ann N Y Acad Sci, 935,* 107–117.

Alschuler, K. N., Theisen-Goodvich, M. E., Haig, A. J., & Geisser, M. E. (2007). A comparison of the relationship between depression, perceived disability, and physical performance in persons with chronic pain. *Eur J Pain.*

Amir, S., Brown, Z. W., & Amit, Z. (1980). The role of endorphins in stress: evidence and speculations. *Neurosci Biobehav Rev, 4*(1), 77–86.

Avitsur, R., Hunzeker, J., & Sheridan, J. F. (2006). Role of early stress in the individual differences in host response to viral infection. *Brain Behav Immun, 20*(4), 338–348.

Biederman, J., Wilens, T., Mick, E., Milberger, S., Spencer, T. J., & Faraone, S. V. (1995). Psychoactive substance use disorders in adults with attention deficit hyperactivity disorder (ADHD): effects of ADHD and psychiatric comorbidity. *Am J Psychiatry, 152*(11), 1652–1658.

Bittman, B., Berk, L., Shannon, M., Sharaf, M., Westengard, J., Guegler, K. J., et al. (2005). Recreational music-making modulates the human stress response: a preliminary individualized gene expression strategy. *Med Sci Monit, 11*(2), BR31–40.

Cabrera, M. A., Mesas, A. E., Garcia, A. R., & de Andrade, S. M. (2007). Malnutrition and depression among community-dwelling elderly people. *J Am Med Dir Assoc, 8*(9), 582–584.

Carmody, J., & Baer, R. A. (2007). Relationships between mindfulness practice and levels of mindfulness, medical and psychological symptoms and well-being in a mindfulness-based stress reduction program. *J Behav Med.*

Cartwright, D. (2002). The narcissistic exoskeleton: the defensive organization of the rage-type murderer. *Bull Menninger Clin, 66*(1), 1–18.

Chapell, M. S. (1994). Inner speech and respiration: toward a possible mechanism of stress reduction. *Percept Mot Skills, 79*(2), 803–811.

Christie, W., & Moore, C. (2005). The impact of humor on patients with cancer. *Clin J Oncol Nurs, 9*(2), 211–218.

Csef, H., & Hefner, J. (2006). [Psychosocial stress as a risk- and prognostic factor in coronary artery disease and myocardial infarction]. *Versicherungsmedizin, 58*(1), 3–8.

Doidge, N. (2007). *The Brain That Changes Itself.* New York: Penguin.

Esch, T., Duckstein, J., Welke, J., & Braun, V. (2007). Mind/body techniques for physiological and psychological stress reduction: Stress management via Tai Chi training—a pilot study. *Med Sci Monit, 13*(11), CR488–497.

Flora, S. J. (2007). Role of free radicals and antioxidants in health and disease. *Cell Mol Biol (Noisy-le-grand), 53*(1), 1–2.

Foote, B., Smolin, Y., Neft, D. I., & Lipschitz, D. (2008). Dissociative disorders and suicidality in psychiatric outpatients. *J Nerv Ment Dis, 196*(1), 29–36.

Flory, K., Molina, B. S. , Pelham, W. E., Jr., Gnagy, E., and Smith, B. (2006). Childhood ADHD predicts risky sexual behavior in young adulthood. *J Clin Child Adolesc Psychol, 35*(4), 571–577.

Gordon, S. M., Tulak, F., & Troncale, J. (2004). Prevalence and characteristics of adolescent patients with co-occurring ADHD and substance dependence. *J Addict Dis, 23*(4), 31–40.

Harris, C. A., & D'Eon, J. L. (2007). Psychometric properties of the Beck Depression Inventory–Second Edition (BDI-II) in individuals with chronic pain. *Pain.*

Hunzeker, J., Padgett, D. A., Sheridan, P. A., Dhabhar, F. S., & Sheridan, J. F. (2004). Modulation of natural killer cell activity by restraint stress during an influenza A/PR8 infection in mice. *Brain Behav Immun, 18*(6), 526–535.

Kjellgren, A., Bood, S. A., Axelsson, K., Norlander, T., & Saatcioglu, F. (2007). Wellness through a comprehensive Yogic breathing program—A controlled pilot trial. *BMC Complement Altern Med, 7*(1), 43.

Klassen, A. F., Miller, A., & Fine, S. (2004). Health-related quality of life in children and adolescents who have a diagnosis of attention-deficit/hyperactivity disorder. *Pediatrics, 114*(5), e541–547.

Krauss, M. R., Russell, R. K., Powers, T. E., & Li, Y. (2006). Accession standards for attention-deficit/hyperactivity disorder: a survival analysis of military recruits, 1995–2000. *Mil Med, 171*(2), 99–102.

Labbe, E., Schmidt, N., Babin, J., & Pharr, M. (2007). Coping with stress: the effectiveness of different types of music. *Appl Psychophysiol Biofeedback, 32*(3–4), 163–168.

Laporte, L., & Guttman, H. (2001). Abusive relationships in families of women with borderline personality disorder, anorexia nervosa and a control group. *J Nerv Ment Dis, 189*(8), 522–531.

Lutz, A., Greischar, L. L., Rawlings, N. B., Ricard, M., & Davidson, R. J. (2004). Long-term meditators self-induce high-amplitude gamma synchrony during mental practice. *Proc Natl Acad Sci U S A, 101*(46), 16369–16373.

Miller, G. E., Cohen, S., Pressman, S., Barkin, A., Rabin, B. S., & Treanor, J. J. (2004). Psychological stress and antibody response to influenza vaccination: when is the critical period for stress, and how does it get inside the body? *Psychosom Med, 66*(2), 215–223.

Mischoulon, D., & Raab, M. F. (2007). The role of folate in depression and dementia. *J Clin Psychiatry, 68 Suppl 10,* 28–33.

Musselman, D. L., Evans, D. L., & Nemeroff, C. B. (1998). The relationship of depression to cardiovascular disease: epidemiology, biology, and treatment. *Arch Gen Psychiatry, 55*(7), 580–592.

Neri, S., Signorelli, S. S., Torrisi, B., Pulvirenti, D., Mauceri, B., Abate, G., et al. (2005). Effects of antioxidant supplementation on postprandial oxidative stress and endothelial dysfunction: a single-blind, 15-day clinical trial in patients with untreated type 2 diabetes, subjects with impaired glucose tolerance, and healthy controls. *Clin Ther, 27*(11), 1764–1773.

NINDS. (2002). National Institute of Neurological Disorders & Stroke Post-Stroke Fact Sheet. *The National Institutes of Health National Institute of Neurological Disorders and Stroke, NIH Publication No. 02-4846.*

Retz, W., Retz-Junginger, P., Schneider, M., Scherk, H., Hengesch, G., & Rosler, M. (2007). [Drug addiction in young prison inmates with and without attention deficit hyperactivity disorder (ADHD)]. *Fortschr Neurol Psychiatr, 75*(5), 285–292.

Schulz, Mona (2005). *The New Feminine Brain.* New York: Free Press.

Sherman, C. (2007). The defining features of drug intoxication and addiction can be traced to disruptions in cell-to-cell signaling. *NIDA Notes: National Institutes of Health, National Institute of Drug Abuse, 21*(4).

Schwartz, J. and Begley, S. (2002). *The Mind and the Brain.* New York: HarperCollins.

Shire US Inc. (2006). Ensuring Appropriate Stimulant Use for ADHD: A Parent's Guide to Being AWARE [Electronic Version], 5. Retrieved January 16, 2008 from http://www.adderallxr.com/about_adderallxr/about-sideeffects.asp

Tarazi, F., and Schetz, J. (2005), *Neurological and Psychiatric Disorders.* Totowa, N.J.: Humana Press.

Tikkanen, R., Holi, M., Lindberg, N., & Virkkunen, M. (2007). Tridimensional Personality Questionnaire data on alcoholic violent offenders: specific connections to severe impulsive cluster B personality disorders and violent criminality. *BMC Psychiatry, 7,* 36.

Thompson, A. L., Molina, B. S., Pelham, W., Jr., & Gnagy, E. M. (2007). Risky driving in adolescents and young adults with childhood ADHD. *J Pediatr Psychol, 32*(7), 745–759.

Wildmann, J., Kruger, A., Schmole, M., Niemann, J., & Matthaei, H. (1986). Increase of circulating beta-endorphin-like immunoreactivity correlates with the change in feeling of pleasantness after running. *Life Sci, 38*(11), 997–1003.

van Stegeren, A. H., Wolf, O. T., Everaerd, W., & Rombouts, S. A. (2008). Interaction of endogenous cortisol and noradrenaline in the human amygdala. *Prog Brain Res, 167,* 263–268.

Index